Coping with Threatened Identities

Coping with Threatened Identities

Glynis M. Breakwell

METHUEN
London and New York

First published in 1986 by
Methuen & Co. Ltd
11 New Fetter Lane, London EC4P 4EE

Published in the USA by
Methuen & Co.
in association with Methuen, Inc.
29 West 35th Street, New York NY 10001

Typeset by Graphicraft Typesetters Ltd
Printed in Great Britain by
Richard Clay Ltd,
Bungay, Suffolk

British Library Cataloguing in Publication Data
Breakwell, Glynis M.
Coping with threatened identities.
1. Identity (Psychology)
I. Title
155.2   BF697

ISBN 0-416-37120-5
ISBN 0-416-37130-2 Pbk

Library of Congress Cataloging in Publication Data
Breakwell, Glynis M. (Glynis Marie)
Coping with threatened identities.
Bibliography: p.
Includes index.
1. Identity (Psychology)–social aspects.
2. Adjustment (Psychology)
3. Interpersonal relations.
4. Social problems.
I. Title.
BF697.B72   1986   158'.1   86-23461

ISBN 0-416-37120-5
ISBN 0-416-37130-2 (Pbk.)

To Dr J.A. Matthews

Contents

Acknowledgements

Many of the empirical examples presented in the book are drawn from the findings of the two research projects: the 'Young People In and Out of Work' project funded under the 'Youth in Society Initiative' by the Economic and Social Research Council and the 'Women in Sexually Atypical Jobs' project supported by the Department of Employment. To both of these organizations I would like to express my gratitude.

Much of the work could not have been completed without the efforts of the research assistants involved in these projects. I would like to take this opportunity to thank Barbara Harrison, Barbara Weinberger, Carol Propper and Ann Collie for all their practical, theoretical and statistical contributions.

I should also like to thank Catherine Mills for coping with the threat of the new technology during the production of this manuscript.

Perhaps unusually, I should like to acknowledge my appreciation to Mary Ann Kernan, of Methuen, for her patience in waiting for me to finally produce this book and for her valuable editorial comments.

Lastly, but hardly least, I want to apologize to my family and closest friends who have suffered the chill of my preoccupied isolation during the writing of this and other books.

1 Varieties of identity-threatening experiences

The purpose of this book is to provide an integrative framework within which identity, threat and coping may be examined. The prime object is to achieve a better understanding of how people seek to cope with experiences which they find threatening to their identity. In such an enterprise it is normal to start with a definition of terms. The constitution of a threat to identity would typically be described at the outset. However, James' caution about the 'circumscription' of a topic in his treatise on varieties of religious experience needs to be considered:

> The theorizing mind tends always to the over-simplification of its materials. This is the root of all that absolutism and one-sided dogmatism by which both philosophy and religion have been infested. Let us not fall immediately into a one-sided view of our subject, but let us rather admit freely at the outset that we may very likely find no one essence. (James, 1917, p. 26)

Instead of starting with a set of formal propositions which circumscribe the structure and processes of threats to identity, the intention is to work towards them by first looking at a variety of identity-threatening experiences. Psychological and social responses to unemployment, abrogations of gender expectations, ethnic marginality, and the transition from school to the labour market are particular focuses in later chapters. These were chosen because research on them is burgeoning and some original findings can be presented here in a context where their theoretical relevance can be acknowledged.

However, this initial chapter will outline a number of case histories typifying aspects of threat to identity. In these, the victims of threat are allowed to speak for themselves about their experiences and feelings. Such case histories illuminate and illustrate the theoretical framework described in later chapters but they are not meant to act in any way as proofs of it. They are used merely to 'make flesh' the concept of threatened identity for the reader and to underline the immense variety of manifestations it can have. They also suggest some components which any model of identity processes must have if it is to be useful as a framework for understanding threat.

There is a danger in using examples to illustrate a theory. All too often the theory is too closely identified with the exemplars. They come to act as metaphors for the abstract formulations and can subvert of trivialize the insights achieved. This is particularly so where the examples entail case histories; the wood disappears into the trees, details of individuals' cases overwhelm the conceptual structure. It is hoped to overcome this by drawing the case studies from very diverse domains and emphasizing the communalities cutting across the specific.

There is a delicate balance to be achieved between the over-simplification and over-generalization in theoretical models, which James eschewed, and the over-particularization and empty detail of dependence upon case studies. Throughout this book, there is an attempt to strike this balance by providing, on the one side, a blend of individual case histories, data from large-scale surveys, the results of manipulative experimental studies, and analyses of changing cultural and societal patterns, and, on the other side, the diverse range of theoretical propositions surrounding identity and coping strategies.

To begin with the case histories: it should be noted that these are based on actual cases but some details have been altered or omitted in order to prevent identification.

Case 1: John

John, 38, married at the age of 24 and had two children, now aged 14 and 10. For most of the time since leaving school at 15 he was employed as a bus driver and lived in a flat on a council housing estate. He was well known in the local community, collected the football pools money door-to-door, and coached the estate's junior football team. Seven years ago he started to dress as a woman. After cross-dressing for twelve months, he declared publicly that he wished to 'change' sex and be considered a woman. He started dressing full-time in women's clothing and sought professional help to get a sex change operation.

John's wife divorced him and took the children. John stayed in the council flat, since he had nowhere else to go. He lost his job and was prevented fromcontinuing as the soccer coach.

John now spends most of his time alone in the flat, venturing out occasionally to the local shops, but then he runs the gauntlet of the local children who call him names and throw stones at him. While he awaits his operation, he is taking a course of hormone treatment which has resulted in the deposit of subcutaneous fat around his nipples, to produce the appearance of breasts, and a marked change in the timbre of his voice. The treatment has had less acceptable effects: vomiting, dizziness and the depression of sexual arousal. John accepts these as costs he must pay for his bodily metamorphosis. He even accepts the possibility of serious side-effects like pulmonary embolism, cancer of the breast or pituitary tumours. These have been explained to him. The painful electrolysis of facial hair is also being undergone.

When questioned about his experiences, John says: 'It's simple, I'm a woman in a man's body. I'm a woman. I think of myself as a woman. I'm changing my body to fit, that's all. I didn't always know I was a woman.'

In John's account, the task is to bring the physical facts into accord with the psychological reality. The evidence of his body contradicts his conception of his real identity. It is a threat to identity but it may not be the central one, since in a sense it is remediable. The body can change. The real problem lies in gaining social acceptance for the revised identity. As John puts it: 'Trouble is other people. They still think of me as I was. The old me. The new me is some misfit to them. They can't fit the old and new together.' This discontinuity of the constitution of identity is vital. John perceives the discontinuity not only between the physical and the psychological but also between the present and the past. He also knows that the community surrounding him focuses on the inconsistency in him.

Of course, there is more to it than that: the community also regards the new identity as aberrant and dangerous. John emphasizes: 'I'm not valued anymore. I've lost everybody. No one wants to know me. Everywhere I turn I am criticized. Even the professionals who are supposed to help. You know, my psychiatrist said he did not think I was serious about wanting the change. Me, that's lost everything. You know why? Because one day I went into his office wearing slacks, not a skirt.' The community response is an attack on personal worth; it threatens self-esteem.

John could move to another area, but if he did so before the operation he feels he might just create the same situation again. So he lives, isolated and depressed, waiting. He confesses himself to being continually threatened psychologically and socially.

John is characterized by the lack of continuity in his identity, by a lack of self-esteem (after withdrawal of community acceptance) and by an unwanted negative notoriety or distinctiveness (he is the only trans-sexual in the vicinity). These seem to be characteristics commonly associated with threatened identity.

Case 2: Jaheer

Jaheer lives in India. Two years ago, when he was 14, he was found to have leprosy. In one way, he was lucky: he was discovered accidentally when a health-education team visited his village to promote basic health care; otherwise he might not have been diagnosed for years. His lesions are relatively minor and the progress of the disease has been halted, at least for the time being. He is, however, restricted to a centre specializing in the treatment of leprosy. Jaheer understands the nature of the place where he lives and acknowledges his treatment, but he refuses to accept that he suffers from leprosy. He persistently denies it. He refuses to assimilate that self-definition into his identity.

Jaheer has been told about the bacteria which cause leprosy. He will not understand this. Instead, he explains: 'Leprosy is visited upon the wicked, evil and sinful as punishment for their sins.' This is the common belief in his home village, as it is in many parts of the world (Vadher, 1983). His proof that he does not have leprosy flows from this belief: 'I am not sinful. I am no leper.' In this case, the social belief system shapes explanations of the facts which lead to conclusions about self-description.

The diagnosis of leprosy threatens the continuity of identity and its distinctiveness; it also attacks self-esteem. The sufferer is removed from his community, his goodness impugned (by the dominant social belief about the causes of the disease), and he is lodged in a setting where others similarly stigmatized reside. The threat to identity is multi-faceted. Jaheer responds by refusing to accept that the diagnosis is correct. The denial changes nothing objectively but, at least, builds a subjective barrier to the attribution of sinfulness. Jaheer is apparently seeking to salvage some part of self-esteem.

Case 3: Josy

Josy is 44 years old. She had a happy marriage until nine months ago when her husband died suddenly in a plane crash. She has no children and no other relatives. Her husband's death left her financially secure but socially isolated; they had only recently returned from a series of postings abroad when he died. Sadness and sleeplessness led her to start drinking. She now drinks an average of four bottles of dry sherry a day, starting at 9 a.m. and continuing until she falls asleep in the early hours of the next day.

Over the months, periods of lucidity and sobriety have been increasingly rare as she is lost in a wash of confusion and, even to her, 'odd' behaviour. When sober she recognizes that her behaviour while drunk is very different to her 'usual' behaviour. She knows that, when drunk, she is aggressive, unpleasant and alienates all who try to help. She is now sufficiently dependent on alcohol to inevitably subside into behaviour each day which, when sober, she tearfully rejects as 'not like' her.

Josy started drinking after her husband's death deprived her of what had been a central part of the content of her identity: she was his 'wife'. As 'wife' she knew what to think, who she was, what value she had and how to behave. Most of her self-defining properties, she derived from him: status; her pattern of movement around the world; her attitudes and beliefs; and even her taste in clothes. With him gone, she felt cut loose. She had no role any longer. The discontinuity in her concept of the content of her identity was drastic. She says: 'I was catapulted into being my own woman. Suddenly. One moment wife, next widow. If it had been a long, slow, lingering illness it would have been better. I could have anticipated all the changes which were required.'

Josy buried herself in the haze of non-identity induced by intoxication. But that too is threatening her sense of self. While drunk she evades reality, yet at the same time it evades her. She recognizes that she behaves out of character and is beginning to wonder which is her true self: the aggressive drunk or the passive wife/sad widow. The drink which was an answer to the threat to identity is now itself metamorphosing into a much more cogent threat. Already she is banned from local shops which sell alcohol and has to take a taxi to more distant sources (she has lost her driving licence). Her neighbours complain of her behaviour. Her GP refuses to allow her in his surgery and a long succession of social workers have found her too difficult to handle. She has lost virtually all of the sympathetic social support her widowhood induced. She is becoming a social outcast. The consequent loss of self-esteem is evident. Again the loss of continuity in self-definition and the reduction in self-esteem are key features of the case.

Case 4: Graham

Graham, aged 20, was the only child of an affluent middle-class family. His mother died when he was 15 and his father, unable to cope with him, had him taken into care by the local authority. In care, Graham was introduced to soft drugs and petty crime. After leaving care, at 18, he sought hard drugs and started to steal in order to pay for them. He was caught by the police, prosecuted, and, after repeated convictions, was sentenced to imprisonment. On his release, he became increasingly out of control, reckless, and dependent on alcohol and drugs. His constant bizarre behaviour finally resulted in him being admitted to a psychiatric unit for treatment and asylum.

Graham in his calmer, more lucid moments, when controlled by psychotropic drugs, describes how he felt when he was taken into care: 'Everything changed. No longer my mother's darling. Just another kid in care. Like all the rest.' Graham emphasizes the loss of distinctiveness he experienced in the hostel, talking about the routines and the depersonalizing rituals. 'I got into the drugs so that I could make a name for myself. Be a big man, but different from the rest. Got hooked, then got caught nicking and put in the slammer. Prison was the same: everybody treated the same, no room for individuality. Institutionalized, I was.... Now I like doing things that make people realize I'm different, not just some grey shadow of a bloke. I don't want to hurt no one, just make them realize I live and breathe and walk this earth too.'

Graham typifies how important distinctiveness can be for the identity. He also shows how, in many social contexts, the search for it can cause trouble and engender other forms of threat to identity dependent upon the withdrawal of social acceptance.

Case 5: Qulsoom

Qulsoom is 11. She was born in Britain but her parents were born in Pakistan. They emigrated to Britain over fifteen years ago but Qulsoom's father has remained a strict adherent of the religious and cultural norms of Pakistan. At home, Qulsoom has to comply with the requirements of the Muslim faith and must perform in the manner expected of a young woman now eligible for marriage. At school, until now, she has been able to pursue her education in the western manner, marked only by her skin and dress. She has imbibed two systems of values and expectations. Until recently she found no difficulty in reconciling the two within herself. Each set of values had quite separate domains of operation and she kept them apart, never looking at their mutual exclusivities.

The problem has now arisen that Qulsoom, being of a marriageable age, should be withdrawn from her school, which is coeducational, prepared for marriage and kept chaste. Qulsoom is now becoming aware of very different demands being made on her by her teachers and her father: they require incompatible behaviour from her. They break the continuity of her self-definition which previously derived sustenance from both of her cultural positions. Her father demands total conformity to the role of a Muslim woman.

Qulsoom's headmistress, aware of the distress the girl is feeling, has attempted to approach the father. She has explained that it is illegal to keep Qulsoom out of school. In response, Qulsoom's father has plans to send her back to his village for immediate marriage.

Qulsoom, being so young, is different from the other cases presented. She has no ability to control what happens to her. This lack of control over changes which are being imposed upon the defining characteristics of one's identity is one aspect of threat. The continuity of Qulsoom's identity is attacked by forces which she cannot control. Perception of this loss of control can itself engender a threat to identity by initiating a loss of self-esteem. Qulsoom, for instance, feeling totally frustrated in her attempts to determine her own future, turns her anger upon herself, castigating herself for her weakness and imperfection. She points out: 'Good Muslims do not have these problems but proper British girls would not accept this.' On both counts, in terms of both cultures, she perceives the reduction in social approval and her self-esteem suffers.

This is not a book specifically about transsexualism, leprosy, alcoholism, drug abuse or culture-conflict; is is a book about what they have in common. The intention is not to go into detailed analyses of the individual cases. These examples are by no means unusual. They represent just a few case studies, that reflect a small part of the infinite variety of experiences which encapsulate threats to identity. The important thing is that they all point to the same sorts of conclusions: the need for continuity in self-definition, the vitalizing effects of distinctiveness and the crucial role of self-esteem. Moreover, they emphasize that threats to identity can only be meaningfully studied in a social context. In all cases, the structure of identity, the nature of the threat and the coping strategies deployed to deal with it, only achieve meaning when related to dominant social beliefs and cultural expectations. Leprosy may have its origin in biochemical changes and may have its immediate impact at the physical level but it becomes intelligible in terms of its effects on identity only through the meaning attributed to it by social processes. The same is true of the other sources of threat described. This means that a framework in which threat can be analysed must encompass a model of the dynamics of identity in relation to social processes and structures. Chapter 2 outlines such a model.

2 Identity and social structure

This chapter is largely devoted to describing the complex network of social and psychological processes which shape the identity of a person. Identity is treated as a dynamic social product, residing in psychological processes, which cannot be understood except in relation to its social context and historical perspective.

The model of identity will be outlined in stages focusing in turn upon each of its parts, but it is important at the end to view the framework as an integrated entity. The method of description used is akin to that which can be employed in operating a cine-camera: it can be focused upon different details in a shifting landscape. It can focus upon the fast car flashing through a panorama, it can pan behind and before the car, but it can also widen the angle of the lens to capture more of the backdrop; and, all the time, the car is moving through its surroundings and they are themselves perhaps changing, if at a less rapid rate. The car changes: losing fuel, acquiring dirt, changing occupants; its location changes; and the location itself changes. The film can record all of this. The camera operator determines where the eye and mind will rest during the ongoing story by shifts in focus. That is what will happen with the description of the proposed model of identity: the film is running, the changes across time and place recorded, but the replay can concentrate upon any spot in the record, any frame in the film, in order to pinpoint connections and grasp an understanding in depth.

The description of the model will thus focus in turn upon:

(i) the structural components of identity in time
(ii) the identity processes and the principles of their operation
(iii) the structures and processes of the social context of identity

(iv) the effects of social change upon identity

(v) the relation of identity to action.

The chapter concludes with a short discussion of the methods available in the study of identity.

Before proceeding to review the structural components of identity, it is probably worth making a small detour. The term identity has been used so far as if it were unproblematic. This is not correct. The term is highly problematic. Theorizing about identity is like traversing a battle-field. Though strewn only with the debris of unconsolidated thought rather than unexploded shells, it is no less deadly. The concept of identity is protean. As Berger *et al.* (1974) said, 'Definitions of identity vary with overall definitions of reality', and they might have added the reverse with equal assurance. At its most expansive, identity has been said to encompass 'all things a person may legitimately and reliably say about himself – his status, his name, his personality, his past life' (Klapp, 1969). At this level, identity joins terms such as character, the self-concept and personality, which are used to connote that unique syndrome of social, psychological and behavioural characteristics which differentiates one person from another.

Indeed, clear and universally applicable distinctions between such terms are difficult to maintain. Where one theorist refers to identity, another will talk about the self and yet both are seeking to understand the same fundamental processes and phenomena. The choice of term is dictated by the philosophical and methodological foundations of their particular theory. For example, the behaviourist employing factor-analytic methods on questionnaire material from large-scale surveys talks about personality; the psychoanalyst or psychodynamic theorist using single clinical case studies might be more likely to refer to the ego or identity; the symbolic interactionist might talk of the self-concept.

Perhaps more significantly, the theory evolved dictates the definition of the term. An abstract and operational definition will depend on the role it has to perform within the theory. In turn, this hinges upon why the theory is developed. In practice, this means that the same term, say identity, can be used by two different theorists and mean completely different things. For Erikson (1968), in the psychoanalytic tradition, identity is a global self-awareness achieved through crisis and sequential identifications in social relations. For McCall and Simmons (1982), from the symbolic interactionist perspective, identities are negotiated performances of the role prescriptions attached to the occupancy of social positions: as such any one person can have many identities depending upon the number of roles adopted. For Biddle (1979), from a role theory standpoint, any label applied consistently to a person may be considered an identity and it does not necessarily have to refer to a social role; so, for instance, a nickname may both create and symbolize an identity, according to him.

Such diversity in definition means that attempts at direct comparisons across theories have nightmare qualities, and meaning is masked by its cloak of words. Consequently, any effort to summarize the multitude of different theories that have been constructed about identity, the self-concept, personality or character at this point would be a difficult and potentially wasteful detour. There are many books whose primary object is to do this (for example, Bavelas, 1978; Burns, 1979; Cattell and Dreger, 1977; Fransella, 1981; Hall and Lindzey, 1978; Harré, 1976; and Holland, 1977).

Instead, the object here is to define the concept of identity through description of its structural components and dominant processes. The model of identity presented is a social psychological one. It seeks to link intrapsychic and socio-political processes and show how both are necessary in the workings of identity. The model is not particularly novel, – it comprises ideas scavenged from various traditions of thought. Its prime purpose is not to provide a reconceptualization of identity: it is to enable subsequent systematic examinations of threat and coping strategies.

The structural components of identity

The biological organism

The development of identity structures has to be seen as a process occupying a person's entire lifespan. Identity structures consequently should be examined in temporal perspective. During a lifetime they consolidate around the basic material of the biological organism. They are a product, initially, of the interaction of the biological organism with its social context; later, they become an inherent constituent of that interaction. The parameters of the biological organism, its physiological capacity, set the ultimate constraints upon the development of identity and provide the capacities necessary for the operation of identity processes. The biological organism is, therefore, seen to run through the core of identity. However, as time accumulates experience and knowledge for the individual, the biological organism comes to be a less and less sizeable proportion of identity. As other aspects of identity grow, the relative importance of the biological organism declines. This obviously does not mean that its role in executing the identity processes becomes any less important. The biological organism's contribution to the identity processes is constant, barring any trauma. The information-processing and storage systems embodied in the identity processes are dependent for their operation upon the physiological and biochemical equilibrium of the organism.

It is worth adding that the biological organism can be considered simultaneously a structure and a set of processes. The physical being dictates the content of identity not only because it provides the means of information-processing. It also has a form which has an appended social significance. The physical being can be male or female, black or white, able-bodied or disabled. Each characteristic of the physical being carries messages about its identity. The messages may be situation- or culture-specific, being decodable only in relation to a particular social system, but they are dependent upon the physical being.

The content and value dimensions

The structure of identity which is accreted around the biological organism is normally conceived of as having two planes: *the content and the value dimensions.*

The content dimension comprises the defining properties of the identity, the characteristics which the individual concerned considers actually to describe himself or herself and which, taken together as a syndrome, mark him or her as a unique person, different in psychological profile from all others. Even where many of the elements in the content dimension are shared with other people, their specific constellation and compilation will be distinctive of the individual.

Many theorists have sought to describe the content dimension of identity. They map the constituent parts of the self. The writing of James (1890), which was in turn heavily influenced by Descartes, Hume, Locke, Kant and Schopenhauer, set the scene for subsequent attempts to compartmentalize the self. James distinguished between the self as subject (I) and the self as object (me) which are merely 'discriminated aspects of the singularity of the process of experience' which comprises the 'global self'. He differentiated four further aspects of the self:

the spiritual self: entailing thinking and feeling
the material self: entailing one's material possessions
the social self: entailing reference to those individuals and groups
                   whose opinions matter
the bodily self: entailing the physical organism

James is, of course, merely listing all those features of existence which distinguish one person from the next: the way one thinks about the world; one's possessions; the social connections one values; and the organic shell one occupies. James is detailing what Allport (1955) later called the 'proprium': 'all the regions of our life that we regard as ultimately and essentially ours' (p. 38).

James considered the process of knowing or experiencing these distinguishing features of the self to be inextricably bound to the process of evaluating them (which comprises the value dimension of identity). According to James, the value of any characteristic can be understood only in relation to the person's 'pretensions'. Such pretensions are basically aspirations and expectations which mould personal criteria of success or failure. Only deficiencies in personal characteristics recognized as failing to meet pretensions have the power to harm self-esteem.

Virtually all the fundamental distinctions drawn by his successors in their descriptions of the content dimension of identity are already present in the writings of James. Largely, these focus upon a number of oppositions:

self-concept *v.* self-evaluation
self-as-object *v.* self-as-subject
social-self *v.* spiritual-self
real-self *v.* ideal-self

Different writers emphasize different aspects of these oppositions. Nevertheless, they each conjure with the idea that the self is both knower and known; evaluator and evaluated; personal and social; and actual and potential. That the self can encompass all of these states of being simultaneously could be considered an insoluble paradox; one which encourages theorists to adopt the Taoist way where contemplation of the paradox is its own answer and resolution of the paradox is unnecessary.

Such defeatism is not entirely justified. The paradoxes are not truly insoluble. The solution lies in coming to understand the social processes which establish and represent the dynamic relationship between components of identity. But this has to be done without relying on mystifying metaphors. All too frequently, having specified their paradox, writers resort to metaphor to produce an answer. Cooley (1902) represents an example. Faced with the problem of the origin of the self, Cooley replied 'self and society are twin born ... and the notion of a separate and independent ego is an illusion.' Since even twins are not born simultaneously, the analogy is misleading but his explanation of their multiple birth is even more mystifying. Cooley introduced the notion of the 'looking-glass self' to describe the development of the self-concept. People, he said, learn about themselves from others. Others act as mirrors reflecting what we are. The metaphor is doubtless elegant but it is also ultimately nonsensical: it entails an infinite regress of mirrors, with everyone acting as one for others, and yet, in truth, two mirrors facing each other can produce no image. The metaphor can do nothing more than mislead unless it is translatable into practical operations (whether social processes or not). The 'looking-glass self' only becomes meaningful ultimately if the processes whereby feedback from others is provided and subjectively interpreted are explained.

Mead (1934) attempted to fill the operational gaps left by Cooley and sought a theory to explain the distinction between 'I' and 'me' which James proposed. Mead considered that the self arises as the result of its relations to the 'generalized other'. The 'generalized other' is really a cognitive entity: the person's image of the reactions and expectations of others who are significant to him or her. Basically, Mead suggests, we learn to interpret the world as others do in order to act as expected.

Mead differentiates between 'I' and 'me' by giving them different contexts in which to operate. 'Me' is focal in exchanges involving group memberships, status, roles and other people. 'I' takes over when the person asserts himself or herself against the situation, emphasizing his or her own capacities. 'I' represents the impulsive, undisciplined, unorganized potential of the individual which is dominant at the start of life and is progressively overcome by societal constraints to produce an ever larger domain of 'me'. In this there are echoes of the Freudian assumptions that the id is translated into action only through interaction with the ego and superego, which are dominated by the reality principle which works within society's restraints. Mead, however, does not assume the existence of an unconscious. In Mead's analysis, 'me' is essentially a social construction, akin to James' 'social self'.

This distinction between social and personal identity has become central to theorizing about the self. At its simplest, the distinction is clear. Social identity is that part of the self-concept derived from group memberships, interpersonal relationships, social position and status. Personal identity is free of role or relationship determinants. Map-minded topographers of the self tend to draw diagrams to represent personal and social identity (Ruddock, 1972; Ziller, 1973; Zavalloni, 1983). Often these comprise concentric circles with personal identity at the centre labelled as the core or nucleus and various aspects of social identity surrounding it. Some make the pattern more complex by breaking social identity down into sub-identities (related specifically, for instance, to gender, religious, family, vocational, etc., roles). Hofman (1983) suggests such a model of the self. These sub-identities, according to Hofman, are arranged hierarchically in terms of their valence (the value attached), their centrality (the importance they have) and their salience (the frequency with which they are called into use). Their prominence in controlling the manifestation of self in behaviour, that is the power that each has to direct action, is dependent upon their hierarchical position. In Hofman's model it is hard to distinguish the notion of a sub-identity from the standard concept of a role. He acknowledges that sub-identities represent the subjective interpretation of the prescriptions attached to occupancy of a social role, so that a person may have as many sub-identities as there are roles available. It becomes difficult then to understand why the concept of sub-identity is imported into the system when role prescriptions would account for behaviour just as well.

More importantly, Hofman's model has a characteristic common to the majority (there are notable exceptions, e.g. Zavalloni, 1983) of those models which represent reality through concentric circles: the processes which link the circles are unspecified. There is no exposition of the way in which personal identity is operationally related to social identity. Hofman argues 'identity is a space' and seems to mean this literally. He treats it as if it were a physical entity that can be mapped two-dimensionally without any incorporation of the psychological processes that are inevitably involved. The spatial representation and the set of spatial metaphors it evokes seem to dominate the model, generating a concept of self which is as static as any geographical terrain caught at one moment in time. Metaphors all too frequently entrap the theorist rather than clarify. It would not harm psychology if the use of metaphor were banned.

The problem in specifying the processes which relate personal to social identity has led to questions about whether both actually exist. Hollis (1977) posed the problem precisely: 'The problem is to make personal identity personal and social identity identity'. In other words, it is difficult to see how personal identity can be defined except in terms of social history and context and how social identity says anything about identity which is unique to the individual, since it is merely a crystallization of a set of roles which could be occupied by any number of people. At one level, the theoretical, the existence of both personal and social identity is merely a definitional trick: an arbitrary boundary can be drawn between them for theoretical purposes and this is perfectly permissable as long as subsequently there is consistency in usage. The real question then becomes: does the theoretical distinction reflect any phenomenological reality?

There is some evidence to suggest that people really do experience both aspects of identity. Turner (1976) found that people do distinguish between times when they behaved according to the precepts of their 'true self' or 'real self' (equated with personal identity) and times when they behaved out of character or purely because of social constraints. The circumstances under which people considered themselves to be their 'real self' differ. Turner found that for some the 'real self' was deemed in control only when they acted on impulse, almost unexpectedly; for others the 'real self' was manifested when they acted out their social obligations. The distinction is there for both groups; it is what is considered 'real' which differs.

Recent work on self-consciousness and self-awareness has emphasized the experiential distinction. Fenigstein, Scheier and Buss (1975) distinguished two aspects of the experience of the self: the 'private self', whose elements are personal in focus, covert and not accessible to the scrutiny of other people, and the 'public self' whose constituents are displayed overtly and recognized as social stimuli to others. Questionnaire studies showed that there is an empirical foundation to the assertion that the dichotomy exists and that self is a combination of the two. Carver and Scheier (1981) have suggested that the values which are invoked at any one time to control action depend upon which aspect of self is being considered by the person at that moment. If the private self is central to awareness, then private values are supreme; public values take over if the public self is focal.

Though they often act in concert, these two aspects of the self can be in conflict, exerting mutually contradictory influences upon behaviour (see Scheier and Carver, 1983, for a summary). It seems that it is at times when they clash that people are most acutely aware that they have both a public and private self. At other times, the distinction is a phenomenological irrelevancy. It also seems that at times of conflict, people tend to exhibit a habitual predisposition to focus on one aspect or the other in coming to a solution. People have habits with regard to which aspect of the self they will allow to dominate. A focus on the private self is correlated with a concern for 'personal' aspects of identity (emotions, feelings, thoughts, goals, aspirations), while emphasis on the public self is closely associated with attaching importance to social aspects of identity (group memberships, social influence, social interaction patterns). In fact, Cheek and Briggs (1982) found a consistent relationship between the tendency to focus on a particular facet of the self and ratings of the importance of that facet to one's sense of identity. In any conflict, the aspect of self habitually considered more important will surface to structure behaviour. In a sense, the conflict reveals the real self because it unveils the facet of self which is primary. This may be why McCall (1977) argues that personal identity can only be revealed in the context of moral decisions, because in them values have to be exposed, and values are the cornerstone of presuppositions about the self.

The data on self-awareness all point to the fact that people can distinguish personal from social identity and that the momentary dominance of one or the other will shape behaviour. This, however, begs the question of the origins of personal identity. The formulations which segment identity like a cake cut into portions never explain the processes which produce a distinctive entity like personal identity. What is really required is a theory of the development of personal identity across time. It is known that at a single moment in time personal and social identity can be separated: the person experiences them as different. The real question is whether developmentally they are separate or whether personal identity is some product of social identity. It could be argued that personal and social identity are merely different points in the process of development.

The person actively accommodates to and assimilates conceptions of the self provided by the social world. Social roles provide a structure for self-description and are hemmed by social values which generate self-evaluation. The individual moves through a sequence of social roles, adopting the social identity appropriate to each sequentially, and sometimes simultaneously, layering them one on top of another. Personal identity could be considered the relatively permanent residue of each assimilation to and accommodation of a social identity. It is what remains when the exigencies of social context that demand acceptance of a particular social identity fade. To this extent it is autonomous of immediate social events but at root fundamentally dependent on them.

Breakwell (1983a) argues that this developmental conception of personal identity does not imply any crude social determinism. There are too many contradictions between social roles and the ideologies appended to them for their effects to be anything but subject to the active interpretation of the individual concerned. Perception of social pressures and adaptation to them selective, and it is an active process. Personal identity may be said to be the residual product of this active process but it is also an inherent part of the process itself; even the principles of selection which guide adaptation are the consequences of past experiences. In real time, the evolution of identity entails this continual and truly dialectical relationship between personal and social identity:

> Current personal identity is the product of the interaction of all past personal identities with all past and present social identities. But the reverse is also true: current social identities are the product of the interactions of all past social identities with all past and current personal identities. (Breakwell, 1983a, p. 12)

This leads to the conclusion that the content dimension actually includes both characteristics which have been considered in the past by theorists to be the domain of social identity (roles, group memberships, etc.) and those which have been regarded as the preserve of personal identity (values, motives, emotions, attitudes, causal schemata in attributional style, and personal constructs). The content dimension ignores the distinction between the elements of what have been arbitrarily labelled personal and social identity in the past because it is assumed that the content dimension is continually present across time and is cumulative. Since the social roles of yesterday are the progenitors of the personal attitudes of today, maintenance of the strict dichotomy of personal and social identity becomes a misleading detour. The content dimension of the structure of identity grows as the person passes through time and the central question concerns the organization of its constituent parts rather than whether they fall into two sorts of identity.

The structure of identity should not be confused with its contents. The actual contents of identity have to be distinguished from the structural properties of their organization. The actual contents of an identity are not static. What is more, the organization of the content dimension should not be seen as static. None of the theorists mentioned assume them to be. The components will shift in relation to each other according to the social context within which the identity is situated. Various suggestions have been made about the organization of the content dimension by theorists (for instance, Liebkind, 1984). But two useful ways of characterizing the organization are in terms of (a) the tightness or looseness of the relations between the components, and (b) the relative salience or centrality of each component. Any constellation of contents can be described in these terms.

There is considerable evidence from various sources (ranging from Kelly, 1955 to Zavalloni, 1983) that people differ with respect to the level of connectedness between components of their self-description or definition. Some have a neat hierarchical arrangement of constituents; others seem to aspire to an identity which resides in a chaos of defining characteristics. As yet, there is minimal evidence as to why people should vary in this way. Variations in the salience or centrality of specific components of the content dimension of identity are more explicable. Salience seems to be highly situation-specific. What is a central component of self-definition in one context at one time will be irrelevant in another. For instance, Waddell and Cairns (1986) examined the effects of situations on the salience of ethnopolitical components of identity in Northern Ireland. For the Catholics studied, situations involving Irish and Anglo-Irish matters elicited prominence of feelings of Irishness. Situations involving the British or 'The Troubles' produced a marked salience of British identifications amongst the Protestants. This situation-specific saliency becomes extremely important when considering the relationship between identity and action later. Here it is sufficient to put up a marker as to the importance of the connections of elements and their relative salience to the model of the structure of identity. To some extent, the organization of the content dimension will depend upon its counterpart, the value dimension.

The value dimension is the second facet of the structure of identity. Each element in the content dimension will have a value attached to it, whether positive or negative, which is attributed to it on the basis of social beliefs and values in interaction with previously established personal value codes. This process of establishing the value of the constituents of identity is considered at some length on p. 98. But it is vital to establish here that no component has a constant value. The values attributed to the self-defining characteristics are subject to perpetual revision, according to social circumstance, which means that the overall value of the individual's identity is in a state of flux.

On both counts, content and value, the identity structure is seen as fluid, dynamic, and responsive to its social context in a way which, it will be seem on p. 98, it purposive. There should be no assumption that the identity is without agency, a mere passive recipient of inputs, just because its meaning is determined by social processes.

Figure 1 depicts the growth of identity across time from its origin in the interaction of the biological organism with social context. The content and value dimension are depicted as expanding over the lifespan, as experiences in the social world contribute to the identity structure. However, it should not be assumed that expansion can necessarily be equated with greater complexity or elaboration in the organization of the content of identity. Many models of cognitive development define maturation as the movement towards higher levels of differentation and the hierarchical arrangement of function (for instance, all those theories deriving from the works of Piaget, – see Piaget and Inhelder, 1966). It may be inappropriate to assume that this is the course of the maturation of identity.

It seems unnecessary to assume any intrinsic drive towards greater complexity or differentiation on the content dimension, let alone the value dimension. Experiences and life-demands may impose a broader and more varied range of content characteristics upon some people but this is not inevitable. Some people have a very simple structure to the content dimension and an even simpler arrangement on the value dimension. It would be possible, as part of a tautological definitional trick, to argue that such people have an immature identity structure, regardless of their age. This seems rather pointless. There is no implication here that possessing an identity which is finely differentiated is in any sense better than the simpler structures; calling one mature and the other not consequently seems to carry too many evaluative overtones.

It is enough to say that the content and value dimensions of the identity structure develop according to experience. Where the range of experiences is restricted, development will be limited and may be halted. This does not mean that the identity then becomes static; identity processes continue but, because they are transmogrifying inputs which are constant, their capacity to modify the structure of identity is minimal. Even under these circumstances, where perhaps changes in the external environment cease, changes in the identity structure may come about as a consequence of relationships between elements on the content dimension being reworked. The identity continues to be a dynamic organism even where it is in a state of equilibrium.

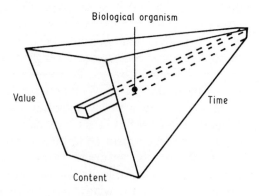

Figure 1   *The structure of identity*

Temporal frame

In describing the growth of identity across time, the nature of time itself needs to be considered. Luckmann (1983) distinguished three kinds of time: *inner time, intersubjective time,* and *biographical time.* The person experiences *inner time* as duration; it is not homogeneous and not a measurable object in space. Inner time dances to the tune of cognitive rhythms; it is the subjective estimate of how long it takes to move from one state of being to the next. The grandfather clock against the wall can tick the passage of a minute while inner time measures the passing of an era. *Intersubjective time* is experienced as the synchronization of face-to-face social interaction. By sharing experiences with others, the interactants come close to achieving a consensual appreciation of their conjoint movement through time. Luckmann suggests that, through reciprocal mirroring, two body-bound inner times are synchronized into intersubjective time and that such synchronization is necessary for effective communication in all social interaction. *Biographical time* is experienced as major spans of meaning, constructed and reconstructed across the entire course of life. The passage of biographical time is presumably marked by the chunking of life experiences into groups which cohere as meaningful entities and which, once passed, represent transitions of importance. The individual's sense of biographical time, Luckmann argues, generates biographical schemes which contain his or her subjective personal history.

Biographical schemes contain a sequential narrative core: the stories that people choose to tell about their lives to themselves which infuse current events with meaning and biographical significance. Biographical schemes not only impose responsibility for actions of the past but also generate objectives for the future. They encompass trajectories for new action, outlining purposes which are compatible with those perceived to have led to the present position.

Luckmann's analysis is valuable because it emphasizes that time is not an objective chronological dimension in the development of identity. Identity development takes place in the arena of subjective temporality. Identity content and value dimensions are themselves instrumental in shaping the perception of time; especially with respect to biographical time, the meaning of which they will dictate in the short term but which will, in turn, be instrumental in determining their structure in the longer run. The fact is that identity which develops through subjective time will also be a fundamental determinant of that subjective temporality.

The weaknesses in Luckmann's analysis of time seem to lie on two fronts. First, he fails to specify the relationships between inner, inter-subjective, and biographical time. This is unfortunate since their inter-action is clearly of importance to any appreciation of the development of identity. Secondly, he largely ignores the existence of time inde-pendent of the individual's construction of it. This is not surprising, given his phenomenological stance towards the construction of reality (Berger and Luckmann, 1975).

Yet, even if chronological time can be ignored, and this is unlikely since the individual will experience biological changes consequent upon its passage, what might be called *social time* needs to be considered. Social time is more than just the reification of inter-subjective time achieved in social interaction, though such exchanges may represent the media through which the individual comes to learn of the passage of social time. Social time is measured in units of meaningful social change. Social time represents a temporal landscape which records significant social events: the start and finish of a war; a momentous technological revolution; changes in legislation; and so on.

Clearly, what happens to be deemed significant will depend upon the interests and purposes of those groups or social categories which have enough power to impose their interpretation of current and past events upon others. This means that, as power relations change, the patterning of social time will be modified. The new sources of power often rewrite the meaning of some events, invent others and conveniently forget even more. Stalin is said to have developed this into an art form. So the shape of social time can be altered. It is important to recognize that this alteration of the past will have implica-tions for both the present and the future: current events take on new meanings in the light of reconstructed pasts and potential events gain different probabilities of actual occurrence.

The flexibility of social time has direct and indirect consequences for the growth of identity. Social reconstruction of the past will modify both the meaning of the existing content of identity and has the potential to transform its value. It may also require the individual to accept new elements of content with their component values. For instance, the Cultural Revolution in China demanded not only the reinterpretation of history, it required individuals to remember their part in it differently and to recant values and beliefs attached to the old order. The dynamics of the social reconstruction of time are considered further on p. 27, in the examination of the relationship between social context and identity development.

The identity processes and the principles of their operation

It is time to turn from looking at identity as a structure whose parts can be dismantled and examined in terms of their form and component materials. It is time to look at identity as a set of processes operating in a principled manner. Just as a computer can be described in terms of its microchip network and in terms of the programmes which put that network to use, so identity can be described in terms of structurral properties and process capacities.

Identity processes

Models of identity, while explicit about its structure, often leave its processes to be inferred or, if they specify processes, fail to delineate the principles which predict their operation. Of course, there are marked exceptions – for instance, Freud. In the interests of parsimony, in synthesizing these implicit statements about processes in order to generate an integrative model of identity, it will be argued that there are two: (a) the process of assimilation and accommodation and (b) the process of evaluation. Most models of identity assume the existence of these processes at some level.

Assimilation and *accommodation*, even though they are distinguishable, are treated as components of the same process, because they are closely interdependent. Assimilation refers to the absorption of new components into the identity structure; accommodation refers to the adjustment which occurs in the existing structure so as to find a place into which to fit the new elements. The process of *evaluation* entails the allocation of meaning and value to identity content both new and old. It is undoubtedly true that both processes could be further broken down into the sub-processes which comprise them, so that one might wish to assert that accommodation entails the rearrangement of salience and centrality hierarchies in the structure of identity. Assimilation would comprise subroutines of memory and general information-processing. Evaluation may require processes of comparison which establish subjective indices of relative worth for potential additions to identity. Many fo these sub-components are examined later when coping strategies for dealing with threat are considered. The coping strategies depend for their form upon the composition of the identity processes.

The two processes do not operate independently of each other. They interact and act simultaneously to change the content and value dimensions of identity. The process of evaluation will influence what is assimilated and the form of accommodation. However, the processes of assimilation and accommodation will establish the values incorporated into identity and will, consequently, erect the criteria of worth against which evaluation must take place. The interplay of both processes across time will produce the content and value dimensions of identity. Just as the structure of identity must be seen to exist in subjective and social time, so must the processes of identity. However, unlike the structure of identity, these processes do not change across time. Their outcomes may change but they themselves do not.

Identity principles

It is debatable whether the principles which underlie these two processes are constant (see the final chapter where their temporal and cultural specificity is discussed). These principles represent the fundamental codes which guide the processes. Basically, the principles specify the end states which are desirable for identity. The operation of the processes of assimilation–accommodation and evaluation can be predicted from these principles. It is possible to arrive at a list of principles which probably guide identity processes on the basis of various studies which have examined how people change their self-definition and self-evaluation. These studies have been founded on varied methods (ranging from introspection, James, 1890, to observation, Kratochwill *et al.*, 1984; psychoanalysis, Fromm, 1939, to laboratory experimentation, Gergen, 1968) but the conclusions seem reasonably congruent. Three prime principles are evident: the two identity processes work to produce uniqueness or distinctiveness for the person; continuity across time and situation; and a feeling of personal worth or social value. In the interests of brevity, these principles are referred to below as distinctiveness, continuity and self-esteem, but the labels are taken to connote all aspects of the three principles.

Past research (Gordon and Gergen, 1968, review both the classical and empirical studies) has shown that all three principles will guide the identity processes. However, there is little known about how these three relate to each other. For instance, it is obvious that there may be occasions when they would be in conflict in their demands on the identity processes: distinctiveness requiring one type of assimilation, continuity another, and self-esteem, perhaps, resisting any. For instance, an individual might have thought of herself for twenty-five years as antipathetic to all sports, convincing herself that she has two left feet and no eye–hand co-ordination whatsoever. One day, she is invited to a social event where a tennis racquet is pushed into her hands and she is obliged to knock the ball about. She finds, to her amazement, that she can play well, better than any of her friends. Her talent is remarkable to them and they start to invent suitably super-cilious nicknames to label her ability. After two or three successful sunny summer afternoons, she has to admit her performance is no chance event. Continuity of the old self-image of ineptitude would indicate the new information about her should be discounted; distinc-tiveness within her peer group calls for a re-appraisal and shift in image. The desire for self-esteem need not precipitate either choice because she was happy with her old image but the new one would in no way hamper self-esteem.

The question in such a situation of conflict is: which principle has priority? In the last resort the question can only be answered empirically on each occasion. However, it seems eminently reasonable, given the dynamic quality of identity itself, to assume that there will be no constant pecking order. The principles will achieve priority according to the social context. Their salience is particularly influenced by intergroup context. For instance, the desire for intrapersonal and intergroup differentiation (i.e. accentuated distinctiveness) is dependent upon the perceived nature of the relationships between the comparitors, whether they be individuals (Festinger, 1957) or groups (Tajfel, 1978). Changes in salience may account for the low correlations between traditional indices of personality traits with behaviour across situations (Mischel, 1968; Argyle, 1976). Where the distinctiveness principle has salience, elements of the content dimension of identity which achieve distinctiveness in the specific situation will dictate action. Where self-esteem dominates, other elements of identity may dictate action. The actual contents of identity do not have to change in order to explain the personality × situation = behaviour equation; only the salience of those principles which call them into play needs to change. Much of the evidence presented later on the effects of threats to identity shows how these principles wax and wane according to situational demands.

It is worth stating explicitly that these three principles may not be the only ones which guide the processes of identity. For instance, Apter (1983) has suggested that the desire for autonomy may be of equal importance in directing identity work. The purpose here is not to provide an exhaustive list but to cull from previous work those principles about which there seems to be considerable agreement, if not total consensus. It may be necessary to include other principles on the basis of future work. In the final chapter, the issue of the cultural, situational and developmental specificity of these principles is considered in an attempt to elaborate the framework presented here.

In considering the processes of identity, besides specifying the principles of their operation, it is also necessary to consider what cognitive abilities are required for them to operate. It is necessary to argue that cognitive processes (for example, memory and learning) are an integral part of identity processes but that they are, nevertheless, theoretically distinct. Cognitive processes required for identity processes would include: memory, learning, consciousness and, probably, organized construal. The importance of cognitive processes to identity is most evident in their absence. For instance, without memory the whole process of assimilation–accommodation takes place in a vacuum; it will continue but it has no grounding and anything it generates is lost after a while. In fact, Kihlstrom and Cantor (1984) regard the self-concept as nothing more than a system of social memory. The erosion of memory which often accompanies ageing is a central plank in the explanation of identity changes in the elderly (Rabbitt, 1985). It seems that greater information is required on the way cognitive abilities relate to identity development; an issue considered in the final chapter.

From cognitive developmental psychology it is already possible to say that cognitive deveopment parallels changes in social understanding (not least in the conception of morality, Lickona, 1976; Weinreich-Haste and Locke, 1983) and, during early infancy, in the conception of the self–other dichotomy (Piaget and Inhelder, 1966). It seems plausible that these connections are maintained throughout the lifespan: growing cognitive powers facilitating the processes of assimilation–accommodation and evaluation. If this is correct, it may be the case that the manner of assimilation–accommodation will alter during the life-span, becoming more differentiated and organized as cognitive development occurs. It may also be true that the process of evaluation would shift during development from concern with largely concrete manifestations of value to a focus upon non-material or ideologically dictated values (Rokeach, 1978). This would mean that the potential content of identity would be valued against different types of criteria of worth as the person develops. In turn, this would result in different contents being assimilated at each stage of cognitive development. As a child, the person assimilates new identity contents which lead to self-esteem measured in concrete terms; as an adult, self-esteem may be achieved through non-material advantages gained by assimilating new identity contents. Basically, cognitive development allows the processes of identity to move from concern with things to concern with ideas. Indeed, a certain level of cognitive complexity is required before it is possible to assume that the identity processes can work at all. For

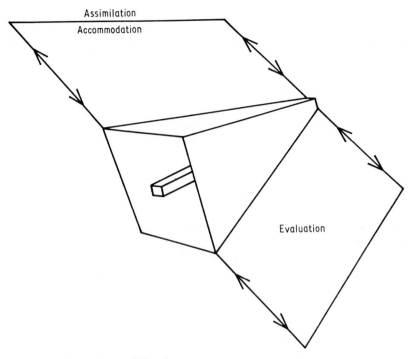

Figure 2 *The processes of identity*

instance, the notion of evaluation requires a certain level of conservation in the Piagetian sense, even at the very concrete level.

The relation of cognitive processes to identity processes requires considerable conceptual clarification before empirical studies would prove fruitful. It certainly seems that the level of cognitive development will affect both the processes of identity themselves and, potentially, the principles guiding their operation. At the moment, for instance, it is impossible to say whether the child has the same principles directing identity processes as the adult. Assimilation–accommodation and evaluation may be constant processes across the lifespan but the raw material with which they operate and the principles which guide them may alter during that lifespan as a consequence of cognitive development. Figure 2 depicts these identity processes in relation to the identity structure.

Structures and processes in the social context of identity

Thus far the focus has been upon the intra-psychic dynamics of the individual to establish an outline of the structure and processes of identity. It is now appropriate to broaden the camera angle to examine in a very simple manner the *social context of identity*. This analysis is founded upon the premise that the social world exists independently of any one individual. It is the ever-changing product of a history of interpersonal and intergroup interactions and their relationship to the physical properties of the world. Clearly, each individual has only a subjective and partial appreciation of the social world but it exists in its entirety outside the individual's consciousness of it. Nevertheless, in discussing identity dynamics it has to be accepted that it is the subjective knowledge of the social world which amtters, not the remainder which is unknown. Although it is then necessary to add a quick and important caveat: the influence of the as-yet-unknown may modify the subjective experience so that the individual becomes ready to recognize it and react to it. The apparent dichotomy between what might be called the objective and subjective social worlds is illusory. They are actually mutually dependent in so far as individual under-standing only develops in social context and that social context is historically a product of the action and thought of innumerable individuals.

Identity as social product

The assertion that identity is the product of the interaction of the individual with influences in the physical and social world is not new. Phenomenological idealist and historical materialist philosophies both describe identity as a social product even though they do focus on quite different social processes in its production: the former on social interaction with other individuals and the latter on influencing con-straints emanating from the macro-social structure.

In his theory of self-knowledge, Hegel (1807) maintained that it is through practical activity that a person 'acquires a mind of his own'. By transforming things in the external world, the person gains self-aware-ness. By observing the changes wrought, the actor achieves some appreciation of his or her own powers and grows to characterize the self in terms of these creations. Objects personalized by the process of interaction are stamped with the mark of the actor. Nor is this process restricted to physical objects, social objects – other people – are also the sounding boards for self-knowledge. People, however, are not mani-pulable like physical objects, according to Hegel. From active involve-ment with others, individuals come to know that they have percep-tions, cognitions, emotions, and intentionality. In recognizing this, the individual comes to understand that other people must see himself or herself as possessing these qualities, too. This appreciation of the mutuality of experience is at the heart of self-consciousness. The person gains self-consciousness by coming to understand how others perceive him or her. Self-consciousness is not, however, any simple passive mirroring of what others see in oneself. The process is dynamic and unending: the very act of recognizing what the other perceives then alters that which is to be perceived. This is the start of the well-known hermeneutical circle with the contributions of both parties to the interaction being transformed by reflection.

Of course, the work of Mead (1934) and Cooley (1902) and, subsequently, the symbolic interactionist school flows from Hegel's propositions. It is worth saying that it shares an important characteristic with that of Hegel. In Hegel's system, self-knowledge is not subject to external or objective validation. The individual stands alone in determining whether the self-knowledge is accurate or not. However, Hegel suggests that inappropriate conclusions about the self are rapidly abandoned because continued interaction with the object, physical or social, which generated them, would point to their internal contradictions (c.f. Kelly's personal construct theory, 1955). Solution of such internal contradictions is said to be the fulcrum of change and development in the self from an undifferentiated whole to a highly differentiated system. Differentiation, equated with maturity, is achieved through a succession of successful navigations of experienced contradictions. Contradictions are overcome by gaining greater knowledge of the object which is their source and by reflection upon that knowledge. Contradictions are deemed practical dilemmas remediable if new information and insight can be achieved. Maturity of self can only be achieved where both active involvement with the social world and personal reflection are feasible. It is a pity that most subsequent psychological theories of self-knowledge, as Markova (1984) has pointed out, do not encompass both aspects of the resolution of contradictions. Mostly, they focus on self-reflection rather than on practical involvement. In examining how people cope with threats to identity later, both tactics are seen to be used in various forms (e.g. reflection being involved in the intrapsychic strategies and involvement in the interpersonal and group strategies).

Hegel, of course, did not specify the nature of the impact of social structure *per se* upon self-knowledge derived in this way. The *traditional symbolic interactionist* framework has also ignored social structure (McCall and Simmons, 1982). It argues that the self is a product of society and in turn a prime determiner of behaviour but the important aspect of society is seen to be the person's interaction with others. Together, interactants construct a meaningful social reality for themselves. Some theorists in roughly this tradition (Gergen, 1982) would argue that social 'reality' is no more than an imposition by individual actors upon inchoate experience and that social structure is merely a fiction of linguistic usage rather than an underlying fact. Shotter (1985) agrees that 'reality is constituted for us by the ways in which we render our activities accountable to one another in our daily lives'. Selfhood, in Shotter's terms, is achieved via this process of social accountability. Gergen (1984a) goes so far as to say that identity is a totally fluid product of moment-by-moment interaction. It exists only in talk, the act of communicating itself to another, and has no existence outside of this. Gergen even queries the memory of self-defining characteristics outside of interaction. It can be seen, then, that against this background the notion that social structure shapes identity would not be readily accepted. Gergen and Davis (1985), in emphasizing the role of interaction, assert that the person possesses agency, the power to create a social being which is not solely the product of social influence processes. Social structure, if it exists, would represent an obdurate social patterning antithetical to the symbolic interactionist belief in the fluidity and constructed character of social experience. Traditionally, symbolic interactionism (Blumer, 1969) has located the ultimate sources of interaction outcomes in interpretative, definitional processes of virtually limitless potential. The existence of a real social structure would clearly curtail the freedom of definitional processes to pattern social life. The introduction of social structure into a theory of identity violates the humanistic emphasis upon the autonomy and the creativity of humanity. Yet, recently, Stryker (1980, 1984) has attempted to do just this.

Stryker has elaborated what he calls an 'emerged structural symbolic interactionist framework'. For him, identities are derived from role positions, so a person can have numerous identities which are arranged hierarchically in terms of salience. Commitment to the role dictates the salience attached to the identity it confers and salience subsequently shapes role performance. He imports large-scale social structural phenomena to explain variations in level of commitment. Social structure, he believes, is manifest in extant lines of differentiation within a society which predispose people who share particular concerns to interact in particular situations and bring to bear particular interactional skills and resources. *Interactional possibilities are thus constrained by social structure.* Since commitment to a role is measured in terms of the important interactional relationships which rely on it, any factor controlling relationships has the power to control commitment. Consequently, through shaping relationships, social structure can be said to shape commitment and thereby the salience of any particular identity in the self-concept.

Clearly, this is a valuable attempt to introduce the effects of social structure into an overall theoretical framework which is highly suspicious of it. For the *historical materialists,* the position is strangely reversed: suspicions being targeted at the individual identity rather than the social structure. Indeed, the historical materialist analysis, typified in Marxist theory, markedly omitted to detail the dialectic between the individual and the social order, whereby the former is socially constructed under specific historical conditions. Sartre (1962, p. 56) turned to existenialism having found that 'Marxism lacks any hierarchy of mediations which would permit it to grasp the process which produces the person and his product inside class and within a given society at a given historical moment'. Since 1957, when Sartre made this criticism, the materialist analysis has been pushed towards the recognition of the central significance of gender relations and of the family in the construction of an individual's consciousness and identity largely by feminist theory (Leonard, 1984). This, in turn, has led to a full-blooded attempt to provide a developed theory of the individual within the materialist analysis.

Leonard (1984) put forward three basic propositions on which a materialist understanding of the individual personality should be founded. Firstly, he argues, human beings are produced by the social relations characteristic of a specific social formation at a particular point in history (acknowledging that this has to work upon a given biological base). Such social relations are focused on economic production and social reproduction, contain contradictions and are based upon class, gender and ethnic domination: 'The individual's life experience and personality structure is determined, in short, by a unique biography situated within a specific set of class, gender and ethnic relations' (Leonard, 1984, p. 109).

Secondly, he proposes that the three major social determinants of personality are *the economy, the family* and *the state. The economy* is a fundamental influence on personality in that capitalist accumulation, and replacement of the labour force on which it relies, requires that the individual engages in socially necessary labour and in desired levels of commodity consumption. Thus, the nature of a person's labour, whether waged or domestic; the level of material sustenance it provides; and the opportunities for time to spend on the development of personal capacities it affords; besides the social value placed upon the consumption of commodities, shape the individual's self-concept and self-needs.

The family household is deemed a significant determinant of individual personality at two levels: it is the actual location in which people are socialized and it provides the core for the 'ideology of familialism', an ideology lauding the value of the nuclear family, the subordination of children and the nurturance of women. Any particular family may be imperfectly representative of this ideological ideal; each has its own idiosyncratic culture and customs which determine the evolution of individuals inside. Within the family, the personality is structured through the individual's resistance and submission to established age and gender hierarchies; family practices which prepare the person for appropriate labour; and those which reflect wider ideologies supporting the status quo and preparing the individual for class or gender subordination.

The third social determinant of personality is *the state*. The immediacy of the impact of the state upon a person's identity will be mediated by his or her class, gender and ethnicity: those with least power being most affected by state intervention. State practices intervene in the genesis of individual identity in a series of ways. They define what is normal and deviant and 'treat' the latter in prisons, schools, psychiatric institutions, and hospitals, not to mention ghettos. They reinforce extant hierarchies of power across age, sex, class and ethnic distinctions by fostering attitudes and skills that fit people to their alloted places. They establish and enforce standards of material subsistence, through social security services, which severely restrict the capacity of the poorest to develop their personal powers fully. They actively discriminate against or stigmatize some social strata or groups and indirectly shape the self-evaluations of their members. Such discrimination is merely part of the overall practices employed to propagate and disseminate the ideology and world view of the dominant societal groups.

The state, family and the economy each have a role to play in generating the individual's identity and their influence is modulated by the social position, in terms of class, gender, ethnicity and age of the person concerned.

The third proposition Leonard makes is that the individual is connected to the social world through two related experiences: of material relations and of ideology, the former being impregnated with the latter. The individual's material activities and exchanges at work, in the family, in the community and with the state, are penetrated by meanings derived from the ideologies through which their class, gender or ethnic group maintains its coherence and makes sense of its social position, legitimating either dominance or resistance to domination. The individual internalizes a picture of his or her self generated from the ideologies transmitted during interaction with others. This process of internalization is reminiscent of symbolic interactionist notions. It is paralleled by the process of identification. Leonard defines identification as a mechanism whereby the individual 'sees' herself or himself in another person. Alignments of this sort presumably generate emulation and provide the subject of identification with power to mould the actions, thoughts and feelings of the individual.

Internalization of the dominant belief systems appropriate to one's class, gender, age and ethnic group and identification with appropriate role models are accompanied by a fair amount of repression. Repression, Leonard says, is an unconscious mechanism which causes the individual to renounce drives and attributes, experienced as pleasurable, in order to comply with social prohibitions which have been internalized. Such socially unwanted psychic urges are redirected into acceptable forms.

It is worth noting here that although Leonard is using words associated with psychoanalytic concepts, in his theory they have a quite different definition. It is, however, interesting that a materialist conception of personality should accept the notion of the unconscious. In fact, this concept is given an even greater part to play where the individual's resistance to social programming is concerned.

The materialist understanding of the individual is founded upon the assumption of the dialectic between the individual and the social order. On the one hand, the individual is moulded, inculcated and penetrated by the social order, its institutions and ideologies. On the other hand, the individual will engage in avoidance of, resistance to, and dissent against the social order. The individual's potential for resistance arises because there are contradictions within and between the social institutions (the economy, the family and the state) which seek to exert control. Freedom for the individual lies at the interstices of these contradictions.

Resistance, according to Leonard, relies upon the individual's contradictory consciousness; unconscious resistance; the development of individual capacities and participation in collective action. Contradictory consciousness arises from the contradictions within ideologies and the struggle between ideologies resulting from the different material interests of different classes and groups. Subordinated individuals become aware of the disparity between dominant ideological conceptions and the actual material circumstances of their own lives and this gives rise to contradictory consciousness which results in acts of deviance.

The person's protest against the social order takes the form of rejection of its values and non-compliance with its rules. Unconscious resistance occurs at the psychological level and is a reaction against repression. The result is internal conflict and, according to Leonard, a common symptom is mental illness.

Leonard claims that the differential class distribution of types of mental illness across socio-economic classes may be explained on this basis. So, the middle class has more incidence of neurosis 'because of the necessarily strong superego development required of an oppressing and exploiting class' (p. 117). Psychosis is the outcome of unconscious resistance in the working class because it entails the construction of an alternative reality which is sheer escapism.

Such descriptions of mental illness are, of course, highly simplistic and the facts are open to a quite different interpretation. For instance, the demographic pattern could be accounted for by discriminating practices in diagnosis and treatment. There is evidence that doctors seeing the same symptoms in two patients will attribute them to neurosis in the case of the middle-class person and to psychosis in a person from the working class (Fielding and Evered, 1980). Alternatively, it may be that the middle class are more likely to seek help for minor ailments. On this, Leonard's conclusions are rather extravagant, given the plethora of other possible interpretations, and need to be treated with caution.

According to Leonard, intrapsychic forms of resistance can be accompanied by more objective efforts. By seeking to develop various skills and knowledge, the individual may develop personality dimensions not specified by the social order. The propagation of personal capacities is seen as a hedge against the dehumanizing effects of alienating wage-labour. Of course, in the materialist tradition, the major means of resisting social controls is seen to be through participation in collective action. Working in unison with others to bring about social change not only gives the individual a public voice, it also has the potential to revise the self-conception to harmonize with the ideology and claims of the collectivity.

Contradictions and free will

Both Hegel and Leonard ultimately argue that identity is both a social product and a social process. Also, they both emphasize the vital role *contradictions* have to play in the evolution of identity. For Hegel they ensure that self-knowledge is validated. For Leonard they insure against sheer social determinism: contradictions give the individual the opportunity to make choices. Identity is born of dialectic within both models and this represents their great strength.

Talk of identity as a social product inevitably leads to the issue of free will. If behaviour is a function of personality and the constraints imposed in the situation in which it occurs and personality is, in turn, a social product, does the individual have any real freedom of action? This is an ageing debate (see Mischel, 1977, for instance). A venerable solution was posed by James (1890) who proffered what he called a weak form of determinism: seen in historical perspective, the behaviour of the moment is understood to have been determined and the individual has no latitude for choice; seen at the moment of action, the behaviour cannot be 'said to be determined by immediate situational constraints. More recently, Harré (1979), from a humanistic perspective, argued that people have 'relative autonomy'. People have the power to shift from 'acting according to one principle, impulse, sentiment or whatever, to acting according to another, whatever the original principle might be' (Harré, 1979, p. 253). He fails to explain how they come to move from one principle to another. A non-explanation would be to claim that this potential was some 'emergent property of consciousness' which appears spontaneously and without antecedents. More realistically, such moves would have to be explained in terms of the operation of complex conceptual processes which are themselves a product of experience (Harré, 1984). If this is correct, the doctrine of 'relative autonomy', that of weak determinism, and the dialectical approach have much in common. All offer the blossoming identity some freedom in the direction of action, even though it is itself socially prefabricated.

A framework for understanding the social context of identity

After reviewing the recent symbolic interactionist and matieralist perspectives on identity as a social product, in order to understand the genesis of threats and the structure of coping strategies, it seems as though it might be useful to have some simple outline of the characteristics of the social context. This outline is in no way meant to represent an attempt to produce a theory of the social system. It is purely used as a heuristic device to gain leverage on how identities are formed and defended.

The social context of identity can be schematically represented in terms of two dimensions: one concerning structure; the other, process.

Structurally, the social context of identity can be said to be comprised of interpersonal networks, group memberships, and intergroup relationships. It would be possible to erect a taxonomy of types of interpersonal networks, groups and group memberships, and inter-group relationships but at this point it is unnecessary. It is sufficient to say that each individual is located within this matrix of networks, memberships and relationships. The content of identity will be assimilated from these structures in the social context. They each provide roles for the individual to adopt. They each generate systems of belief and value, which specify acceptable behaviours and attitudes. By establishing codes of value and morality, they also provide the criteria against which the evaluation process in identity must make its comparisons.

There are two things about the structure of the social context which need to be clarified. The first concerns the use of the term 'group'. The notion of social groups as a unit of analysis has been largely restricted to use by social psychologists over the last forty years. Sociologists prefer to talk about what are perceived as larger-scale social categories: gender, socio-economic class, ethnicity (see, for instance, Leonard's 1984 exposition). The distinctions between human groups and social categories have been expertly discussed elsewhere (for instance, Tajfel, 1981a). For the purposes of the present discussion they appear relatively unimportant. The functions which they serve in terms of identity can be seen as similar in so far as both generate role prescrip-tions and belief systems imbued with value. Nevertheless, it is also true to say that social categories may prove more influential in identity development since they have historical continuity and social signifi-cance not equalled by many smaller-scale groups. Indeed, many small groups are predicated upon social category dynamics. This argument indicates the need to include social categories, such as gender, class and race, as structural components of the social context of identity. It also emphasizes the second point about structure which needs clarifica-tion: the structural components of the social context do not exist independently. It may be nearer the truth to say that they are nested within one another. Intergroup relations shape group boundaries and membership; group or social category memberships predispose the creation of certain interpersonal networks. Moreover, the process of influence is not unidirectional: interpersonal networks may remodel group structure. The relationships between the components in the structure of the social context are dialectical.

At this point it is worth emphasizing that this description of the social context is concerned with the types of component structures which comprise it, rather than the complex superordinate structure which their interconnection creates. That particular elaboration of the framework is not possible in this volume. However, it is important to state that the types of component structures differ in their relative power, particularly in their ability to dominate the social influence processes which generate the second dimension of the social context.

Though these types of component structures characterize the social context throughout time, the substantive incarnations of each obviously differ across history. For instance, specific groups which existed a century ago may now only linger on in what remains of their impact upon individual identities and the ideologies embodied in culture. Alternatively, a particular constellation of people may come together for the first time today to become an interpersonal network; interpersonal networks *per se* have always existed, but this specific one is new. This means that although the social context is perennially comprised of these types of structure, it can change its appearance. The character and purposes of the particular groups may differ, but the existence of groups *per se* is a constant. When social change occurs, it can, therefore, be manifested at one of two levels: firstly, it can comprise the formation or dissolution of interpersonal networks and groups; secondly, it may consist of a reorganization of the power relationship between existing networks and groups. Such social change clearly has ramifications at the level of social process.

The second dimension of the social context consists of *the process of social influence*. While the structure of the social context represents its material existence, the process generates its ideological substance. Interpersonal networks and groups comprising the structure of the social context of identity manipulate their relative positions through attempts at influence. Each group arrives at an interpretation of reality which suits its own interests and intentions and then it tries to convert other individuals or groups to its view.

The process of social influence finds expression in many forms of activity (education, persuasion, coercion, propaganda, polemic and rhetoric, for instance) and the techniques are based on various assumptions about what will induce change (reward-punishment; rationality with informed argument, etc.). All conspire to create a multifaceted ideological context for identity development.

The social context contains many vying ideologies: systems of explanation and evaluation of social affairs which prescribe the need for specific changes and the methods for bringing them about. These ideologies are reified in social representations (Moscovici, 1976; Herzlich, 1973; Farr and Moscovici, 1984); social rules, rituals and orthodoxies (Deconchy, 1984); stereotypes (Hamilton, 1979) and social attributions (Hewstone, 1983). These manifestations of ideology are

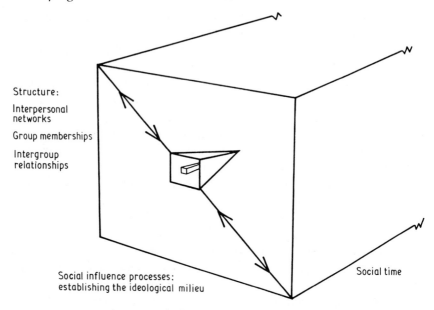

Structure:

Interpersonal
networks

Group memberships

Intergroup
relationships

Social influence processes:
establishing the ideological milieu

Social time

Figure 3   *The social context of identity*

examined in some depth in later chapters in so far as they pertain to threats to identity.

The inconsistencies and conflicts between ideologies reflect the differing interests of their originators. The individual identity is, therefore, faced with a social context which is most frequently presenting contradictory prescriptions for action and exhortations to belief. At any one moment in time, the individual has to make choices between different ideologies. The process of assimilation and accommodation, guided by the principles which control their operation, will filter alternatives and take maybe part, but not all, of one or several of them. The precise nature of that which is accepted will be determined by an interaction between what is on offer and the prior structure of identity to which it must be assimilated.

Movement of the individual in the social context

It would be an error to conceive of the individual as occupying a static position within the matrix of social context, structure and process. The individual moves within this matrix as he or she shifts from one group membership to another or from one interpersonal network to the next. The individual may also move simply because he or she is a member of a group which moves its position. This movement may sometimes be imposed by external forces (the man who is made redundant shifts from the category of the employed to that of the unemployed) or can be volitional (the woman who resigns paid work also joins the unemployed but by a different mechanism). Such movement between structural components of the social context has the effect of changing the relationship between the individual and the ideological milieu. A change of group membership may mean a whole new belief system and moral code that is designed to influence the new member. Equally, it means moving away from the remit of influence of the ideology of the previous group. *Any movement in the social matrix will require the individual to process potential new contents and values for identity.* It is not inevitable that the processes of assimilation–accommodation and evaluation will actually lead to changes in identity structure but they will be required to go into action, regardless.

The act of the individual who apparently initiates movement from one group to another or one network to the next, is explained in terms of the search for self-esteem or a positively valued identity (Tajfel, 1978). The implication is that the process of evaluation has led to an unsatisfactory result, that is, an abrogation of one of the guiding principles of the identity processes; the process of assimilation–accommodation is then set into motion to incorporate elements into identity which will result in a more positive self-regard or to eject those which are deflating self-esteem. In so far as this results in alterations of group memberships and interpersonal networks, the processes of identity, operating in accordance with the principles which guide them, can be seen to be directing the action of the individual in the social world. Tajfel (1978) has suggested that when exit from a group or category is not possible and so self-esteem cannot be protected through individual attempts at mobility through the social matrix, the person may seek to induce social change. Such social change would involve the individual in efforts to influence the relative power and status of the group concerned. By achieving greatness for a group one cannot escape, one achieves a reflected grandeur for the self. Tajfel and others (for instance, Lemaine, 1974; Billig, 1976; Taylor and McKirnan, 1984) have suggested that this may be the spur to the creation of new militant subgroups, the development of new rhetoric and various forms of social creativity. The thwarted, dissatisfied individual identity seeks to transform both the substantive content of groups and networks and the ideological products (beliefs and values) of influence processes. This may result in a picture which over-emphasizes the role of the individual in generating social change. In fact, individual action is only one source for social change. Moreover, it is emphasized here largely to counterbalance any impression which may have been developing that the individual identity is the mere recipient of inputs from its social context.

The effects of social change upon identity

So far it has been suggested that the individual may shift position in the social matrix and that this will lead to a changed pattern of influences which impinge upon the identity. It has also been suggested that the individual may seek to bring about a change in the structure or processes of the social context by one means or another in order to satisfy identity needs. But it is also true that social change can occur independently of the particular individual and the identity is subject to the effects of such change. In this case, the idea is that the individual does not move within the social matrix, rather it moves around the individual, transforming the meaning of the position he or she occupies.

Within this model of identity, social change is considered to have occurred whenever there is: (i) a reconstitution of the structure of the social context either in terms of the units of its composition (i.e. the number or size or constitution of groups or networks) or in relation to their arrangement (i.e. power hierarchy, alliances, nestings); and/or (ii) a revision of ideologies generated by the influence processes. Although it might be interesting, it is not necessary to engage in the harassed debate on the structural or functional origins of social change here (see Smith, 1973, for the arguments). For the purposes of the current exposition of the model of identity, it will be assumed that social change is an intrinsic, inevitable and continual characteristic of the social context. Social change should be considered the norm since the social context is never static.

Since social change is constant, the individual will be faced continually with fluctuating information for assimilation into the identity. Clearly, the principle of continuity which guides assimilation-accommodation will resist any haphazard response to such fluctuations. The individual is highly selective about which minor social changes merit response. The identity can even be barricaded against major social changes, at least in the short-run (methods for doing so are considered in Chapter 4). Whether the rejection of the altered reality can be maintained over time without serious consequences for identity is discussed later with regard to responses to threat. Yet it seems unlikely; to the extent that the social changes are not acknowledged and mirrored in modified self-definition and evaluation, the person is failing to orientate subjectively to an objective reality. This may lead to inappropriate coping strategies.

The extent and speed of identity modifications following social change are likely to depend upon:

a) *the degree of personal relevance of the social change.* Where the changes involve groups, networks or categories central to the existing identity content, it has greater personal relevance. Low personal relevance would be hypothesized to result in little identity change. However, high personal relevance does not necessarily produce high levels of accommodation. For instance, the individual may reduce the personal relevance rather than accept the change. For example, the person might leave a group which is very important to her but which has suddenly lost status or power. Personal relevance is a necessary but not sufficient condition for change.

b) *the immediacy of involvement in the social change.* Where the changes require the individual to act in new ways, there is a higher level of involvement. This demand for revised action would be hypothesized to be associated with speedier and more extensive modifications of the structure of identity: the disparity between action and previous self-conception pointing the necessity for change. There is considerable evidence for this assertion (e.g. Gergen, 1971). Under such circumstances, changes in identity are not inevitable but resistance is more difficult and more traumatic.

c) *how much revision of identity content and value is demanded.* It seems likely that the greater the revision required, the longer it will take to achieve and the slower will be its onset. Strategies to resist change, which are detailed in later chapters, will be called into play. Only if they fail will change occur. Even positively regarded, changes will take longer if they are extensive, and extensive changes are less likely to be regarded positively anyway.

d) *how negative the change required is deemed to be.* Where the change required abrogates the principles of continuity, distinctiveness or self-esteem which normally guide the process of assimilation, it will be considered to be negative. Such a change is predicted to threaten the integrity of identity and will be wrought only after all alternatives have been rejected as unworkable. It therefore occurs only after delay and when accepted is likely to be minimized. Many of the examples of threats to identity discussed in later chapters typify the nature of these delaying tactics.

These propositions have the status of hypotheses. However, all are testable. A central element in the regulation of responses to social change lies in the mechanisms which control the conscious recognition of the fact that change is occurring. Given that social change is continuous, the individual, in the interests of guarding against information overload, pays only selective attention to the nature of that change. Any one person will be aware of only a small fraction of the social changes which are ongoing and will largely be concerned only with those which have meaning according to his or her beliefs and attitudes, intentions and aspirations. Social changes which fail to gain access to conscious awareness do not have the power to reframe identity.

However, access to conscious recognition is not an all-or-nothing affair. It seems that one may become aware of a social change only very gradually as its sedimentary accretions grow in one's consciousness. This seems to rely upon the individual assimilating separate bits and pieces of information which may be taken as relevant to identity over a period of time, and which are only later recognized as relating to each other to form the basis for a substantive shift in the meaning allotted to self-definition or evaluation. In such a circumstance, the identity is responding to social changes which are not consciously labelled as such. Recognition comes later and with it the ultimate meaning of the identity changes which have been accumulating. Toch, 1966, describes this phenomenon in relation to conversion experiences. This pattern of identity revision is also echoed by something parallel in attitude change. Recent studies (Ajzen and Fishbein, 1980) have shown that sharp and apparently unanticipated changes in attitudes, which have previously been considered inexplicable conversions, do most frequently have a long history of minor, sequential and unacknowledged modifications in attitude preceding them. It is as if the individuals move inch by imperceptible inch to a new position which, once recognized, proves how far they have travelled.

Both the gradual recognition of social change and the remodelling of identity it entails can have this quality of surprise. The individual may suddenly become aware of a social change only after having absorbed a large amount of information about it over time. Moreover, the consequent changes wrought in behaviour and identity may be further delayed in recognition. The classic example of this has to be culled from the realm of changes in interpersonal networks: one of the partners in a marriage fails to recognize the changes which occur in the pattern of the relationship until faced with some overt and unmistakable symptom of marital breakdown but then in retrospect all of the small alterations become evident. It may then be only after much emotional turmoil that it becomes obvious that, throughout the decline in the marriage, changes had occurred in the identities of both partners. Consciousness of the social change goes hand-in-hand with consciousness of the identity change.

The relation of identity to action

Action is the social expression of identity. The only route of access to the identity of another is through his or her action, whether verbal or not. Since identity comprises emotions, beliefs, and attitudes it is a prime motivator of action. Identity directs action. This is not to deny the importance of situational constraints and stimuli in determining behaviour. It is simply to reaffirm that these situational determinants gain their meaning only through interpretation within the individual's system of beliefs and values; their implications for purposive action rather than unintended behaviour are, therefore, mediated by identity.

Thus, the content and value dimensions of identity specify appropriate action. Moreover, the identity processes, guided by the principles which dominate their operation, will also direct action. In search of continuity, distinctiveness and self-esteem, the individual seeks to move across positions within the social matrix. In this way, action is precipitated by the requirements of identity.

However, it would clearly be an error to represent identity as in some way the prime or ultimate determiner of action. Identity is itself a product of social interaction. It is not a simple product in that it has the power to moderate its own development through the principled operation of assimilation-accommodation and evaluation. Yet it is totally dependent upon that interaction. Identity and action are dialectically related. This assertion leads full circle to the statements about the genesis of identity across subjective time with which the description of this model began. In one frozen moment in time, identity may motivate action but the direction of causality is more apparent than real; an artefact of the artificial and purely imaginary cessation of the march of time. In the next arbitrarily and hypothetically sliced moment in time, action could generate identity changes. Action and identity, in time, are dialectically related.

Some concluding remarks about the framework

The integrative framework outlined simply represents one way of hanging a series of different assertions which are commonly made about identity within a single framework. It is not original in its constituents, only in the manner of their arrangement. Also it is not exhaustive. It is meant as a preliminary guide to identity in social context. Many of the components of the model are not fully explained here. For instance, the nature of social influence processes and the mechanisms through which ideologies are expressed are not thoroughly described. The intention in this chapter is merely to signal where such components fit in the model. Later chapters elaborate upon them further and explicitly examine their relevance for threatened identities.

The framework serves as a structure within which the nature and effects of threat can be systematically explored. The framework offers a means of generating coherence and order to the evidence of the effects of threat generated in diverse contexts. Equally importantly, the case studies in Chapter 1 of the impact of threat to identity represent examples of the assertions made in the model. They pinpointed the vital role of the social context in generating threat and emphasized the importance of distinctiveness, continuity and self-esteem in the subjective experience of threat to identity.

Methods for studying identity, threat and coping

The methods used to study identity have been diverse and have reflected the theoretical preconceptions of their originators.

During the history of the endeavour to understand identity, methods have included everything from introspection, through psychoanalysis, to the behavioural record of minute action segments (Ginsberg *et al.*, 1985). Yet it is only recently that the methods have been used in conjunction. Methodological liberation has lain in the acceptance that it is legitimate to use different approaches in unison. There is now a shift from the sole use of personality trait lists to elicit a person's self-description (Butcher, 1972; Kline, 1983). Contemporary researchers are more likely to rely upon a combination of multi-dimensional scaling and longitudinal autobiography or diary records (Ericsson and Simon, 1984). They do not shun in-depth interviews (Brenner *et al.*, 1985) or extensive observational studies (de Waele, 1985). These methods simultaneously provide information about the content and value of the identity structure and data on its variations across social context or spatial and temporal location. They echo the changed emphasis in theorizing about identity where there has been a move from centring explanation upon psychic dynamics to focusing it upon social processes.

The framework suggested here should push the targets for investigation still further from the pure cognitive process or motivational and affective regimes. In proposing the social origin of threat and the social determinants of coping, the model points to the need to explore social influence processes in a shifting social matrix. Social representations, shared social beliefs and social attributions need to be studied in order to understand the form of threat and the viability of the various coping strategies. These social processes may be only rarely amenable to examination through the use of manipulative experimental methods. Most frequently, they will demand other methodologies: account gathering (Brown and Sime, 1981), textual and content analysis, ethnography (Hammersley and Atkinson, 1983), and observational techniques (Forgas, 1979). To test an integrated framework for identity, threat and coping, it is necessary to employ an integrated set of methods. Each method may provide information at a different level. The equivalence of all data need not be assumed for all of it to contribute to the understanding of identity.

In describing the nature of threat and the variety of coping strategies in the remaining chapters, data collected by means of the complete range of methods will be cited: from case studies to large-scale surveys; from introspection to participant observation; from unobtrusive to highly manipulative interventions. The target for understanding is both the individual and ideological system. There is no pretence that all of the material discussed has the same status in terms of reliability but it is all instructive as to the dynamics of identity. The survey results in terms of means and standard deviations on Likert-scaled self-report checklists can reveal things which the verbatim transcript of a single case study taped over months cannot. But the reverse is also true. Methodological myopia is as bad as theoretical tunnel vision.

3   The structure of threats

The origin of threat

The central purpose of this book is to examine how people evolve strategies for coping with threatened identities. The temptation to start in Chapter 1 with a definition of threat was resisted. Following the advice of James (1917), some of the experiences associated with threat have been described prior to imposing closure through its formal definition. However, even James ultimately resorted to circumscription of his subject matter. Consequently, it seems justifiable here to develop a clear and comprehensive definition of what constitutes a threat to identity. Also, it seems reasonable to follow the lead of James in focusing upon the individual. James defined religion as 'the feelings, acts and experiences of individual men in their solitude, so far as they apprenhend themselves to stand in relation to whatever they may consider divine' (p. 31). The conception of threat to identity needs to be similarly lodged in the individual consciousness.

Threats to identity are manifested in many different forms and a taxonomy of the events and experiences which have acted as such would prove interesting but would be essentially uninformative at the theoretical level. Threat cannot be adequately characterized merely in terms of its form. The definition of a threat must be derived from its implications for identity. Many types of experience can act as threats. They may share nothing in their outward form. The communality, and the justification for labelling them all threats, lies in the structure of the predicament they all pose for identity. *A threat to identity occurs when the processes of identity, assimilation-accommodation and evaluation are, for some reason, unable to comply with the principles of continuity, distinctiveness and self-esteem, which habitually guide their operation.* The reason for this obstruction of the processes of identity constitutes the threat.

The immediate origin of the threat can be either internal or external. A threat can originate internally where the individual seeks to alter her or his position in relation to the social matrix, changing group membership or interpersonal network, in accordance with one principle guiding the operation of the assimilation-accommodation process, only to find that the move conflicts with the requirements of one of the other guiding principles. For instance, continuity might drive the person to join a new group which is compatible with existing memberships but self-esteem might resist that allegiance if the grouping has a mostly negative contribution to make to social status. Such a threat may arise for the man who has been made redundant and has come to regard himself as long-term unemployed. To join a group of men similarly unemployed and attend a drop-in centre designated as a meeting place and, perhaps, training workshop might be congruent with the self-definition imposed by continuing unemployment. However, attendance there could also be perceived as a signal of defeat if the centre is seen locally as a hideout for failures or those too lazy to gain work. By attending the centre under such circumstances, the man creates a threat to identity: the continuity of self-definition and the achievement of self-esteem through social approval are at variance. Such a threat has an internal origin only in so far as the individual initiates the change in his group memberships which generates the conflict between the dictates of the identity processes. In such a case, the principles orientating the process of assimilation are demanding mutually exclusive changes in identity. This type of source of threat emphasizes the vital importance of developing a theory which will predict the relative salience of each principle and the situational factors which moderate their impact.

Alternatively, a threat can originate externally with a change of some sort in the social context. The change can consist of a modification in the size or number of groups or interpersonal networks available; or in their relationships in terms of power; or in the ideologies they generate to maintain their influence. In fact, any sort of social change may act as a threat to identity so long as it obstructs the principled operation of the processes of identity. Basically, threats demand changes to either the content or the value dimensions of identity which would be inconsistent with the continued integrity of identity. It is important to note that not all changes are threatening – only those which challenge the principles underpinning the integrity of identity. On the content dimension, threats challenge either the continuity or distinctiveness of self-definition. They query whether you can continue to be what you think you are and/or whether that is in any way unique or differentiating. So, for instance, a threat emanating from a challenge to continuity might arise where someone who defines herself as compassionate and generous is told that everyone thinks her cold-hearted and mean. In contrast, the same woman might find the threat initiated through an onslaught on her distinctiveness if her critic instead of challenging her compassion and generosity simply insisted that these were common characteristics possessed by every ordinary person and so not a means of achieving individuation or uniqueness. On the value dimension, threats challenge self-esteem. They query whether what you are is any good. In this case, our compassionate and generous lady would be acknowledged as such but would be informed that such qualities are a sign of weakness, a fatal flaw of character in the modern world. Often the threat attacks both the content and value dimensions simultaneously: denying you qualities you believed to be your own and condemning you for failing to possess them. In this attack, the compassionate generous woman would be told she was neither and it would be explained to her how important it is to be both.

The example used tends to imply that threats revolve around challenges to individual qualities. This is not always the case. The threat often concerns group memberships. These threats tend to fall into two categories: articles which repudiate an individual's claim to be a member of a particular group and attacks upon the value of a group in which the individual's membership is acknowledged. The first category of threat impinges upon the content dimension of identity. For instance, a young woman born in Britain with parents born in Pakistan may regard herself, justifiably, as British. However, she may also have her claim challenged, without any legal justification, by any racist who chooses to use more prejudiced criteria for acceptance as British. The second category of threat concerns the value dimension of identity. This type levels a refracted slur on an individual's self-esteem by denigrating the group. If the person gains much self-esteem through association with groups which have social status or acceptance, any detraction from a group's value will diminish the member's value and consequently act as a threat to identity.

In relation to threat, the emphasis placed earlier upon the distinction between the occurrence of social change and its conscious recognition is important. Social change which has the potential to be threatening may not be consciously perceived. Without admission to conscious awareness, its power to act as a threat is minimized. For instance, a woman may not know that a distant but very important relative has died for some time after the death. The death itself may result in the effective collapse of an interpersonal network within the family and may ultimately radically revise the roles that the individual has open to her within the family. This may represent a serious threat to identity. But the threat cannot become manifest until the woman is aware of the death and appreciates its implications. The same is true in the context of group memberships. Eviction from an important membership may be a potentially damning blow to identity but it cannot operate until the individual becomes aware of the expulsion. Of course, it is then worth noting that consciousness of a threatening social change may be resisted. Avoiding the conscious acknowledgement of the threat may actually be a strategy adopted for coping with it. This process, often referred to as denial in the clinical literature, is considered further in the chapter on self-protection. Nevertheless, it is worth consideration here that the whole notion of denial actually assumes consciousness of the threat at some level or else how could it be excluded from consciousness as a means of defence.

The point here, of course, is that the perception of a 'threat' may be modified by the very processes designed to cope with threats to identity.

Situations, which in objective terms might be deemed threatening, may sometimes fail to be identified as such subjectively. This is partly, undoubtedly, because coping strategies can cut in very rapidly in threatening situations. It may also be because the threat has to be viewed within the overall structure of the identity. Some identity patterns (i.e. content/value configurations) may be more responsive to threats than others.

This supposition derives some support from the research upon depression by Brown and Harris (1978). They were concerned with social factors in the aetiology of psychiatric disorder. Earlier research (Leff, Roatch and Bunney, 1970; Paykel, 1973) had shown that most depressions are preceded by stressful life events such as failure at school or work, divorce, redundancy, illness in the family or of the individual concerned, and rejection by a loved one. However, many people (90 per cent in the Brown and Harris study) suffer such trauma and do not become depressed. Brown and Harris were concerned to establish what factors increased vulnerability to depression following a stressful event. They interviewed women in the working-class borough of Camberwell in London and found that 15–20 per cent were at least moderately depressed but were not receiving treatment. Vulnerability to depression following either acute stressful events or chronic stressful difficulties was increased for those women who had lost (through separation or death) their mother before they were 11 years old. Even so, only half of the women in this category became depressed. The others shared characteristics which militated against vulnerability: they had an intimate, confiding relationship with a spouse or lover; or a job of some sort outside the home; or fewer than three children still at home; or a serious religious commitment. Rosenhan and Seligman (1984) suggest that what these 'invulnerability' factors have in common is that they enhance self-esteem and a sense of self-control which ward off the feelings of generalized hopelessness which characterize depression. Effectively, they militate against the 'cognitive triad' which Beck *et al.* (1979) identified as part of the mechanism generating depression: negative thoughts about the self, about ongoing experiences and about the future. Such negative thoughts conspire with 'errors in logic' to generate despair. According to Beck *et al.* there are five varieties of such errors in logic: arbitrary inference (drawing conclusions in the absence of evidence); selective abstraction (concentrating on parts of information not the whole); overgeneralization (from small specific occurrences global inferences are drawn); magnification, and its counterpart minimization (errors are grossly exaggerated, successes ignored); and personalization (unrealistically taking responsibility for unpleasant events). Brown and Harris showed that low self-esteem and 'negative thinking' precede the onset of depression, and may be considered a causal influence, rather than simply being regarded as the product of it, though it is undoubtedly also true that a loss of self-esteem may be an outcome of depression.

For the current purposes, one of the values of the Brown and Harris discoveries is to underline the fact that the pre-existent identity configuration (level and source of self-esteem and content of self-definition) will influence whether stressful events are treated as subjectively threatening. It will certainly dictate whether they ultimately overwhelm the strategies evolved for coping with threat and result in depression. Beck's theory contributes a further strand to the argument which is that individuals will differ in the logical (or illogical) heuristics they employ in information processing. Three differences are related to self-esteem levels and will modify the perception of a threatening event.

The experience of threat

Abstract formulations of the nature of threat may be necessary for conceptual clarity but they give none of the real feeling for the experience of threat. They give no inkling of the phenomenological development of the threat or its subjective impact. The purpose of the remainder of this chapter is to explore two examples of threat to identity in order to develop some concrete understanding of it. They are chosen because the author has conducted extensive studies, using integrated methods of data collection, of threat and coping in these two domains. They are also reasonably topical.

The first example shows how and why unemployment threatens identity. The second explores the threat posed by employment in a sexually atypical job. Both examples are basically concerned with threats derived from social category membership. In the case of unemployment, the threat is generated by movement into a social category which is socially stigmatized and materially deprived. In the case of sexually atypical employment, the threat emanates from the individual's failure to comply with gender role expectations.

The structure of the threats to identity in the two examples is different and the difference is explored below. However, it will be evident that the threats have an impact upon identity by challenging continuity, distinctiveness or self-esteem and are the products of social influence processes set into motion by the changing pattern of inter-group relations over long periods of time. Both examples involve a movement of the individual within the social matrix which results in new pressures being brought to bear upon identity. Whether the actual movement of the individual is determined by prior social change is a moot point. Social and economic changes will be what propel most people into the dole queue, but others choose to resign. The development of equal rights and opportunities legislation will be what encourages most of the women who go into what has been traditionally 'men's work' to do so, but a minority of women have always sought such sexually atypical employment. Yet, the extent of social change underpinning the modification in the individual's social position will be an important ingredient in the recipe for threat. If large numbers of people become unemployed simultaneously within a single community, for instance with the closure of the local pit or steel foundry, the nature of the threat changes. It might be predicted that, under such circumstances, unemployment would be a less isolating and socially demeaning experience; less of an attack on self-esteem, at least. Coping strategies would also supposedly change: shifting from the individualistic to the community-based. The veracity of these assumptions is examined in later chapters (Kelvin and Jarrett, 1985, discuss many of these issues). Here, the intention is merely to signal that in considering threat generated by social category membership, it is necessary to examine just how far it is received collectively. In considering sexually atypical employment, the threat is seen to operate at a highly individualized level. So few women or men actually breach gender roles that the collective threat is unlikely (Tropp Schreiber, 1979; Hoiberg, 1982).

Clearly, threats do not emanate solely from problematic category memberships. Any change of position in the social matrix which results in demands for assimilation-accommodation and evaluation to breach the principles of continuity, distinctiveness or self-esteem constitutes a threat. Consequently, disruption of interpersonal networks (as in divorce, breakdown of close friendships, death of a relative, etc.) or group memberships can generate threat. Changes in the ideological milieu which require adjustments of either attitudes or values can equally attack identity. However, the unemployment and sexually atypical employment examples are chosen because they encompass changes across a broad area of the content and value dimensions of identity. Unemployment and sexually atypical employment both have the power massively to transform the individual's interpersonal network, group memberships and perception of ideological structures. They have such wide-ranging implications for all areas of living that it is possible to examine within their remit other roots of threat. In later chapters, other examples are described but it is worth emphasizing here that the same processes of social representation, stereotyping, attribution, and struggles for power reappear time and again in definitions of threat. Understanding them in relation to unemployment and sexually atypical employment primes more general understanding of threat.

Unemployment

It is hardly novel to suggest that the experience of unemployment constitutes a threat to identity. There is now an extensive body of data which shows that, in the majority of cases, unemployment leads to significant psychological turmoil. This is manifested in increased anxiety, depression, insomnia, irritability, lack of confidence, listlessness, inability to concentrate and general nervousness (Warr, 1983). Both cross-sectional and longitudinal studies (Banks and Jackson, 1982; Cohn, 1978; Feather and Barber, 1983; Perfetti and Bingham, 1983; Fagin, 1979; Brenner, Brenner and Bartell, 1983; Feather, 1982) point to the struggle which unemployment can incite in both the content and value dimensions of identity, revising either self-definition or self-evaluation and often both. The fact that unemployment acts as a threat to identity is undeniable. The main question now is how and why does it generate such threat. An answer to this is an essential precursor to any understanding of how people seek to cope with that threat.

Jahoda (1979, 1981, and 1982) has suggested that work is a person's strongest link with reality, demanding a pragmatic orientation to the environment which precludes the excesses of fantasy and emotionality. Work, consequently, has psychological advantages independent of any material profits it purveys. Paid employment, the dominant variant of work available in modern industrialized societies, has, according to Jahoda, both manifest and latent benefits. The manifest benefits are obvious to all and revolve around the monetary rewards for work. The latent benefits are less obviously associated with work in the minds of the majority but become painfully evident when work is no longer available. A job normally defines a person's status, establishes a network of social interaction with co-workers, provides an area in which competence can be shown and praised, specifies what goals need to be attained, and, not least, determines a timetable for the day, giving it structure and meaning. These are some of the latent benefits of work, withdrawn during unemployment. Deprivation of these latent benefits is said to account for the debilitating effects of unemployment.

Jahoda's explanation of the psychological effects of unemployment has been interpreted to have relatively clear policy implications. In an era of mass structural unemployment, when policy makers deem reinflation of the economy and the recreation of jobs inadvisable, Jahoda's analysis has been taken to imply that the latent benefits of work should be provided for the unemployed without providing them with work itself. The symptoms of this interpretation of Jahoda's work can be seen on a number of fronts. Firstly, in schemes to develop drop-in centres for the unemployed which are designed to provide alternative social networks and contacts while simultaneously offering a substitute timetabling for the day's activities. Secondly, it can be seen in community projects which encourage the unemployed to volunteer their skills in the pursuance of goals deemed valuable to the community. Thirdly, it is evident in the recent reconstrual of the meaning of leisure: it is no longer a waste of time, there is now a movement afoot to educate people for their leisure, presumably to show them what they should be doing when not working. Much of the activity that these three manifestations exemplify is premised on the assumption that the negative effects of unemployment can be ameliorated, if not banished, by some surrogate which provides the latent benefits of work. To some extent the assumption may be correct; however, it ignores the properties of unemployment itself.

Jahoda explains the effects of unemployment only in relation to the loss of the positive implications of employment. Unemployment and employment may well be two faces of the same coin but, just like the head and the tail, they have different defining characteristics. The problems consequent upon the loss of work may not simply hail from the withdrawal of the concomitant benefits of employment, they may be generated by the social experience of unemployment itself. To become unemployed is to be consigned to a different social category which has a character and social position of its own. The unemployed, as a social category, have a series of social beliefs and attitudes which encircle them and which determine the experience of unemployment and responses to it. It would be possible to argue that in predicting the psychological effects of job loss, not only the latent and manifest benefits of work need consideration, but also the covert and overt costs of unemployment. The lost benefits of work and incurred costs of unemployment are not synonymous.

The social representation of the unemployed

The theory of social representations has assumed considerable importance in social psychology of late (Farr and Moscovici, 1984), promising to elucidate the social processes involved in the active construction of an understanding of the world. According to Moscovici, social representations are 'concepts, statements and explanations originating in daily life in the course of inter-individual communications' (1981, p. 181). Their character is essentially collective; members of a social group will share many representations. They provide a system of interpretation, labelling and exchange which orient people appropriately in their particular social context. However, the precise nature of social representations is a matter of fierce debate (Potter and Litton, 1985; Moscovici, 1985; Semin, 1985; Hewstone, 1985; Jaspars and Fraser, 1984). They are accused of being indistinguishable from schema, or stereotypes, or beliefs, or, indeed, attitudes. They are accused of being unsullied by association with a systematic body of theory. They are accused of being inaccessible to empirical study. All these accusations are repulsed by the followers of Moscovici: they are unique in being collective and interactive, they are tied to propositions about their appearance and function; and they have *been* studied (Herzlich, 1973; Di Giacomo, 1980; Hewstone, Jaspars and Lalljee, 1982).

So far, the method of choice in studying social representations has been content analysis of utterances or cultural artefacts. This has been

highly criticized since it requires arbitrary decisions about what constitutes collective agreement. Alternative methods are now being
explored (for instance, the use of Smallest Space Analysis and Cluster
Analysis). This augurs well for the solution of the methodological
difficulties.

Thus, social representation is essentially a construction of reality. It
reflects dominant systems of belief and value in presenting an acceptable interpretation of objects, persons or events. When applied to
people, the social representation has two roles: firstly, to attach to
them a definite form by locating them within a social category with
distinctive characteristics; secondly, it acts as a template prescribing
how their actions should be explained and interpreted. The social
representation of the unemployed will, therefore, effectively erect a
stereotype of them which depicts their psychological and social
qualities. It will also explain how they come to be unemployed and,
most importantly, how they should be evaluated. The social representation of the unemployed is manifest in various forms. It finds
expression through the mass media, through legislative procedures,
through cultural artefacts (novels, art, pop records, etc.), through jokes
and so on. It also resides in the attitudinal and belief systems of
individuals. The social representation, being a product of extensive
social interaction in the context of specific material circumstances, is
independent of any one individual's representation. However, the
reverse is not true. The social representation is the backdrop to the
individual's attitudinal and attributional development. This may mean
that the individual echoes totally or only partially the dominant social
representation. Either way, the individual cannot claim autonomy of
belief. In a sense, this is merely to reiterate the old maxim that social
reality determines, to a large extent, personal reality (Berger and
Luckman, 1975).

For any socially important phenomenon, like unemployment, there
will be competing social representations, originating in disparate ideologies held by groups with conflicting interests. However, the
dominant social representation of the unemployed is quite evident and
fundamentally negative. The development of countervailing positive
social representations by minority groups may be envisaged as one
means of alleviating the damaging impact of unemployment but, as
yet, this seems a distant possibility. The existing dominant social representation simply serves to stigmatize the unemployed. It does this on a
number of fronts.

Kelvin (1984) describes the historical roots of the social representation (though he does not employ the term social representation) in the

early legislative responses to unemployment and the evolution of the Protestant Work Ethic. He traces the derogation of the workless back to the 1349 Ordinance of Labourers. Passed at a time of great labour shortages, after the Black Death had decimated the workforce, the Ordinance differentiated between the 'deserving poor' and the 'sturdy beggar'. The 'deserving poor' were to receive aid in their distress but the 'sturdy beggar' was to be shamed and starved back into gainful employment. This dichotomy was maintained, embodied in various legislation, over six centuries. In 1905, the Unemployed Workmen Act provided assistance only for those who were without work but actively seeking it. The same premise underpins the allocation of social security benefits under the current Welfare State: the person has to be available for work, should any appear, to be eligible for the dole. Repeated failure to accept work offered may result in withdrawal of benefits.

The legislation has, over the centuries, reified the existence of two types of unemployed person: the unfit and the undeserving. From the viewpoint of the unemployed themselves neither option is appealing. They can opt for being unfit, an incapable or indequate character only good enough to be a charity cases. Alternatively, they can conceive of themselves as undeserving; social parasites, scrounging from the State. Neither representation offers much sustenance to identity; both attack the very heartland of self-esteem.

This social representation of the unemployed has its origin in economic necessity: generated in an era of labour shortage, it was designed to propel people back into work. The applicability of either stereotype in a time of fearsome structural unemployment is clearly suspect. With high levels of unemployment internationally (see Ashton, 1986), the collapse of traditional industry in the face of new technology, and the restriction on reinvestment and growth under monetarism, it is not only the inadequate and the feckless who become unemployed. There are simply not enough jobs for all those seeking them. In 1984, in Britain, there were 3,101,000 people unemployed (an unemployment rate of 12.9 per cent) but only 156,000 jobs vacant (CSO, 1985).

Yet the social representation has been six centuries in the making and is hardly likely to change quickly or quietly. This is particularly so because it capitalizes upon a fundamental tendency in social attribution. There is a consistent bias in attribution; that is the process whereby reasons are allocated to occurrences, which results in the victims of misfortune being deemed to be the originators of their own fate. This is tied to what is called the 'just world hypothesis' which proposes that basically people get what they deserve (Rubin and

Peplan, 1975; Wagstaff and Quirk, 1983; Lerner *et al.*, 1976). If what they get is unpleasant, that must be what they deserve. In the case of the unemployed, the just world hypothesis tends to support the derogatory social representation fed from legislation. They are not seen as the hapless victims of economic recession but rather as social miscreants (scroungers) who have failed in some way to comply with society's requirements and are being legitimately chastised through the loss of paid work.

The second root for the negative social representation of the unemployed emanates, according to Kelvin, from the so-called Protestant Work Ethic (PWE). It is commonly argued that with puritanism, which followed the Protestant split from the Catholic Church, came a belief in the absolute value of work, independent of its instrumentality, as an overt expression of religious dedication and involvement with the well-being of the community. Hard work, like cleanliness, was next to Godliness. Whether, in fact, the Protestant Work Ethic was ever anything more than the propaganda of a small section of the community which wished to motivate the workers to work harder and longer to swell the coffers of their employers and masters is now openly debated. Kelvin and Jarrett (1985) argue cogently that, even in the period just following the Civil War in England, it is doubtful whether the masses were particularly religious or particularly assiduous in their devotions at the alter of the workplace. The large number of tracts written to castigate the indolent who failed to turn up for work except when in financial need evidences both the absence of the PWE in the workers and its self-interested relevance for their employers. As Kelvin and Jarrett (1985, pp. 102-3) point out, 'for at least the last 500 years, there is steady and consistent evidence of late coming to work, long breaks at work, early leaving of work, downing of tools at the first opportunity and the like disdain for work'. Accordingly, Kelvin (1984) suggests that it is inappropriate to assume that the PWE is an internalized psychological construct which can be used to explain the negative consequences of unemployment. People do not suffer when unemployed because they are unable to comply with the Protestant Work Ethic which has become part of their personal belief or value system. The masses never assimilated the PWE in the first place, much to the consternation of those whose interests it might serve.

Kelvin's argument that the masses were and are sadly lacking in religiosity and sadly remiss in their affiliation for intrinsically unrewarding work, while interesting, should not be seen to minimize the role the PWE plays in shaping the threat represented by unemployment. The notion of the PWE is still a central strut in the structure of the social representation of the unemployed. The unemployed, being either stigmatized as inadequate or parasites, are depicted as lacking the normal quota of the PWE. For the purposes of the social representation, the facts are irrelevant. It hardly matters that most people in truth appear to lack the PWE as it was classically defined. The mythology of the PWE is a support for the derogation of the unemployed.

In a sense, the myth of the Protestant Work Ethic through its infiltration of representations of work has been made flesh. The rhetoric of the coalition of clerics and entrepreneurs has, over centuries, changed public conceptions of work such that it is now possible to measure how far an individual actually adheres to the PWE in his or her own value system (Furnham, 1984). There is considerable evidence that a strong belief in the intrinsic value of work is associated with conservative political views (Furnham and Bland, 1983), negative attitudes towards the unemployed (Furnham, 1982), and beliefs that recipients of social security benefits are lazy and dishonest (Furnham, 1985). People do differ fundamentally in their orientation to work and this is tied to a whole array of other social and political beliefs if not to religiosity or worship. This implies that 'Protestant' may be a misnomer leading to misunderstandings. It may be tied to particular views of economic activity and social structure rather than religious belief (Furnham and Lewis, 1986).

No matter what their label, assessments of the value of work mediate the psychological impact of unemployment. The more the individual is personally committed to gaining work, and the more central its importance in his or her life, the greater the distress during unemployment (Stafford, Jackson and Banks, 1980). The person who has actually accepted the PWE, with or without its religious overtone, suffers most when unemployed. The irony here lies in the fact that, while unemployed, the person may still be subject to rhetoric designed to foster a belief in the intrinsic merit of paid work. The unemployed, because they are stereotyped as either undeserving or incapable, are exhorted to become more work involved. For instance, much of the philosophy underlying government schemes, like the Youth Training Schemes, designed for the unemployed revolves around the need to inculcate 'good work habits' and the 'right attitude towards work'. It seems likely that, if successful, such programmes may result in the adoption of a belief system which will, should the person remain unemployed, incite psychological distress. After all, young people who know they have acquired the 'right attitude' because they have been told so by YTS tutors, but who cannot get work subsequently, will continue to be told that their unemployment has its roots in their individual inadequacies. These cannot be inadequacies of attitude of experience because they have supposedly been rectified by the YTS programme. A logical conclusion for the young person to draw would be that they have some deeper inadequacy. There is evidence to support this inference. In a study of young people on government training schemes in Britain, Breakwell *et al.* (1984b) found that after leaving the schemes they responded even more negatively to unemployment. One young lad explained that on the scheme: 'they made me feel I was worth something, taught me something, had something to offer. Couldn't get a job though. Know now I'm no good. No use. Nobody wants me. It's real important to have a job. Bit o' money. The scheme made me get the right idea about work. I'm tidy when I do get a job. Suck up to the gaffer. I just don't do it right. I'm no good.' Stafford (1982) examined the impact of participation in a similar scheme upon job prospects and psychological well-being (as measured by the General Health Questionnaire). She found prospects of employment improved for 16-18-year-olds after taking part in a scheme but the beneficial psychological effects of participation fade if work is not found and a backlash effect occurs.

The social representation of the unemployed, with its roots in legislation and the Protestant Work Ethic, can be seen to be mirrored in the attitudes of individuals towards those without paid work. When asked to rate 'the unemployed' and 'the employed', as if they were two distinct and internally homogeneous groups, on a series of bipolar adjectival dimensions people will do so. Their descriptions of the unemployed are significantly more negative than those of the employed on every possible dimension of comparison, whether it be intelligence or sociability, cleanliness or kindness, laziness or sporting ability (Breakwell, Collie, Harrison and Propper, 1984). The unemployed are deprecated, demeaned and derogated in every comparison with the employed regardless of the relevance of the descriptive domain to employability or employment status. The negative social representation of the unemployed has thoroughly permeated the attitudes of individuals and the stereotype they hold. Though these data pertain to British samples, there is no reason to believe that in other parts of the world where the negative social representation exists, people would be any more resistant to it as individuals.

More interesting still, is the grip which the social representation has upon the minds of the unemployed themselves. In the same study, Breakwell, Collie, Harrison and Propper (1984) found that British 16-19-year-olds who were unemployed held significantly more negative stereotypes of the social category to which they belonged than of the employed. However, they expected other people to have an even more condemning view of the unemployed and a more glorifying picture of the employed. In fact, it was shown that these young unemployed expected others to be even more polarized in their attitudes than they actually were. Other people do criticize the unemployed and laud the employed but the gap is not as great as the young unemployed expect it to be. Nevertheless, they are correct in thinking that others differentiate between the employed and unemployed more than they personally do.

The evidence now supports the conclusion that people, whether employed, unemployed, on job-creation schemes, or still at school, consistently deprecate the unemployed and value the employed (Kelvin and Jarrett, 1985; Jahoda, 1982). The psychological effects for the unemployed person of accepting this negative stereotype cannot be overestimated. To acknowledge it and adhere to it is to strip away personal self-esteem. Even to recognize that others despise and deprecate the unemployed is a shattering blow to the self-concept without going on to concur with them which is what the unemployed do. It seems reasonable to suggest that the psychological effects of unemployment do not simply result from the withdrawal of the latent benefits of work. The social representation which attacks self-esteem, and threatens identity, could account for much of the depression, insecurity and anxiety experienced during unemployment.

Shifting some of the burden of explanation for the effects of unemployment from the highly individualized level of the cognitive and interpersonal benefits of work to the broader societal level of the dynamics of social representation and attitude formation has policy implications. It suggests that policy responses which focus on the replacement of some, if not all, of the latent benefits of work at the individual level cannot hope to rectify the psychological distress and social dislocation experienced. It suggests that efforts should equally be directed at modifying the social representation of the unemployed. A social representation produced in a period of labour shortages, consequent upon the Black Death, is hardly appropriate to those experiencing unemployment at a time when there are simply too few jobs for the number of people seeking work. It is commonly thought that the community at large is sufficiently aware of the macro-economic processes which have generated mass structural unemployment and that attitudes which vilify the individual without work will shrink. The evidence seems to assert the contrary: the unemployed are still blamed for their unemployment. The victims are victimized. It seems possible that attitudes would eventually change but they have been six centuries in the making and are congruent with well-established attributional biases operative in other areas of social understanding. Rather than relying on the natural erosion of the social representation, positive steps could be taken to eradicate it. Policy which re-educated both the public, and more specifically the unemployed themselves, about the causes of unemployment would transform its psychological and social impact.

Threats to identity created by unemployment

The purpose of this discussion is to set the scene for an examination of coping strategies by exploring how unemployment acts as a threat to identity. Unemployment is not a homogeneous experience, despite the way it is often characterized in psychological literature. People become unemployed in different ways and this will determine what effects it has upon identity. For instance, at the most obvious level, there is the distinction between those who choose to leave their previous job of their own accord and those who have no option – they are sacked or made redundant. Self-imposed unemployment has a different implication for identity to involuntary unemployment. Being thrown out of work can attack all three guiding principles of the identity processes. It represents a sharp chasm in continuity: previous interpersonal networks, goals, roles and activities are expunged, often suddenly, sometimes after thirty years with little warning at 4 p.m. on a Friday afternoon. It challenges distinctiveness by withdrawing the opportunity to display unique skills, removing a definitive social position, and depositing the person in the undifferentiated category of the unemployed. It overwhelms self-esteem by attaching a stereotype which reeks of social repugnance and, certainly not least, by probably eradicating financial independence or security. Choosing to leave work may represent a lesser threat to identity in some respects since it is less likely to confront continuity or distinctiveness. The person who chooses unemployment is likely to be desirous of a breach in continuity and an alternative source of distinctiveness or else the job would be retained. For the voluntarily unemployed, the major threat is against self-esteem, particularly since they are most likely to be viewed by others as scroungers or layabouts, being deprived of the more socially acceptable excuses for their status.

Even among those who are involuntarily unemployed, it is necessary to differentiate the redundant with a wealth of work experience from the young person who has never had a real job. The unemployed young person has had no opportunity to develop what is sometimes called an occupational identity. Within the model of identity suggested here it would be safer to say that these young unemployed have never had the experiences which would result in the assimilation into the identity structure of any self-definition in terms of work. Unemployment for them, unlike for the older person who experiences redundancy, is not a threat to continuity; it is not a disjuncture with the past, except in so far as they may have harboured expectations of careers while at school. Furthermore, it represents a threat to putative, rather than achieved, distinctiveness. Its primary power to molest identity-function lies in its effects on self-esteem through the impact of the dominant social representation and the financial and material deprivation it imposes. As one young woman interviewed as part of the Breakwell *et al.* (1984b) study said: 'I've never had a job. I can't call myself a worker. I left school and wanted to be a hairdresser. I'd had Saturday work in a hairdressing salon. But nobody wants to train kids. I feel bad about not getting a job because the family needs the money. In any case, neighbours think I'm a layabout. You know, like the papers say, I'm lazy and thick and useless. Me mum know I've tried but it's hopeless.'

Employed and unemployed people have been compared in an examination of the effects of unemployment upon physical and mental health. The evidence is equivocal. However, generally speaking, the consensus of such studies is that unemployed people are less healthy, happy and well-adjusted (reviewed partially in Furnham and Lewis, 1986). This is just as true for school-leavers as for older groups. Donovan and Oddy (1982) studied matched groups of British employed and unemployed school-leavers. Those unemployed were more depressed and anxious, had lower self-esteem and poorer subjective well-being (i.e. self-reported sense of security), and showed a greater incidence of minor psychiatric morbidity. The close relatives of the unemployed also suffer. Liem and Atkinson (1982) report that the wives of men unemployed for over three months are more likely to be depressed and anxious than those with working spouses.

Given that the experience of unemployment is not homogeneous and the threats it poses to identity are differentiated, it should come as no surprise that people do differ in the intensity of their psychological response to unemployment. Age, sex and socio-economic class are, to some extent, predictive of differences in response and seemingly mediate the nature of threat posed by unemployment. At least among men, age appears to be curvilinearly related to a negative psychological impact of unemployment. Middle-aged men experience greater distress than either those younger or those older (Hepworth, 1980; Jackson and Warr, 1983). Contrary to common misconception, women do not, as a sex, cope better with unemployment. In fact, for women who are single or the principal wage-earners in their family, the consequences of unemployment do not differ from those for men. However, where a woman is unemployed because she is engaged in child-rearing the negative effects are alleviated. The psychological benefits of having paid work for a woman with young children seem to accrue only for those in the working class (Warr and Parry, 1982) where the additional income and variety of social contacts generated by a job outside the home proves very valuable. Unemployment for men as well as women in the working class generates greater psychological problems than for the middle classes. For them unemployment is associated with greater financial hardship and more constraints upon activities, both of which are known to precipitate psychological distress (Payne *et al.*, 1983).

Variations in responses to unemployment, according to age, sex and class, may be due either to the fact that the threat to identity constituted by unemployment differs across these social categories or to the differences between the strategies evolved by them to cope with the threat. In reality, it is likely to be a product of both. For the middle-aged working-class man, unemployment may attack identity on more fronts and he may have less material resources with which to resist the onslaught. Of course, this is not inevitable and within the generalization about these broad social categories there should be allowances for individuals who react in ways which are not predictable purely in terms of their social-category memberships. In some ways, these exceptions are fundamentally interesting for the identity theorist since it seems likely that they use coping strategies which are atypical and may be illuminating about the hidden dynamics of identity. Variations in coping strategies are considered in the next chapter.

Sexually atypical employment

Sexually atypical employment is a clumsy phrase and sex-inappropriate work is still worse since it carries normative overtones which could be deemed offensive in an era of equal opportunities legislation. However, they are the two labels most frequently used to describe the situation of someone who holds a job traditionally or stereotypically associated with a member of the opposite sex. Men doing 'women's work': the male midwife, the boy typist, the Mr Mop; women doing 'men's work': the female engineering technician, the lady financier, the woman Captain in the Merchant Marine; all are in sexually atypical employment. All have occupational roles which are inappropriate according to the sexual division of labour dominant in the western industrialized world.

The sexual division of labour operates horizontally and vertically. Horizontal segregation is reflected in the fact that men and women have different types of work. Women congregate in the administrative and clerical jobs and in the service and health sectors of the economy; men in the production industries (CSO, 1985). Vertical segregation is evident in the status of the jobs held by men and women. Even where they do the same type of work as women, men are infinitely more likely to gain the influential and high-status positions. For instance, in the teaching and nursing professions and in the social services where women form the bulk of the workforce, men dominate in the senior posts (Martin and Roberts, 1984).

It is fashionable to assume that the sexual division of labour is in decline; that the enactment of the sex discrimination legislation and the establishment of the Equal Opportunities Commission will banish occupational segregation. Indeed, there is some evidence (Martin and Roberts, 1984) that the pattern of employment for women is changing: women spend more of their lives in paid work, return to work quicker after having their children, and are seeking jobs of greater status and in a wider range of industries. However, there is equally strong evidence (Chiplin and Sloane, 1982; Hoiberg, 1982; West, 1982) that women are still disadvantaged in the labour market: they earn less than men even in the same type of industry; the range of jobs available to them is more restricted; and the opportunities of promotion remote. Women, or for that matter men, doing sexually atypical work are still relatively rare.

Various explanations for the sexual division of labour have been proposed and, rather than being mutually exclusive, tend to be complementary; differing in the level of analysis adopted. The first type centres on the differential psychological and biological capacities of the sexes. At its crudest, this explanation proposes that women are physically weaker and so precluded from some types of work; it suggests they are more emotionally labile and thus unsuitable for other types of work; it argues they lack aggression and drive which accounts for their failure to gain jobs at the top; and it claims that they have intrinsically inferior mathematical and spatial abilities which make them incapable of still more forms of work. The evidence for the existence of such sex differences is tenuous and suspect (Archer and Lloyd, 1982). In reality, there is far greater overlap in the psychological and physical abilities of the sexes than there are differences (evidence in the extensive review of the sex difference literature reported by Maccoby and Jacklin, 1974). Those minor differences which exist at that level are inconsistent across people and are far too weak to explain the sexual division of labour. Instead of explanations, it might be argued that in the absence of empirical evidence to support them, they represent rationalizations used to justify the existing system of occupational segregation. Sayers (1982) presents a lucid appraisal of the role of biology in explanations of sexual inequality; her book represents a good source for those wishing to examine this issue further.

The second type of explanation focuses upon the socialization process (Chetwynd and Hartnett, 1978). It claims that the sex differences in occupational aspirations and suitability are learnt rather than the product of innate cognitive or biological predispositions. It states that children learn what behaviours, emotions and beliefs are acceptable in each sex. They learn what jobs, at home and at work, are expected of each sex. The family, school and mass media, through explicit instruction and through the provision of models to be emulated, specify the parameters of appropriate action and thought. In this way, the child comes to know that there are distinct sets of rules and expectations applicable to the two sexes. The child arrives at the concept of gender differences. Sex differences and gender differences are quite distinct notions: the former refer to differences between men and women which are biologically determined, for instance the secondary sexual characteristics; the latter concern the differences between the images of the two sexes created by social processes. Gender differences are socially defined; conceptions of masculinity and femininity are not direct reflections of biological imperatives, they are completely dependent upon time, place and culture. The child acquires a version of gender differences appropriate to his or her culture and generation.

The image will include prescriptions and proscriptions about work (Deem, 1980; Chetwynd and Hartnett, 1978). Children as young as 5 years of age are able to describe what work a man should do and what he should not do; which jobs are right for a woman and which not permissible. At that age, they appear to have no idea that the woman doing 'men's work' would be unable to do it, they simply regard it as wrong and they consider the woman concerned to be strange and not likeable. The justificatory assumption that men do not do women's work (cooking, cleaning, etc.) because they are less good at it only comes later. Breakwell and Carter (forthcoming) have interviewed forty 6- and 7-year-olds, equally divided by sex, who were told a number of stories about people doing their jobs. Three types of work were described: secretarial, car repairs and household chores. In half the presentations, the person doing the work was male, in the others female. The children therefore heard some stories where the sex of the worker was at variance with that expected traditionally of the person doing that work. The children were asked to say how good the individual, in each case, would be at their work, whether it was 'right' that they should do it, and whether it was usual for a person of that sex to do the job. The children, both girls and boys, thought that people should not and would not normally breach sex role stereotypes. However, they did not believe that people in sexually atypical jobs would be less capable of doing their work well. Interestingly, it was only in relation to the household chores that boys and girls differed in the direction of the biases expressed. Both sexes felt that members of their own sex would be better at household chores, despite both sexes reckoning that it is women who do and should actually perform these tasks. It is important that at this young age children make gender prescriptions about jobs but they do not assume that the people who breach sex roles are incapable of doing the jobs properly. They seem to have to learn later the explanation in terms of innate inabilities which legitimates the sexual stratification of labour and supports prior beliefs: not an uncommon phenomenon in the development of discriminatory attitudes (Davey, 1983).

The child learns to discriminate before understanding why. Having learnt the lessons of discrimination well, the child is loathe to breach gender role expectations in choice of leisure interests, educational pursuits or occupational aspirations. Appropriate choices in these domains are vital if the child's masculinity or femininity is to be confirmed. To ignore these constraints is to challenge the properties which delineate one's gender. Most people, in their choice of career, avoid the challenge by conforming to the traditional gender expectations. This explanation of the sexual division of labour is fundamentally a social psychological one, founded upon the processes of social influence. The third type of explanation shifts from the pressures impinging upon the individual to the societal level.

The third explanation for the sexual division of labour is concerned with the economic processes which underlie it. It points to the fact that in the main women take the poorly paid, part-time, insecure jobs in the industrialized, capitalist economies. This suits the women because, by and large, they fit their work around their familial commitments. They take part-time work because they need to be at home when the children are not at school and because running the home requires much time. They take poorly paid work because they are less geographically mobile, tied by their husband's job, and because they are less likely to have acquired a skill or higher qualifications due to the structure of apprenticeship schemes in the past. This suits the employers because they need the 'reserve army of labour' represented by women. They need a fluid labour force which can be set to work or laid off according to economic exigencies. The men may be the hard core of their workforce but women comprise a secondary resource: cheaper and more malleable because mostly non-unionized and part-time so provided with minimal support from the legislation protecting employment. This description of the role of women in the workforce is sometimes known as the dual labour market theory (Roberts, Finnegan and Gallie, 1985). It essentially argues that the sexual division of labour is structurally determined, developing historically as the joint product of the position of women in a patriarchal familial system and the requirements of capitalism (Burman, 1979). It is interesting that it views women only within the nuclear family system. Women alone disappear as if they do not exist within this theoretical perspective. Women alone, without husband or children, would presumably not be subject to the same pressures to accept poor pay, poor prospects and insecure employment.

The gap between the second and third explanations is bridged by a fourth, concerned with the processes of schooling and selection which reinforce gender stereotypes learnt in childhood and funnel the individual into acceptable employment (Kaplan and Sedney, 1980). Overt sex discrimination in schooling is now illegal in Britain, just as it is in the process of selecting between candidates for a job. Yet it is clear that at both levels discrimination still takes place (Chiplin and Sloane, 1982). At school, boys may now have equal opportunity to choose cookery and girls to do woodwork with the rearrangement of the manifest curriculum. However, it has been suggested (Chetwynd and Hartnett, 1978) that there is a hidden curriculum which operates to direct the sexes into their appropriate gender roles. The attitudes held by teachers are subtly transmitted to their pupils. Teachers with traditional views of gender roles may be 'educating' their students in those roles without either explicitly trying to or even knowing that they are doing so. Recent work with young children has shown that teachers of both sexes pay more attention to boys in the classroom, are more positive about their successes, and encourage them more in scientific and technical enterprises (Wheldall, 1985).

Beyond the microcosm of the classroom, the hierarchy in the school itself is likely to purvey covert messages to its inmates. The fact that

Table 1 *Percentage by discipline and level of full-time students who are female*

	Post-graduate	Under-graduate	Other higher education
Medical, Dental, Health	37.8	48.3	83.3
Engineering and Technology	8.0	7.4	6.8
Science	21.6	33.7	27.3
Language and Literature	44.4	69.6	47.4
Arts	29.4	56.0	57.2

Source: derived from 1984 Education Statistics, HMSO.

girls will not see many women in positions of authority or teaching subjects in science or mathematics means that they are provided with no role model to emulate which would lead them to aspire to status or to science. Of course, boys have a similar absence of models in subjects entailing home economics, sewing, and, increasingly, the languages.

At first sight, the hidden curriculum may appear a relatively minor problem. It is not. It shapes the subject choices young people make at school which can determine what work is ultimately available to them. Girls are turned off science and technology at school and a major source of originality and skilled labour is shut down. This is reflected in a series of statistics. Table 1 shows the percentage of students in the five broad discipline-bands who are female at postgraduate, under-graduate and on other higher educational courses.

These figures represent the latest picture of a gradually changing situation. Over the last fifteen years in Britain, for instance, the influx of women into engineering and technology degree courses has been 2.25 per cent per five years. The rate of change in physics and chemistry has been even slower (1956: physics 6 per cent, chemistry 10 per cent; 1982: physics 12 per cent, chemistry 25 per cent). The rate of change clearly needs to accelerate if the needs of new technology industries for more science graduates are to be met. The Butcher Committee Report predicted that between 1984–89 there would be a 56 per cent overall increase in the graduates who would be needed. Given the drop in the birthrate and the increase in the entry requirements for higher education, the only source of this generation of technocrats will be those who traditionally opt for arts or humanities degrees and these are preponderantly women.

Entry to science, engineering and technology at degree level is very largely dependent upon gaining the correct O and A Level passes. It is interesting to examine the statistics on success in GCE/SCE and CSE for signs of changing patterns in the aspirations and expectations of young women. Table 2 shows the percentages of children gaining O Level or CSE grade 1 in a range of subjects. Table 3 gives the same information for A Levels.

It is evident that the same pattern of imbalance is present at both O and A Levels, though it is not so marked as it is at higher levels of education. There seems some scope for encouraging those girls who currently opt for science subjects to continue with them at university or in polytechnics.

The O Level figures reveal that it is not science *per se* which girls shy away from but most especially physics. This is vital because physics O Level is now a basic requirement for many science and engineering degree courses. Table 3, because it amalgamates the science subjects as a single category, fudges this issue for the A Levels. Table 4 gives older but more instructive information. It can be seen that a greater proportion of the physics A Levels are now gained by girls but the rate of change is very slow – slower than for any other science. Clearly, the 'hidden curriculum' at school is still functioning.

Industry compounds the inadequacies of the education system. The careers officers and personnel managers responsible for selection of people for jobs still hold the traditional stereotypes of male and female work (Hartnett, 1978). They discourage and actively prevent people from taking sexually atypical employment. Careers officers explain to young women who want to become engineers that it is a dirty job, too masculine and that they would not like it (Breakwell and Weinberger, 1983). Personnel managers believe that women cannot cope as middle managers and operate unofficial vetting and exclusion policies (Chetwynd and Hartnett, 1978). The way the system operates to control the flow of men into sexually atypical jobs (like midwifery or certain clerical-secretarial roles) is less well documented. Doubtless because, for some inexplicable reason, their plight arouses less outrage. It is no less real for that and needs study.

The four levels of explanation for the sexual division of labour fit together to create a virtually seamless garment which would predict the continuance of the system in perpetuity. Yet some people do evade it. Some people do cross the great divide and take employment which is sexually atypical. The individual choosing this course of action breaks with tradition in either type of work or status attained, breaching either horizontal or vertical segregation. This creates problems for the individual and for his, or more often her, family, workplace and community. It represents an affront to gender role expectations which cannot be ignored. It threatens the status quo:

Table 2 *Percentage of pupils leaving school in Great Britain with GCE/SCE O Level (Grades A-C) and CSE (Grade 1), 1982–3*

	Male	Female
English	34	46
History	14	16
French	11	20
Music, Drama	11	17
Maths	34	29
Physics	22	9
Chemistry	16	11
Biology	12	20
Other Science	19	3
Geography	20	14
English and Maths	26	26
English/Maths/Science	23	19
All leavers	460,000	442,000

Source: derived from 1984 Education Statistics, HMSO.

Table 3 *Percentage of pupils leaving school with two or more GCE 'A' Levels or three or more SCE H, 1982–3*

	Male	Female
English	28	52
Maths	53	30
Geography	23	18
Science	38	17
Arts/Social Science	30	49
Mixed	32	33

Source: Department of Education and Science.

Table 4 *GCE A Level passes: percentage gained by females*

	1956	1980
Maths	11.3	25.8
Physics	11.9	19.2
Chemistry	15.3	32.7
Computer Science	—	19.8

Source: Department of Education and Science.

disrupts the predictability of things, outrages social norms. It is, in fact, an act of rebellion which can be voluble and violent but is more often quiet (Breakwell, 1985a), a personal affair with untold social consequences. The implications for identity are extensive.

Threats to identity created by sexually atypical employment

This section addresses how sexually atypical employment has the power to threaten identity on all three fronts: continuity, distinctiveness and self-esteem. Doing such work queries *continuity* in relation to gender roles since it is fundamentally inconsistent with compliance with gender expectations. A woman who fails to conform with gender prescriptions in job choice calls into question her femininity. She becomes sexually suspect. If she happens to be good at her job, the doubt becomes stronger. Being a good worker in this case can be equated with being a bad woman. The social representation of her attacks her own continuing conception of her representation of her womanhood. It seeks to ferry her into an uneasy limbo between masculinity and femininity. If she happens to have either a husband or children, she is even more vulnerable: she can be castigated as a bad wife or mother. Essentially, the disapproval meted out to the woman who rebels in her choice of work imposes a form of discontinuity across her other roles. She is told that they cannot continue as before. Her new occupational activities preclude it. It is important to recognize that this may be completely untrue. The woman may perform all her other roles in precisely the way she did before: good woman, good wife, and good mother. However, her performance gains new social meaning by association with her new occupational role and this is what disrupts continuity. In a sense, the woman has no control over this disturbance in continuity. Once she makes her choice regarding work, the rest follows inexorably. Of course, she can use various strategies to resist the social representation and the attributions levelled at her and these are discussed in the next chapter.

The challenge to continuity may not be restricted to the abstract representation of the woman. Her work may indeed transform her relationships in her family and with friends. It may so alter her material resources and the timetabling of her day that continuity in the old style would be impossible. Increased income and decreased time at home would encourage changes both in the content and value dimensions of identity. In some senses, the discontinuity in how she is regarded by her family and friends may be greater than the disruption in her conception of herself. She may have harboured the desire to work in a 'man's job' for years and have grown accustomed to the implications such a move might have for her identity. To that extent, there is the possibility of anticipatory changes in identity. The same might be true in the case of unemployment where redundancy is an ominous possibility for some time preceding firm confirmation that it will occur. In both instances, the individual has time to begin the readjustment of identity in anticipation. Yet, in both cases, the actual move may be quite different from expectations. The woman, or indeed man, taking sexually atypical employment may fail fully to predict the familial and community consequences. The woman doing 'men's work' not only has to keep her own doubts in check, she also has to quieten those of her relatives and friends. They can be more sensitive to the breach with social expectations and certainly more horrified by the affront to gender role than the woman is herself. They can, therefore, resort to attempts to rectify her behaviour and may act as the most salient agents of social control, reinforcing the messages the woman will already be receiving from the world outside about her aberrant activities. There are many examples of husbands insisting that their wives should stay at home with the children, or of parents dissuading their boys from taking a job which would impugn their masculinity. The disruption of the place held in the family or in a network of friends can represent an indirect threat to continuity in identity structures resultant from the shift to sexually atypical employment.

The threat to identity can emanate from modifications in *distinctiveness*. The principle suggests that people value being unique, different from others. But the distinctiveness has to be in ways which are positively valued. Choosing a job defined as sexually atypical can certainly exaggerate a person's distinctiveness (for example, being the first woman Prime Minister is distinctive). The central question concerns whether such hyper-distinctiveness is actually desirable. If it is not, it can be considered a threat to identity; something which requires remedial action. If it is desirable, then it may necessitate considerable accommodation of existing content and value dimensions of identity but it will not constitute a threat via the abrogation of distinctiveness. In fact, in such a situation, the threat would be evident only through the disjuncture in continuity of the content of identity that it would entail and this might be easily remedied, especially if anticipatory reorganization of the structure of identity had occurred. Since vertical and horizontal segregation normally result in women occupying low status, low paid, unskilled jobs, it seems reasonable to predict that women breaking out of the straitjacket of their gender roles will gain distinctiveness which does have features which are clearly positive. Taking 'men's work' means gaining greater status, better wages and more skills; all are socially valued. For the man taking 'women's work' the situation is reversed. In most cases, he will be losing rewards normally socially prized since 'women's jobs' rarely carry social status or high earning potential. The man is sexually atypical employment gains distinctiveness, even notoriety, but it has little kudos.

The focus on the value of distinctiveness leads naturally to the issue of *self-esteem*. The impact of sexually atypical employment upon self-esteem has to be equivocal. It will depend on a number of factors. Firstly, it will depend on the precise nature of the social representation of the person who breaks gender expectations in a particular job. Thus far, sexually atypical employment has been treated as it if were homogeneous and this is clearly false. A woman Prime Minister, a female professor of physics, a lady coalminer, a girl nightclub bouncer, are all examples of sexually atypical employment. But the women doing these things are not imagined to share similar attributes and are not subject to the same criteria of evaluation simply because they are all doing 'men's work'. The expectations and status normally appended to the job will vibrate with gender expectations to produce a strange concoction that will establish the social representation of a woman in that job. Social representations will vary in their positivity and thus in their power to damage or contribute to self-esteem. As a general rule, it seems likely that the social representation will be most derogatory where the qualities attached to the job are maximally differentiated from those archetypically associated with the gender of the intruder. Secondly, the threat to self-esteem will depend upon the actual status, material and intrinsic rewards of the work done. A good income with a great deal of job-satisfaction and social status will militate against any diminution of self-esteem despite the sexually atypical nature of the work. Of course, job-satisfaction is not simply tied to the pleasure gained from the work itself, it also arises from the pattern of contacts with other workers. For the man or woman who breaches gender role expectations, relations with workmates may generate enough extra friction to quell or obliterate job-satisfaction. This may be another prong in the attack on self-esteem. Finally, for self-esteem the fact that the decision to take a sexually atypical job was volitional may be vitally important. When a person ignores gender-prescriptions deliberately, he or she has little option but to take full responsibility for the choice. Accepting that responsibility may result in the threat to self-esteem being more dangerous. Having accepted responsibility, the individual has no cover when the family and friends, and society more generally, begin to condemn and question. In considering coping strategies in later chapters, some emphasis is placed upon the ability to reallocate responsibility for failures and successes.

Given that sexually atypical employment does have the power to threaten identity on all three fronts – distinctiveness, continuity and self-esteem – it seems that for those who take such jobs something in the socialization process has gone wrong; they have failed to learn their lessons well. This sort of assumption underlies studies which have sought to tie patterns of parenting to atypical career choices in their children. But this has been as fruitless as the hunting of the snark. It is true that some generalizations have been produced. For instance, working mothers are more likely to have daughters who choose 'men's work'; families with no sons are more likely to have daughters who go into heavy industries as skilled workers and are more likely to have daughters who go on to further education; and men choosing 'women's work' are marginally less likely to have had a man living in their home when they were children (Cooper and Davidson, 1982; Lewis and Cooper, 1983). None of these factors are totally predictive and it seems that there is certainly no single cause for the breach in gender expectations. Moreover, the breach in respect of work choice is unlikely to be extended into other domains of the gender role, except those directly determined by work.

A less simple answer to the question might suggest that some people cannot tolerate the restrictions of gender roles because their talents and abilities drive them outside. Such an answer is complex because it begs so many further questions – such as, what determines their talents and how do they come to be aware of them. Notions of psychological androgyny are relevant here and will be examined in later chapters (Cook, 1985; Kaplan and Sedney, 1980).

Within the model of identity proposed here, it is not too difficult to explain why an individual would choose to threaten identity by choice of work. Preferences in relation to work will be determined by both past and current ideology assimilated by the individual, filtered through the distorting mirror of the communication systems of the groups and interpersonal networks to which he or she belongs. Existing identity structures will dictate what work is deemed preferable but only in relation to new incoming information about what is available and socially valued. The resultant choice is the product of a whole biographical history. It may not be anticipated that it will threaten identity. If it is, it may be considered worthy of the risk as long as the advantages for identity are predicted to be greater than the costs. This non-material and material cost-benefit analysis will take account of the resources available to cope with the incipient threat. If anticipated, the threat will only deter movement into the sexually atypical work if it is considered to be beyond the power of the individual to cope. Of course, the individual may be in the worst position to calculate that power accurately.

Communalities across threats to identity

In order to understand how any movement of the individual in the social matrix or any social change gains the power to threaten identity, it is necessary to examine its social and personal meaning. The examples of unemployment and sexually atypical employment illustrate that the movement of the individual gains meaning only within its historical context. Being unemployed attacks self-esteem because of the social representation of the unemployed developed over six centuries. It also attacks self-esteem for other reasons (loss of income, status, etc.) but even these are dependent upon ideological structures to become meaningful. For instance, poverty would not attack self-esteem in a society where poverty was lauded though it might have other negative effects. Sexually atypical employment is socially defined and its implications are established in social representations. Other examples of threat can be given, such as marginality, ethnic minority group membership, bereavement, or changes consequent upon ageing, but they share many characteristics. They represent threats because they abrogate continuity, distinctiveness or self-esteem but they have the power to do that because social influence processes append specific social meanings to them. The ideologies, generated by groups and social categories, manifested in rhetoric and propaganda, define the meaning of movements of the individual in the social matrix (Althusser, 1985; Donald and Hall, 1986; Eccleshall *et al.*, 1984). If the nature of the threat, and the coping strategies which can be used against it, are to be understood, the ideologies which contextualize them must be understood too. This stipulation applies as forcibly to threats whose origins lie in changes in interpersonal networks as it does to those produced by movement in group or social category memberships. So, for instance, the social meaning of divorce has changed in western culture in the last fifty years (changes embodied in legislation) such that the implications it has for the identities of those involved have altered no matter how tragic they remain.

This is why the descriptions of unemployment and sexually atypical employment focused on their ideological backdrop besides examining the changes in material circumstances they bring about.

Ideologies may establish the social meaning of a move which is potentially threatening but the personal meaning of the move to the individual concerned will depend upon belief systems and values assimilated into the identity throughout life. The personal meaning of a current threat will be a function of both its contemporary social meaning and judgements of it on the basis of well-assimilated structures of identity. In predicting coping strategies, both the personal and social meanings of the threats need consideration. Having established something of the social meaning of unemployment and sexually atypical employment, in describing coping strategies later they will be used as prime examples and more of their personal meaning becomes evident. However, throughout it is important to remember that these are treated as examples; other threats share the same essential structural ingredients.

4 Self-protection at the intra-psychic level

The purpose of this and the next two chapters is to outline the range of options open to someone seeking to cope with a threat to identity. Each coping strategy is presented with examples of its usage, outcomes and drawbacks. The main object is to examine how the array of logically possible strategies for coping relate to each other. This chapter focuses primarily upon strategies of self-protection lodged at the intra-psychic level. The next two chapters are concerned with coping at the interpersonal and intergroup levels.

The transience of threatened identities

Before discussing coping strategies, a distinction needs to be drawn between residing in a threatening position and the experience of threat to identity. The individual may occupy a potentially threatening position for an extensive period. A person may remain unemployed or in sexually atypical employment for years; the congenitally physically or mentally handicapped are likely to remain so for ever. They occupy a threatening position in the social matrix which is stable and con-tinuous but the threat to identity it creates is inevitably transient. Threats to the structure of identity are short-lived because, as soon as they gain conscious recognition, the individual will initiate strategies designed to obliterate them. Consequently, residence in a threatening social position is not coterminous with the experience of threat.

Occupancy of the threatening position may be chronic; experience of threat is rarely so.

Since the experience of threat is dependent upon the efficacy of the coping strategies used by the individual, it can be recurrent. Strategies designed to eradicate or ameliorate may fail or succeed only briefly, in which case the experience of threat would return. This periodic recrudescence of threat is important in explaining some apparent inconsistencies in the actions of victims and their switch from one coping strategy to another. As long as the person remains in the threatening position, the strategy for containing its threat must be maintained. Yet there is no assurance that it will remain effective over time, even if it proves so initially. When the erosion of its power becomes evident, a new tactic will be employed sometimes in tandem with the old, sometimes as a replacement. Therefore, in considering coping strategies, it would be inappropriate to regard them as mutually exclusive alternatives. They are all part of the arsenal of self-protection possessed by the individual and can be used in collusion.

The effective operation of coping strategies ensure that the experience of threat is normally transient. However, on occasion, the threat can still be considered chronic even though it erupts into consciousness only spasmodically. Where the threat so disrupts the processes of identity that very central and highly salient elements in the content or value dimensions of identity are challenged, coping strategies can be mere palliatives. They do not banish the threat, instead the effort to control its implications takes over the individual's whole life. Threat of this form which shapes the person's every move is chronic. The energy devoted to keeping it in check is so great that there is little left over for anything else.

What constitutes a coping strategy?

Any activity, in thought or dead, which has as its goal the removal or modification of a threat to identity can be regarded as a coping strategy. Threat itself has been defined in terms of subjective experience rather than in relation to a constellation of objective circumstances. A threat exists where the individual perceives the disruption of the principled operation of identity processes. A coping strategy requires a similarly cognitive definition: *anything the individual believes to be done in order to expunge threat, constitutes a coping strategy.* The cognitive definition is concerned with the intention which precedes the strategy: an act or thought becomes an attempt at coping if it is intended to remove the threat. The cognitive definition is not concerned with the outcome of the strategy: it remains a coping strategy even if it fails.

This type of definition has an obvious weakness in that there may be occasions when the threatened individual is employing a coping strategy but is unwilling to acknowledge that the intention is to deal with the threat. For instance, the person who is using denial as a defence against the threat is hardly likely to admit that denial is intended as a means of self-protection; such an admission would vitiate its efficacy because it would mean accepting that the threat existed. Therefore, in order to make the definition comprehensive, it has to have a further element: *any thought or action which succeeds in eliminating or ameliorating threat can be considered a coping strategy, whether it is consciously recognized as intentional or not*. This means that an observer may know that an individual in a threatening position is implementing a coping strategy even when its user is either unaware of it or unwilling to admit it. The observer's task is considerably aided by the fact that there has been much written about how people respond when faced with threat or trauma. Action which fits into the taxonomy of coping strategies that can be constructed is reasonably likely to be functioning as an attempt at coping.

Coping strategies can have any or all of the following targets:

   (i) the removal of aspects of the social context, at the material or ideological level, which generate threat;
  (ii) the movement of the individual into a new social position which is less threatening;
 (iii) the revision of identity structures, on the content or value dimensions, which enables the identity processes to operate again in accordance with the principles of continuity, distinctiveness and self-esteem.

The strategies used to engender such changes are pitched at a number of different levels: intra-psychic; interpersonal; and intergroup. In discussing those at each level, it is worth noting that strategies at one level will have repercussions for events at the others. This domino effect is particularly apparent operating from the intergroup level down to the interpersonal and intra-psychic. For instance, strategies involving the genesis of intergroup conflict or discrimination cannot fail to have an impact upon interpersonal and intra-psychic configurations. Yet the effect can occur in reverse, if less noticeably at first. For example, the actions of a single individual or a small coterie can bring about massive movements in group relations, as is evidenced by the

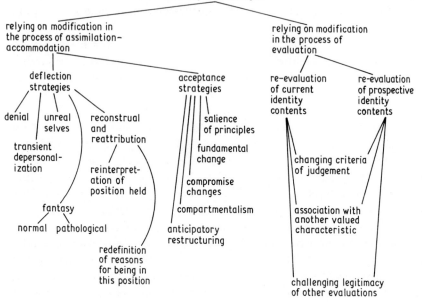

Figure 4   *Intra-psychic coping strategies*

impact of terrorist activity. For the purpose of clarity in the analysis, these three levels will be described independently in this chapter and the next.

Intra-psychic coping strategies

The range of intra-psychic coping strategies is depicted in Figure 4. Intra-psychic coping strategies operate at the level of cognitions and emotions rather than in terms of action, although they may have very serious implications for subsequent action. They rely upon the processes of assimilation-accommodation and evaluation.

Strategies relying on the process of assimilation-accommodation

Basically, strategies relying on assimilation-accommodation cluster into two groups: those which deflect and those which accept the identity implications of the threat. Deflection strategies entail the refusal to modify either the value or content dimensions of identity in the direction required by the threatening position occupied. Acceptance strategies result in the revision of one or both of the dimensions of identity in a manner congruent with the threat; changes which create a break in continuity, a loss of positive distinctiveness, or a reduction in self-esteem.

Deflection strategies
There are a range of deflection strategies commonly used.

Denial Denial is a well-documented response to stress (Lazarus and Folkman, 1984): the distressing reality is simply denied; the existence of the threat to identity is not acknowledged. Denial can be a complex strategy with a number of stages. First, the facts are denied, then their relevance, then their urgency, then the need to act, then the emotions aroused and, finally, the importance of these emotions. The strategy can be seen in its most virulent form in responses to news of a grave illness. The man who is told that he has two months to live at one level may accept this information, discussing the implications for his family with calm rationality, but at another level may refuse to accept that the information has any relevance at all and may, within a few minutes of discussing the trauma for his family, start to talk about a holiday he will take them on in five months' time. It is as if the mind, having perused the full horror of the situation, censors the information. Sometimes the outcome is partial amnesia and the person is simply not able to remember the information which has horrified (Lazarus and Longo, 1953; Lazarus and Alfert, 1964). At other times, recall of the information is retained but it is refused attention; the person cannot concentrate upon its meaning (Maher, 1970; Goodwin and Guze, 1984; Rosenhan and Seligman, 1984).

In relation to a threat to identity, four sequential layers of denial are feasible:

(i) denial of the fact of occupying the threatening position: for instance, the man who is made redundant may simply refuse to believe it.

(ii) denial that being in that position is threatening: for instance, an unemployed person may acknowledge the fact but reject the idea that it represents a social stigma.

(iii) denial of the need to change identity structures despite recognizing that the position is threatening: for instance, the unemployed person may feel the stigma and suffer the loss of the latent benefits of work but refuse to change either the content or value dimensions of identity, denying that continuity, distinctiveness or self-esteem are breached.

(iv) denial of the emotional implications of a change to the content dimension of identity: for instance, the unemployed person may revise the self-concept to assimilate the derogatory stereotype attached to his or her employment status but may deny that this causes anger, despair, or any other emotional reaction.

An individual may use all four layers of denial when facing a threatening position before the strategy crumbles. Denial is, at best, a temporary, holding strategy. It attacks the individual's effective orientation to reality, preventing action appropriate to the predicament. The person who is busily denying his unemployment may fail to make the necessary effort to regain a job. Denial of the facts to oneself, upon occasion, may be accompanied by strategies at the interpersonal level to delude others. The man who becomes redundant may act out elaborate performances to persuade others that he is still at work: leaving home each morning at 7.30 a.m. to catch the train, dressed for the office, returning at 6 p.m. still carrying his briefcase, but spending all day in the library, hiding from knowledgeable eyes. Such denial and deceit serve only to bend reality and, while they may be short-term palliatives, are counterproductive in essence.

However, in evaluating denial as a coping strategy it is important to consider its four distinct layers separately. Denial of the fact that one occupies a threatening position is inevitably disadvantageous in the long run because it isolates the person from a reality which is unlikely to go away and may get progressively worse if ignored. Denial that the position is threatening, rejecting the need to change identity, and dismissing the emotional implications of any modifications made, may all act as staging posts to the use of other coping strategies. These layers of denial can be precursors for other tactics; for instance, the evolution of a conscious attack upon the legitimacy through a reconstrual of the situation which might serve to justify and rationalize denial. Denial and reconstrual should not be confused: the former is essentially irrational, a departure from reality and its rules of logic and fact; the latter is the creative interpretation of fact within the broad boundaries of rationality.

To the extent that denial can be used almost as a tactic to buy a psychological time-out before resuming the struggle with an unpleasant reality, it can be productive but only in so far as it is a transient component in the battle against threat. Unfortunately, denial can become an habitual strategy. Whenever faced with threat and for as long as it remains, the person employs denial. As long as the strategy is reinforced with some sort of success it remains the automatic response. Habitual denial, often because it encompasses many realms of the person's life, severely damages the ability to deal with reality.

Occasionally, the results can be tragic. The case of a woman who committed infanticide illustrates this point. As a girl of 16, she became pregnant. She had the child but since she was unmarried and so young, the child was taken into care and then adopted. At 18 years of age she was cohabiting with a man much older than herself, became pregnant by him, but consistently refused to acknowledge the pregnancy. She had a miscarriage. Nine months later she was pregnant again and throughout the pregnancy persistently denied that she was having a baby. She refused to visit her GP and would not go into hospital for the delivery of the child. The baby was born at home with only the father in attendance. The woman denied that the child was hers just after the birth. She was at first passionate in her rejection of the baby but then became quiet and appeared to accept it. When the man left her to get some rest, she was holding the child. When he returned to the room some hours later, he intended to get ready for work. He opened his wardrobe, pulled out a drawer and found a black dustbin liner containing the child's body. The woman, when inter-viewed by the police, claimed never to have been pregnant and denied all knowledge of the child.

There is one form of denial which is particularly interesting since it appears to be a developmental phenomenon. Children of ethnic minority groups, between the ages of 4 and 10 years, at various historical times have been found to deny that they belong to their own racial group. Children are aware of racial differences from about 4 years of age and as soon as they can distinguish one race from another they start to learn the attitudes which the wider society has towards each race (Pushkin and Veness, 1973; Milner, 1984). For the children of ethnic minorities this means, in the main, learning a negative stereo-type of one's own group. Stevenson and Stewart (1958) showed that black Americans, between 4 and 7 years of age, were more likely than their white peers to perceive members of their own race as aggressive, bad, fearful, mean and unsuccessful. In Britain, Milner (1973) reported that West Indian and Asian immigrants were significantly more likely than children of the indigenous population to consider members of their own races to be 'bad', 'ugly' and not 'nice'. However, Breakwell (1974), in a more exhaustive study, found that 9-year-old children, born in Britain, of Afro-Caribbean parents, were not universally negative about their own group. They were no more critical of black people than white children were of white people. As one little black boy said, 'Blacks is better than whites, more friendly like and nice to you.' He was followed a few minutes later by a white lad of the same age, who had not heard his statement, who said: 'Whites are easier to get on with than blacks. They're nicer.' Yet the children seemed to have a differentiated view of racial groups. Typically, the children commented that 'not all whites are bad, not all blacks are bad – there are good and bad in both'. But black girls were significantly more critical of their own race. For instance, when asked to choose the race of characters for a story about the heroic capture of a wicked thief, these black girls designated the hero white and the villain black. Black boys, on the other hand, nominated a black man as the hero and a white man as the thief.

This gender difference is interesting. It may also be theoretically important because it shows that, in responding to the task, the children did not simply reiterate what they were seeing at that time on the mass media – at least, the boys did not. This finding may be explained in a number of ways. Firstly, it is possible that the lads are less sensitive or more resistant to stereotypes of their ethnic group received through the mass media. Secondly, it is feasible that black girls as women and black believe themselves to be in a doubly disadvantaged position and so have twice the reason to express criticisms of their own group. There are a number of other potential explanations of the finding. However, they are all merely speculative since the data do not permit validation of any of them.

It is important to consider the timing of these studies since it may explain the differences in their results. Societal attitudes towards ethnic minorities have changed over a thirty-year period and the data from the children reflect these changes. The children of ethnic minorities become less deprecating of their own group as society in general moves toward the eradication of the stigma attached to the group. Certainly, there has been a parallel change in the incidence of denial by these children.

Clark and Clark (1947) first showed that black children in the USA were subject to 'ethnic self-misidentification'. They gave children the task of saying which of two dolls, one white and one black, they most resembled. Black children were significantly more likely to misidentify themselves than white children, choosing to say that they were most similar to the white doll. Morland (1963) replicated the finding and showed that the children were well aware that the dolls represented the two races. The methodology of these early studies was heavily criticized (Greenwald and Oppenheim, 1968) since it could be argued that the light-skinned black child was making a valid claim in saying that the white doll was more similar to his or her own skin pigmentation than the black doll. This resulted in the use of more subtle instruments to measure ethnic identification. For instance, Jahoda, Thompson and Bhatt (1972) in Britain used an identikit task where the child built up a self-portrait from a diverse range of component parts representative of the physiognomy and pigmentation of the races involved. Yet, even these more carefully constructed tests showed significant levels of self-misidentification in the children of ethnic minority groups (Hraba and Grant, 1970, in the USA; Milner, 1973, in Britain).

Ethnic misidentification of this sort does seem to be tied to holding negative attitudes towards one's own group. For instance, in Breakwell's 1974 study, the black girls who held a more negative stereotype of black people were the only ones to exemplify a self-misidentification. When asked to indicate which a series of pictures (representing a range of skin tones and hair colours) most closely resembled themselves, only the black girls in the sample failed to pick a portrait reflecting their own race. This finding is compatible with the notion that membership of an ethnic minority will challenge self-esteem if the individual has accepted the dominant negative stereotype of that group. Having assimilated the negative image of their own race, these 9-year-old black girls were protecting their self-esteem by denying to themselves and the rest of the world that they belonged to that group. Interestingly, the misidentification extended to their relatives too: they represented their mother, father and siblings as white. Evasion of the group membership could not be attained if the rest of the family was accepted to belong, so they are also transmuted. The black boys did not engage in such denial.

Why there should be this sex difference is unknown. It is possible that the strong dichotomy of gender roles in black families and communities would result in marked differences in the socialization pressures experienced by the boys and girls; with the girls gaining less self-esteem as a consequence of their position within the group. This could explain why they are more willing to deny their ethnic origin; they have less to gain by maintaining it.

Ethnic self-misidentification represents a form of denial but it also comprises a form of psychological mobility. Actual social mobility is impossible: these young girls cannot exit from their race in reality. They take the next best option: they exit subjectively. It is, however, a short-lived phenomenon. None of the studies have found that ethnic self-misidentification persists into adolescence. There are too many occasions when the misidentification can be disconfirmed for it to be maintained or for it to retain its power to salve self-esteem. As the child grows older, the pressures of realism overcome wish-fulfilment in conceptions of the self.

Transient depersonalization Goodwin and Guze (1984) describe depersonalization as a 'disturbing sense that one's body has changed or become distorted' which is often accompanied by derealization where the physical world begins to feel so changed that it is totally alien. Depersonalization in its most extreme forms is a hallmark of anxiety neurosis. Rosenberg (1984) extended the definition of the term to encompass reference to feelings of having lost one's personal identity, becoming strange and unreal. Depersonalization which is severe and chronic occurs frequently in the schizophrenias. However, Rosenberg suggests that 'transient depersonalization', the fleeting momentary experience of feeling estranged from oneself, is a common occurrence, not indicative of psychiatric disturbance. Anyone can experience transient depersonalization; in its grip they do not recognize themselves, stand outside of themselves and observe themselves in a detached, disconnected way.

Rosenberg's studies of adolescents showed that up to 70 per cent of those people investigated had experienced transient depersonalization. Its occurrence was tied to the experience of some threat to the individual's sense of continuity. Unanticipated changes in the physical or social environment precipitated depersonalization. Violations of self-expectations were also strongly associated with the phenomenon. For instance, a failure to act in accordance with firmly held beliefs or behaviour which was dissonant with attitudes were often precursors of depersonalization.

It seems, then, that depersonalization is a response to threats to identity. The question then becomes: is it a coping strategy? Depersonalization which is transient, rather than chronic as in the case of psychosis, can act to anaesthetize the individual from the initial pain of the threat but its effects will wear off rapidly. Where the threat is chronic and the depersonalization transient, the respite is momentary. As a coping strategy, it consequently has severe limitations. The most serious of these is that it does not appear to be under conscious control. People do not decide to depersonalize and then do so; it is something which happens to them, seemingly beyond volitional interference. It seems to happen when the process of assimilation is faced with new information about the self which is so disruptive of continuity, distinctiveness and self-esteem that it cannot fit it anywhere into the identity-structure and treats it as if it were about some other creature. But the cut-out in the assimilation process is apparently automatic, not prefaced by a decision to reject the change. Depersonalization is thus experienced as different to denial because of the strange sense of other-worldliness it encompasses but they are similar in that both delay acknowledgement of the change needed in the identity structure.

Real selves and unreal selves Depersonalization has a less dramatic counterpart in the tendency, documented by Turner (1976, 1978, 1984), Turner and Schutte (1981), and Turner and Billings (1984), of people to distinguish between their real self and other unreal selves. Turner argues that the subjective sense of self is context specific: situational variables highlighting the salience and continuity of some rather than other elements in the self-concept which are reified as self-images. For Turner, the self-conception is stable and generalized, self-images are transient and specific to the social context giving rise to them. The self-image of the moment is evaluated against the standard set by the self-conception; self-images at variance with the self-conception are regarded as inauthentic or unreal. Their relevance for the real self-conception is rejected, they have no power to change it. Turner quotes the example of a young man who became Rag King for a week and behaved in a manner congruent with the expectations of the role: appearing in drag, flirting with everyone, highly extroverted, boozy and frenetic. But he claimed that this was no reflection of his real and enduring self. He felt that this was an unreal, inauthentic image of himself. He experienced the conflict between the transient self-image and his stable self-conception. In the terminology of the current model, he experienced threat to continuity and his coping strategy was to deny the credibility of the information incoming about his identity. His behaviour was attributed to the constraints of the situation and its relevance for his notion of his identity was rejected. The result is the experiential division between the real self and unreal selves.

Acting in an inauthentic way has parallels with the phenomenon of transient depersonalization but it is not experienced as a loss of control of the body. The judgement that the behaviour cannot be attributed to the real self often happens only in retrospect. There is no sense of other-worldliness at the time. The person decides that the behaviour, thought or feeling was so much at variance with his or her abiding self-conception that it has to be attributed to an aberration. Labelled aberrant, inexplicable, or unreal, it is deprived of its legitimate demand for assimilation into the identity structure. Assuming that the aberration is not then recurrent and that other people do not challenge its assumed irrelevance, this type of coping strategy can work. People have a remarkable facility for cordoning off information about themselves and for refusing to assimilate it. Unwelcome facts can die in quarantine, as long as nothing intervenes to release them.

Fantasy   Fantasizing can be used as a strategy for blocking a threat to identity. Fantasy can range from whimsical speculation, through daydreams, to full-blooded visions which totally occupy the person's life. Research on fantasy has tended to focus upon that which touches upon sex and violence. Friday (1981) describes raunchy and pitiful examples of women's sexual fantasies which envelope most varieties of and contexts for sexual activity. She outlines the many functions which sexual fantasies serve in relationships and out of them. Not all fantasies derive from threats. They can be used to heighten pleasure and anticipation in non-threatening situations. Where they are used in response to threat, they typically represent only a temporary escape, taking the form of wishful thinking.

Fantasy has the power to wish the threat away and replace it with a more acceptable form of reality. The unemployed man has visions of himself as managing director of his own firm; the woman, recently widowed, imagines extensive conversations with her dead spouse; and the child bereft of friends after a move to a new town conjures up a bevy of close mates who are purely imaginary. Fantasies vary in duration and complexity. They can be single, fleeting mental images designed to boost morale and revive self-esteem: seeing oneself as the winner of the Le Mans after just hearing that one has failed the driving test for the fourth time. They can be coherent and well-developed tales that one tells oneself under stress, or at any spare moment, about one's skills and talents, attractiveness and future achievements. They do not necessarily have any immediate resemblance to the threatening context. The fantasy need not deal with to problem which generates the threat. It may simply shift the individual into another parallel psychic reality. For instance, one young man of 19, who had been unemployed for most of the time since leaving school and who had a difficult time dealing with his widowed mother, fantasized that he had a prize-winning bull terrier dog. His fantasy entailed nothing to do with getting a job or resolving his problems with his mother. The fantasy, which occupied most of the time he had alone, consisted of caring for the dog: what he would feed it, how it should be exercised, and when it could be mated. Such stories can live on in the imagination for years and be subject to updates and revisions. For instance, by the time the young man with the fantasy bull terrier was nearly 21, the dog had been blessed with puppies and further competition successes;

the lad was considering the financial viability of setting up a breeding kennel. It should not be thought that this young man had deluded himself into believing the dog actually existed. He knew the fantasy for what it was but it developed and matured as he did.

Clearly, there is a fine line between the fantasy which acts as a temporary salve to identity, barricading it from a reality which attacks, and a delusion or hallucination which might serve the same purpose. Essentially, fantasy is largely under conscious control. The individual knows when a fantasy is in progress and can turn it off as easily as switching off a radio. The person controls the fantasy, not the reverse. There is no such control over delusions and hallucinations. However, even fantasizing can become habitual; resorted to at the least sign of threat. Like all of the coping strategies described so far, fantasy can erode the ability to relate to reality appropriately. Also, like them, it can protect the identity temporarily from threat and allow time for the evolution of more effective strategies. All of these strategies generate a common danger: they can trap the unwary, preventing the individual from appreciating the need to develop reality-oriented strategies. So, fantasy may be benign but only when employed within strict limits.

Psychotherapists make the distinction between normal and patho-logical fantasy; the latter being distinguished by its unavailability to conscious control and, often, by the socially unacceptable nature of its content. Psychotherapy makes use of fantasy to access the origins of pathology and to intervene. At the individual level, Cox (1978) suggests the therapist should use free-association to unearth 'fantasies of incest, penis envy, the dentate vagina, the frustrating breast....' (p. 64). Cox uses these fantasies to enrich his knowledge of the psycho-dynamics underlying the individual's psychosis. He points out that such fantasies are not always rooted in fear and failure. Some are reflections of memories of success and celebrations and these offer equally valuable insights into the individual so long as the therapist can resist feeling threatened by the client's pleasure in these fantasies of achievement. The implication is that fantasy, once made public, has the power to threaten the therapeutic relationship if it triggers doubts or weaknesses in the indentity of the therapist. Cox points to the vital fact that therapy is two-edged and the therapist may be threatened by what happens within it. If this occurs, he suggests that the therapist will try to protect his or her own identity by re-structuring the therapeutic process. Cox cautions against this being done except in the full knowledge of the motives for it.

Psychotherapists for many years have argued that the fantasies people have are not particularly individualized or unique. Fantasies feed off popularly held beliefs and shared desires, common practices and consensual experience. Thus, group psychotherapists (Bion, 1959; Jacques, 1955) argue that participants in therapeutic groups should be encouraged to reveal their fantasies to each other and begin to appreciate, as they discover that their fantasies are similar, how far they share common problems. In reviewing this literature, Kellerman (1979) suggests that this process of sharing fantasies can result in much greater cohesiveness for the group and increased therapeutic change may result. Seen in the framework of the model of threatened identity being presented here, this finding from pscyhotherapeutic practice can be explained. The argument would be: a threat elicits fantasy as a coping strategy; finding the fantasy to be one shared with others allows, firstly, the fantasy to be normalized and, secondly, opens the potential for re-examining the threat subjectively; within the group there is the opportunity to discuss the threat with others known to share the initial response to that threat; and, finally, the group represents an arena for forging and testing new responses to the threat. The individuals in the group may respond to different threats with different fantasies. This is not really relevant to the argument. The main point is that the fact of fantasizing is normalized but then there is the chance to go beyond fantasy in generating coping strategies. The group is a buffer protecting the individual who experiments with other strategies. It may even suggest alternatives.

Reconstrual and re-attribution   Occupation of a social position has the power to threaten only if it has implications which breach the principles guiding the identity processes. The individual may seek to reconstrue the situation or its implications in order to eliminate its power to do this. There are a number of tactics which can be used within the reconstrual strategy.

(i) *Re-definition or re-interpretation of the properties of the position occupied.* This may involve any or all of a series of sub-routines:

   ignoring some aspects of the situation or, at least, deprecating their importance

   introducing information from a wider context which modifies the meaning of the position

   inventing properties for the position which previously did not exist.

For instance, an unemployed man might use all three sub-routines in reconstruing his situation. He might ignore the financial hardship consequent upon unemployment or claim it is unimportant for him. He might emphasize that unemployment will give him time to develop new skills which will benefit him subsequently. He may insist that his unemployment has to be understood against the backdrop of mass unemployment in his particular community or industry. He may suggest that unemployment is, for him, equivalent to early retirement since he is 55 and does not expect to find another job. All of these gambits represent creative re-definitions of the position in which he finds himself. All of them serve to dampen the threat of the position. They exemplify how assimilation can be purposive and that accommodation is likely to be generative.

This suggestion that construal of a situation is active and creative and driven by personal needs or motives is hardly novel. As Bertrand Russell (1930) pointed out, 'popular induction depends upon the emotional interest of the instances' and a host of psychological experimentation upon inference processes and social judgement (for instance, the work reviewed by Nisbett and Ross, 1980) has served to prove him right. Nisbett and Ross conclude that the source of many errors of inference lies in two tendencies: 'the overgeneralization of certain generally valid, intuitive, inferential strategies and the under-utilization of certain formal, logical and statistical, strategies' (p. 15). These intuitive strategies include the application of 'pre-existent knowledge structures' – schemas, beliefs, and theories – and the utilization of 'representativeness' and 'availability' heuristics. This means that people's interpretations of events are 'often unduly influenced by prior beliefs' and thus distortion of experience and memory occurs. In relation to identity threats, this work on inference processes supports the notion that situations which are threatening will be reinterpreted. Existing belief systems about the content and value of identity will cut in to distort inferences to be drawn about identity from information incoming from the situation.

(ii) *Re-definition of the reason for being in the position occupied.* Normally this involves a change in the pattern of attributions (i.e. explanations) made for one's own actions and those of others. Upon finding oneself in a threatening position, one tactic of re-attribution would be to deny responsibility for being there. The shift would be from an internal to an external locus of control. The victim attributes his or her position to external constraints or forces beyond individual control, whether they be fate or chance or macro-socioeconomic processes. Re-attribution of this sort can protect against the threat. Even though occupancy of the position may contravene the dictates of continuity, distinctiveness and self-esteem, it may possess no power to alter identity structures if it is deemed inescapable. Its relevance to identity is minimized since being there is not volitional. If not self-determined, its importance to self-conception can be contested. This ties back into Ralph Turner's work on unreal selves: when people saw their actions as determined by institutional constraints, they felt they were not acting as their 'real selves'; the real self acted on impulse, disregarding the situational context. When people engage in re-attribution, they effectively move the threat away from the real self. Of course, in some instances, re-attribution can serve to acquire a set of actions for the real self. For instance, where the actions have positive implications for self-esteem and continuity, they may be claimed to result from personal premeditation and effort or talent, rather than the individual admitting their roots in temporary circumstances.

To propose that such re-attribution tactics are used when threatened is to suggest that the original theory of attribution is inadequate. In Kelley's (1967) formulation of the theory, people were said to act rationally in attributing causes for events, coming to conclusions after analysing co-variations in information available. Kelley's only concession to the possibility of irrationality or bias lay in his claim that, in the absence of relevant information, people use prefabricated sets of beliefs, labelled 'causal schemata' about the reasons for events which have been developed on the basis of experience. More recently, there has been greater emphasis upon the social origins of many causal attributions (Hewstone, 1983; Jaspars, Fincham and Hewstone, 1983). Jaspars has suggested that social groups create social attributions which individuals learn and use, short-cutting the deductive process envisaged by Kelley. In addition, there is a vast literature (see Fiske and Taylor, 1984, and Higgins, Ruble and Hartup, 1985, for reviews) on the biases which normally operate in relation to attribution. All of this evidence suggests that people do not use formal rules of logic in making attributions. They are nothing like naïve scientists performing analyses of variance unendingly in their heads. They operate according to social dictates and self-interest. Self-interest rules where the identity is to be protected from threat. Attributions are revamped and revised to support consistency, distinctiveness and self-esteem.

Re-attribution which shifts the responsibility from the individual to the external circumstances may have serious implications for subsequent efficacy in dealing with the threatening position should it be maintained. Having rejected responsibility for being in a position, the person may feel incapable of moving out of it. A nice example of this emanates from Eiser's (1982) work on smokers. He found that many smokers account for their continued use of cigarettes in terms of addiction. They regard themselves as addicted, no longer in control of their own actions, and are much less likely to be able to give up

smoking even when they try. It is interesting that, in accepting themselves as addicted, they are colluding with one of the dominant social
attributions for smoking. For some people, re-attribution in face of
threat will mean acting in defiance of social attributions. For instance,
the unemployed man who explains his inability to get work in terms of
a nationwide economic recession rather than in terms of his own
inadequacies will be contradicting the still dominant social attribution
for unemployment which places the blame firmly on the shoulders of
those who are unemployed.

Resisting the social attribution is difficult and the re-attribution is
only likely to persist as long as the individual is receiving some social
support in it. Where a group of unemployed people can get together to
be mutually reinforcing in their rejection of the blame for their jobless-
ness, there is a greater likelihood that the re-attribution can be maintained. Getting such a group together necessitates strategies which
operate at the interpersonal level and it represents an example of how
a coping strategy which is lodged at the intra-psychic level initially may
evoke others at the interpersonal level.

Acceptance strategies
Denial, depersonalization, unreal selves, fantasy and reconstrual are all
coping strategies which rely upon deflection of the threat while
resisting change in the identity structure. There is, however, a further
batch of strategies reliant upon the assimilation-accommodation
process which act to modify the identity structure in ways demanded
by the threatening position despite the damage done to self-esteem,
continuity or distinctiveness as a consequence. The purpose of these
acceptance strategies is to bring about change with the minimum
amount of damage. At first sight, acceptance strategies may seem more
like capitulation to the threat than coping with it. However, this is an
erroneous impression; they represent creative adaptations which may
rely upon preliminary redefinition or re-attribution tactics. The acceptance is rarely wholesale, mostly it reflects a compromise negotiated by
some psychic tribunal between the change demanded by the threat and
the status quo required by the principles supporting the structure.
There are a number of tactics available to the acceptance strategy:

Anticipatory restructuring Where the potential threat is evident some
time before becoming acute there is room for anticipatory restructuring
of the identity. For instance, when a young woman decides that she
wishes to become a skilled engineer while still at school there is time
for her to evolve gradually a self-conception which is congruent with

the demands of the job. She will anticipate much and experience some of the discrimination that she will encounter in her chosen work while still at school. She will learn that female engineers should not be sexy or feminine, butch or aggressive, technical whizz kids or leaders of men.

Anticipatory restructuring entails incorporating at least some of these characteristics into the identity structure on the content dimension before taking the job. By doing this, the young woman is not faced with a sudden demand for a disjuncture with her established identity. The established identity has been evolving gradually in directions which acknowledge what is required of a woman in that sort of work. As one 18-year-old woman training to be an engineering technician explained: 'I knew that I wanted to be an engineer ever since Dad let me help repair an old motorbike when I was 10. I liked getting oily and seeing the thing work when we'd finished. But I knew from the reaction of my sisters that it wasn't quite the done thing. It bothered me but I liked the work too much to let it put me off. So I spent a lot of time messing with mechanical things. I got a reputation as a tomboy. I also got a reputation as being willing to try to fix anything and mostly produced the goods. I learnt it is results that count. Once they realize you are serious. I learnt not to hide behind my femininity and not to have a chip on my shoulder. It took time but I knew what to expect when I started my training and the bit of difficulty the lads gave me didn't really hit me. I'd worked out what to expect. I don't think of myself as unusual or different now.'

Of course, the efficacy of anticipatory restructuring is premised upon two assumptions: firstly, that the demands which will be manifest in the threatening position are known in advance; and, secondly, that these demands do not destroy self-esteem. Anticipatory restructuring may obviate potential threats to continuity and distinctiveness but not those to self-esteem. A change which deflates self-esteem will do so whether introduced gradually or not. However, even the impact of the threat to self-esteem can be somewhat controlled through anticipatory restructuring, since the change introduced may result in a shift of focus between elements in identity such that the newly incorporated element gains less salience and thus its total power to deny self-esteem is contained.

Compartmentalism   Occupying a threatening position may lead to changes in the content dimension of identity. The unemployed youth may come to accept that unemployment is one of his or her defining characteristics. However, the implications of the change can be minimized through the use of the compartmentalism tactic. This simply involves drawing a strict boundary around the dissatisfying addition to the identity structure. It is not permitted to contaminate the rest of the identity. In so far as this is feasible, assimilation occurs without accommodation. A teenage girl, having accepted that she is now an unemployed person, continues to behave in the way she always has, refusing to modify anything else about her view of herself. As one young girl of 17 said: 'I've been unemployed since I left school. I'm not looking for work. I don't think about being unemployed. I just do what is expected of me at home.' This girl was to some extent unusual. She was born in Britain of Pakistani parents; she was still unmarried, which her parents considered unusual, and they exercised severe control over her behaviour – she was not allowed to attend the interview unless accompanied by her mother. For her, unemployment was a fact but not a central characteristic in the identity structure. The behaviour of her parents and their cultural socialization facilitated compartmentalization of this facet of identity.

The capacity for compartmentalism is quite startling in some cases, where completely mutually exclusive self-definitions are held simultaneously. There are case histories of women committed to imprisonment or psychiatric treatment after killing their own child. At one level, these women will acknowledge the infanticide and recognize themselves as killers. At another level, this self-definition will be ignored and they will hold the view of themselves as good, caring mothers. Compartmentalism can erect impenetrable walls between the two aspects of identity; their incompatibility is then never perceived because they are never directly compared.

The process of compartmentalism can be used to assimilate and then segregate a component to identity in such a way that it remains static for years. In its prison, that component of identity does not grow and change. It remains atrophied, incommunicado, so that the rest of identity may continue and flourish. Yet, obviously, this tactic can only function effectively if circumstances conspire to let sleeping dogs lie. If the threatening position is continuously occupied and if it makes demands for relevant action, then the wide implications of the modification in the identity structure will not be amenable to psychic boundaries. Once the initial change to the identity structure is wrought, compartmentalism may be only a temporary hedge against accommodation to the change throughout the identity structure.

Compromise changes Rather than making the change to identity required by the threat, a common response is to make an alternative modification. This alternative revision of the identity content is a sort of compromise, compatible with the threat but salvaging everything possible· in terms of continuity, distinctiveness and self-esteem. An example of the compromise change in identity can be seen in those unemployed who adopt the sickness role. Instead of defining themselves as unemployed, they will claim that they are off work because of some long-term ailment (Fagin and Little, 1984, report several of these cases). Adoption of the sickness role is often accompanied by very real physical debility (Warr, 1985), so it is by no means an easy option but it is considered preferable by some to the stigma of unemployment.

Defining the self as ill serves to alter the meaning of the position. It will not eradicate the threat predicated upon the loss of the latent benefits of work but it certainly fends off the abuse associated with labelling oneself unemployed; some scraps of continuity and self-esteem are retained. Defining the self as ill can also precipitate illness. One GP in an area of high unemployment in the Midlands reports how he has had a number of cases of redundant men who come to his surgery claiming to have high-blood-pressure symptoms but when tested their blood pressure is normal. However, over a period of weeks, with repeated protestations of symptoms and tests, their blood pressure rises to confirm their own 'illness representation of the self'. This anecdote should hardly surprise those who have seen biofeedback used to enable people to control autonomic nervous system responses.

Fundamental change   When other tactics fail, the individual may allow the process of assimilation-accommodation to bring about a fundamental change in the identity structure. If the threatening position challenges continuity, distinctiveness and self-esteem, the person may sacrifice any or all of them in order to assimilate the new components into identity. The unemployed, middle-aged man who considers his chances of regaining work negligible may accept 'unemployment as a way of life'. Continuity is abandoned, distinctiveness reduced, self-esteem negated but the threat, with the anxiety it generates, is also over. Once the change to identity is wrought, the threat is passed. The threat only remains threatening as long as changes to identity which breach the principles guiding assimilation are resisted. As soon as those principles are abrogated and the change instituted, the experience of threat dissipates. Hayes and Nutman (1981) suggest that this 'acceptance of unemployment as a way of life' is the final stage in a series of adjustments to unemployment. These begin with shock at losing the job and active attempts to find another while remaining optimistic about doing so; then, with successive failures, the person becomes pessimistic, anxious, and distressed; finally, this gives way to fatalism, inertia and acceptance of joblessness as a way of life.

The stage-model of response to unemployment has received equivocal empirical support. The overwhelming fact is that people do not all respond to unemployment in the same way. This would be predicted on the current model of identity. However, some do respond by accepting 'jobless' as a total definition of themselves. Interestingly, where they do, anxiety and depression recedes. This also would be predicted on the basis of the present model of coping strategies. Capitulation to the threat by changing self-definition actually removes the conflict which is causing the distress. The incompatibilities between old self-definitions and current situationally determined definitions are eradicated. The situational definitions dominate; the subjective conflict lifts and anxiety decreases. As a coping strategy, such capitulation, therefore, has an obvious attraction.

Capitulation has equally obvious problems: an identity which has lost distinctiveness, continuity and self-esteem is hard to tolerate. The individual will be motivated to act in ways which will revive all three. Assuming that the person is still in the same position which originally eradicated them, this is impossible. If the individual strives to recapture them, the threat is reconstituted. As soon as the unemployed man says 'I really want a job' and starts to look for one, the threat reappears because he is no longer accepting the definition of himself as inevitably unemployed.

It is possible, of course, that the fundamental changes in the identity structure initially wrought in response to the threat actually change the baseline on which the continuity, distinctiveness and self-esteem principles operate. For instance, acceptance of unemployment as a way of life may constitute an initial break with the past but, after a time, it has a history of its own. It is possible, then, that the continuity principle would hold the person to unemployment since this has become a stable, long-term component of identity. Similarly, self-esteem may be lowered by the experience of unemployment but, once it is stabilized at this new lower level, subsequently unemployment itself will not cause self-esteem to fluctuate. So the threat constituted by unemployment may be resolved by a fundamental change in the identity structure which revises the parameters on which the identity processes must work. The threat cannot then arise phoenix-like from the flames: the dynamics which underpinned it are radically changed. An identity which has been restructured to accommodate the implications of a threatening position can no longer be threatened by occupancy of that position.

Salience of principles   There is one further option sheltering under the umbrella of the acceptance strategy. This entails the revision of the relative salience of the three principles guiding assimilation. So long

as the threat is not contravening all three principles, it is possible
to rearrange priorities between them, shifting emphasis from the
threatened to the unthreatened. This can mean that a change which
abrogates continuity may become tolerable because continuity is attributed less importance than, say, self-esteem.

Switching focus between the three principles undoubtedly happens;
people in threatening positions are able to recount their subjective
experience of the shift. One young woman who had decided to take a
job as an officer in the Merchant Marine reported how, when she got
her First-Mate's ticket, she knew that she had finally broken with her
past; she was a different sort of person and she experienced regret but
she was quick to counterbalance this with her deep satisfaction at
having succeeded. She described how her job cut her off from many of
her erstwhile relationships (with boyfriends and relatives alike) and
she knew that she was losing contact with her past self. However, the
rewards in terms of self-esteem outweighed the costs in terms of
continuity; she gave self-esteem more priority and the losses in
continuity weighed even lighter. Clearly, this tactic can only work so
long as one of the principles remains unthreatened.

Strategies relying on the process of evaluation

Fundamentally, strategies involving the process of evaluation concern
either the re-evaluation of the existing content of identity or the re-
evaluation of the prospective content. Both are largely designed to
make the identity changes required by the threatening position more
palatable and ultimately less disruptive.

The value attached to the various contents of identity is socially
determined: the individual learns their social worth through interaction
in the context of dominant ideologies. As Tajfel (1981b) pointed out,
individual values cannot be independent of social stereotypes. This
is partially how threat arises, when the individual learns that a new
social position carries a negative social value. But the individual's
self-evaluation is no simple and accurate reflection of the socially
constructed value placed on the concomitant memberships and characteristics. Tajfel, together with Doise (1978) who argues a similar case,
is not suggesting a sociological determination of individual values.
They both offer a social-psychological determinism: the processes of
individual cognition interact with the processes of social influence,
which establish dominant ideologies, to produce personal beliefs and
values. The personal evaluation process, once established in this way,
is selective and purposive: ignoring or diminishing the importance
of negative inputs to identity, creatively revaluating information in

accordance with previously internalized value systems and beliefs which need not be concordant with currently dominant social values.

The latitude of freedom available to the evaluation process hails from two sources. Firstly, it is rare indeed for a single value system to dominate a society. Different social groups and categories, in generating ideologies which satisfy their corporate interests, create conflicting value systems. The individual, in evaluating constituents of identity contributed by group memberships and interpersonal networks, consequently normally has available a number of different value systems from which to choose. In defending against a threat, the individual gravitates to the value system which maximizes the chances of salvaging self-esteem.

Secondly, some degrees of freedom emanate from the fact that the actual value of an identity element is not absolute, it is relative. Dominant ideologies may hold that a characteristic is odious; so possession of that characteristic is demeaning. Yet just how demeaning it becomes depends on a series of comparisons open to the individual. These comparisons can be between the past and current content of identity or between oneself and other people. It is possible to retrieve self-esteem or to secure against its disappearance by choosing comparitors wisely. In a situation where the characteristic is socially unacceptable, a comparison which showed the current identity to possess it to a lesser extent than in its earlier development would prove a positive boost to self-esteem. Similarly, a comparison which showed that others possess it to a still greater degree would militate against self-castigation. Thus a characteristic which is, in some global social sense, negative can become a source of satisfaction when viewed relatively. The process of evaluation is destined to view all identity contents relatively; none have a single fixed value, they are all interdependent.

The process of evaluation most frequently entails social comparisons to establish personal worth. Festinger (1954) first formulated the theory of social comparison processes, arguing that people establish the validity of their beliefs and attitudes by comparing them with those of others. Beliefs about the value of the self were claimed to be similarly subject to social confirmation through the continual process of comparison. Judgements founded upon comparison are, nevertheless, highly subjective. They require subjective interpretations at several levels: of the characteristic to be compared; of the extent of differentials, and of the actual value attributed to the characteristic. Such subjectivity in interpretation is the root of the freedom available to the process of evaluation.

The process of evaluation also involves sub-routines wherein present identity structures are compared with past and potential structures: a process of intrapersonal rather than social comparison. Comparison of the present with past identity is self-explanatory, the same is not true for the comparison with potential identity. The potential identity is not yet in existence; it is an end state for identity which is deemed desirable and attainable. In so far as it is realistically attainable, it is distinct from the notion of the ideal self.

Markus and Nurius (1984) have postulated the concept of 'possible selves' which parallels the notion of the potential identity. They argue that possible selves represent individuals' ideas of what they might become, what they would like to become, and what they are afraid of becoming. They therefore link cognitive and emotional elements relating to the self. Markus and Nurius suggest that possible selves are important because they function as incentives for future behaviour, being targets to attain or avoid, and they provide an evaluative and interpretative context for the contemporary view of the self. Both the notion of possible selves and potential identity share the common assumption that the current identity is capable of planning its own future and, presumably, working towards achieving it.

This perspective emphasizes that identity is no mere product – it acts purposively to its own ends in accordance with its guiding principles. In terms of the process of evaluation, this means that current identity is comparing itself with the planned end-state and coming to conclusions about what still needs to be done. The absence of movement towards the potential identity may result in a sense of failure, perhaps despite apparent success in overt social terms, and a consequent slump in self-esteem. The outcome of such negative intrapersonal comparisons can work on two fronts: attempts to modify current identity or modification of the potential identity. Where relevant changes in the current identity structure are not feasible, the potential identity may change in order to eradicate the affront to self-esteem or, alternatively, it may remain the same but become less associated with reality, shifting towards an image of the ideal self which is desirable but unattainable.

So, for these reasons, the process of evaluation has some autonomy from the social value systems which encircle it. This means that, when faced with a threatening social position, the process can act to defend the identity. It does this by employing two standard tactics: re-evaluation of the existing content dimension of identity or re-evaluation of the prospective content imposed by occupation of the threatening position.

Re-evaluation of the existing content dimension of identity
The threat to identity will either require an existing component to
be removed or some new component to be added. Whichever is
demanded, the individual can respond defensively with one of a
number of tactics.

(i) Where the threat demands a change in the existing structure one
way to minimize the negative effects upon continuity, distinctiveness
and self-esteem is *to devalue the element of identity which is to be excised.*
For instance, the man who loses his job can claim that it was a badly
paid, no-hope situation, that he has done well to get out of it, and he
never wanted to be a university lecturer anyway. This process of
exorcism and retrospective devaluation is most evident in the case of
some women who have sexually atypical work. The nature of the work
militates against feeling themselves to be feminine. They respond by
rejecting their own femininity and decrying its value. For example, one
woman who had, after considerable struggle, been accepted on the
shop-floor as an engineer, commented: 'Being feminine gets in the
way. I consciously decided not to be feminine at work. Now I find it
difficult to be feminine anywhere! What's the point of it anyway? It just
makes men believe you are weak, frail and dependent. I'm glad not to
be thought feminine.'

(ii) Where the threat challenges self-esteem directly, pouring scorn
upon some previously valued, existing identity characteristic, an alternative tactic is to simply *refocus attention upon some other element of
identity and inflate its value.* The value of the characteristic attacked is
not explicitly modified by the evaluation process, but the characteristic
itself is no longer allowed to occupy the centre of the identity stage;
another quality is brought to the fore instead, invested with greater
value, and self-esteem is maintained through this circuitous route. An
example of this tactic comes from the cases of those who are socially
mobile, gaining, through education or financial acumen, access to a
higher socio-economic class. They often report finding that their
working-class background, in Britain at least, constitutes a serious
disadvantage, despite the recently arrived social acceptability of
regional accents. They seek to eradicate all trace of their background,
focusing upon their educational or business achievements. They may
actually get converted and begin to hold to negative attitudes towards
the working class; even if they do not, they tend to put their allegiance
into cold storage from whence it emerges only occasionally to put in a
guest appearance at safe venues. Having working-class origins is not

allowed to play a significant role in the calculation of self-esteem, it is superseded in that equation.

Of course, not all the socially mobile respond in this way. There are notable examples of people who parade their class origin as if it were a badge of office, legitimating their pronouncements about, and critiques of, their class of arrival. But this is again merely an alternative example of the way elements in identity can be rearranged and re-emphasized to bolster against the loss of self-esteem.

(iii) Where the social position occupied threatens self-esteem, the individual may *engage in the exercise of self-efficacy* in order to regain self-esteem. Gecas and Schwalbe (1983) have argued that the 'looking glass self', which suggests that self-conception is a reflection of the way the person is conceived or perceived by others, has led to an overly passive view of human beings. They suggest that the self-concept is also based upon the person's own understanding of his or her actions in the world, especially efficacious actions. Gecas and Schwalbe, following the philosophical tradition of the symbolic interactionist school in sociology, argue that human beings are characterized by agency: intentional and creative action. They, therefore, introduced the idea of self-evaluation based on efficacious action. Self-esteem is generated by action which is judged as effective by the actor. Self-knowledge is garnered from the consequences of our actions upon the material and social world. When actions achieve their desired ends, they are deemed efficacious and have the power to instigate self-esteem.

Efficacious action as a basis for self-esteem is different in principle from esteem, which is base dupon the perceived opinions of others or derived from the occupation of a particular position within the social matrix. Franks and Marolla (1976) call the former 'inner self-esteem' and the latter 'outer self-esteem'. Inner self-esteem derives directly from the experience of oneself as an agent who can make things happen in the world and of effectively realizing one's intentions, regardless of obstacles. In some cases, of course, the achievements which give rise to inner self-esteem will also initiate outer self-esteem because they elicit praise or social rewards. But the overlap is by no means complete and when faced with serious threats to outer self-esteem, compensations can be achieved through manoeuvres which enhance inner self-esteem.

Gecas and Schwalbe postulate that achieving efficacy-based self-esteem is dependent, to a great extent, upon the nature of the social contexts within which the individual functions, because it will, in varying degrees, affect the organization of practical activities. Three features of the context are influential in determining the possibility of efficacy: the degree of constraint on individual autonomy; the degree of individual control; and the resources which are available to the individual for producing intended outcomes. In addition, the actual possibilities for efficacious action are a function of the relationship between these contextual resources and an individual's capacity to mobilize them. In order to achieve self-esteem through efficacious action the individual must have the resources and be capable of using them so as to gain a sense of self-determination. Having made a free decision to pursue a course of action, to succeed is to become aware of oneself as self-determining.

Success is not an objective state. Bandura (1982) argued that self-efficacy is not dependent upon the degree of actual success so much as upon the degree of perceived success. He suggests that judgements about the extent of success are dependent upon what types of cues people have learnt to use as indicators of personal efficacy. These cues, and the inference rules attached to them, are components of the attribution schemes which give action meaning for the individual and establish or undermine the experience of self-efficacy. These attribution schemes, in turn, will be dependent upon ideologies dominant within the culture, as we have seen earlier. This means that the perception of self-efficacy is doubly controlled by the social context which, firstly, delimits individual autonomy and available resources and, secondly, establishes the criteria against which the success of action is measured.

The use of the exercise of self-efficacy as a coping strategy when facing a threat to self-esteem, therefore, will depend for its success upon a relatively benign social context. To be useful, it must be possible to evolve self-efficacy in an area of activity which the individual has learnt to consider to be of social value. Occupancy of some threatening positions may prevent activity in areas of social value. For instance, having been labelled a criminal may proscribe many subsequent activities which would have the power to establish self-efficacy. Furthermore, the threat may act to immobilize the person's belief that they can achieve anything through their own efforts. For example, being unemployed is so threatening to identity at a time of mass structural unemployment because individual efforts to gain work seem pointless. Unemployment attacks the individual's perception of self-efficacy directly in only one realm of action but, indirectly, it can generate a pervasive conception of the self as incapable and ineffective. Many unemployed are reported to become progressively de-skilled not just in relation to their erstwhile job but in all central areas of activity. One of the most consistent findings across studies of the unemployed is that their activity levels decline; they sleep longer, they watch television longer, and their social activities decrease (Bunker and Dewsberry, 1983). This mode of adaptation to unemployment reduces the opportunities to experience self-efficacy.

It is possible to view the provision of community-based work schemes for the unemployed as an arena within which self-efficacy might be retrieved. Building a good adventure playground for the local children could be seen as an achievement which might engender pride and some self-esteem. Yet whether it would be interpreted in this light by the unemployed themselves is questionable. It would depend on two factors. Firstly, they would need to see their involvement in the scheme as voluntary; preferably, the scheme should be their own idea. Secondly, the achievements represented in building the playground would have to be socially valued. Currently, in community-based projects for the unemployed, it is rare for either of these two conditions to apply. They consequently offer little scope for coping with the threat to self-esteem through heightened self-efficacy.

Re-evaluation of the prospective content of identity

A social position may be threatening because it requires an addition to the content dimension of identity which will deplete self-esteem. The prospective content has the power to attack self-esteem because it is negatively valued by social ideologies. Normally, the individual will accept the value attached to a characteristic by social processes even where this is to the individual's personal detriment. Examples of this abound in the literature on ethnic minority groups, where members of the minority are found to assimilate and apply to themselves the derogatory attitudes about them which pervade their society (Milner, 1984).

People can resist the socializing pressures whcih tie negative appraisals to their identity characteristics, however. Sometimes, they cope with the threat by refusing to accept that the characteristic should be deemed worthless or demeaning. They can exercise autonomy in instilling the characteristic with some positive connotation. To do this as a solitary individual is difficult. The re-evaluation remains idiosyncratic and purely subjective. An alternative strategy would be to persuade others to join in the re-evaluation but this could not be considered an intra-psychic coping strategy. Where coping remains at the intra-psychic level, some individuals do resist social value systems and establish the personal worth of socially reviled characteristics. This revision of the evaluative status of a characteristic can be achieved through a number of tactics.

(i) *Changing the criteria against which it is judged.* In this, the threatened person is telling himself or herself 'never mind the quality, feel the width'. The rest of the world may claim the characteristic is worthless because they are judging it against, for instance, a financial criterion of value. The threatened individual can claim it is immensely valuable because the criterion chosen is the contribution it can make to, perhaps, community welfare. Society and the individual are using different rulers against which to measure value. An example of this tactic hails from the studies of young people who are temporarily employed on youth training schemes or the community programmes funded by central government. A lad, working on building a local children's adventure playground, said: 'Me mates think I'm barmy, working these hours for peanuts. They really take the mick out of me. Even me old man reckons I'm draft 'cos I'm getting no trainin'. But I think it's better than the dole an' I'm helping to do something for the kids. The way I look at it is this: it's not the money that counts, it's the satisfaction from building something that's goin' ta get used. Better than pushin' papers about or serving in a shop. That don't give no thingy ... you know.'

(ii) *Associating the characteristic with another positively valued characteristic.* In this, the threatened person argues that it is impossible to have one characteristic without the other; the nice is dependent upon the nasty and the nasty has a value as a consequence. In this way, identity characteristics gain reflected acceptability. For instance, being seen to be a workaholic is reprehensible in circles of western industrialized society. The workaholics' self-defence relies upon tying hard work to financial success and power. Only workaholics who flop need fear reductions in self-esteem as a result of their addiction.

This type of tactic is used by some women in non-traditional jobs. It comes to be particularly useful with spouses who are starting to feel neglected or unfairly responsible for domestic tasks. A woman, who at the time was achieving considerable success in publishing, suggested, when interviewed, that recently she was coming to feel that the pressure of work was overwhelming her home life. She was coming to feel herself a bad wife, a feeling accentuated by the fact that, although in her late thirties, she had no children. Her thoughts were turning to abandoning her job. Yet, whenever she got to this point, she explained that she started to enumerate the advantages which accrued, not just to her but also to her husband, because of her hard work and success. Sometimes she regaled him with the list. More often she simply explained it to herself: the positive was dependent upon the negative.

(iii) *Challenging the right of other people to make judgements about the characteristic.* In this, the threatened person contends that other people, who do not know what it feels like to be in the threatening position, have neither the ability nor the right to make pronouncements about the value of the characteristic. This is often accompanied by the assertion that people would soon alter their evaluations if they did have experience of the position. The tragic response of the young unemployed, when chastised for not getting a job, is typical of this sort of self-defence; they ask, 'what would their inquisitor feel like and do if he (sic) lost his job?' Implicit in this sort of tactic is the belief that the judgements of others are not legitimate or valid unless they can claim personal experience of the position.

Breakwell (1985b) asked young people who were unemployed to explain how they would respond if criticized for their unemployment by their father, a prospective employer, and a stranger in the street. There were two dominant responses: they would ask the attacker how he would feel in their place and they would explain it was not their own fault, there was nothing they could do to get work which they had not already tried. In a sense, they sought empathy and resorted to fatalism. But both responses actually challenge the legitimacy of the attack. They imply the attacker has no right to judge because he has insufficient understanding of the situation or an inadequate appreciation of how much the young person has sought to overcome it. Of course, this tactic does not require that the person criticized actually verbalizes this illegitimacy to the attacker. As a mechanism of self-defence it is sufficient that it occurs at a purely subjective level. The individual merely has to believe the attack is illegitimate; there is no need to prove it to the attacker.

All three tactics essentially achieve a subjective revision of the evaluation of the characteristic which overrides the value attached by others. Such a subjective evaluation will be continually challenged by inputs from the outside world. One method used to bolster the subjective evaluation is to shift from intra-psychic coping strategies towards interpersonal strategies, garnering support for the personal interpretation by converting other people to your view.

In relation to these coping strategies relying on the process of evaluation, it can be seen that action becomes an increasingly important corollary of re-appraisal. It is most evident in attempts at self-efficacy and in challenges against the legitimacy of social value systems. As coping strategies shift from the process of assimilation-accommodation to the process of evaluation and back again, it becomes obvious that those at the intra-psychic level will interact with those at the interpersonal and group levels, if only because they orientate the individual's action in the social and material world.

Coping powers

It is worthwhile speculating upon the relationship between the failure of intra-psychic coping strategies and various forms of psychiatric breakdown. It is well established that there is no simple direct correlation between the occupancy of a threatening position and psychiatric disturbance. Stonequist's (1937) original notion of the 'marginal man' predicted that threats to identity would be associated with psychiatric instability, higher levels of deviance, and more restlessness. The 'marginal man' is a person who finds himself or herself in a hinterland between cultures (the first generation offspring of immigrant parents who experiences the culture of the old country at home but that of the new country at school) or straddles two distinct parent groups (the mixed-race child or the child of parents from two different and conflicting religious sects) (Watson, 1977). The marginal is threatened by anomy or normlessness and by rejection, potentially, by both parent groups.

Empirical work on marginals showed that Stonequist's predictions regarding psychiatric disturbance and criminality were fundamentally inappropriate (Antonovsky, 1956, Goldberg, 1941). Psychiatric breakdown occurs only where the marginal position generates threats to identity which overwhelm the available coping strategies. The capacity of the individual to tolerate threat without psychiatric collapse depends upon that person's coping powers.

Individuals differ in their ability to evolve coping strategies and mobilize them against threat. They also differ in their understanding of how and when they should employ particular strategies. In some cases, the strategies take over, moving outside the individual's control. This can be seen to be so where an individual exhibits habitual or apparently compulsive and indiscriminate denial. When taken to extremes, many of the strategies comprise recognized symptoms of psychiatric instability. For instance, transient depersonalization and the perception of unreal selves are both symptomatic of schizophrenia (Wing, 1978; Willis, 1976). Coping strategies can only be valuable as long as they are under the individual's control. The individual's coping power consists not only of the ability to create a strategy but also the capacity to delimit its sphere of influence. Where intra-psychic coping strategies fail, they instigate greater vilification of the threatened person and add to the pressure already experienced. Attempts at coping are hazardous enterprises, particularly for those with limited coping powers.

It may be an error to think of the availability of coping powers as simply some function of individual differences in intelligence, knowledge, experience or whatever. The coping powers of the individual at the intra-psychic level are, in part at least, dependent upon the social networks and group memberships he or she has. The support available from interpersonal networks and group memberships may be instrumental in enabling the person to feel confident enough to use the intra-psychic strategies of re-evaluation or re-definition. For instance, the marginals studied by Antonovsky (1956) and Goldberg (1941) were not overwhelmed by the threat implicit in their position; they did not become psychiatrically unstable, show greater criminality or commit suicide more often, largely because they comprised tightly knit communities which buffered individual members from the full force of the rejection of mass society and encroachment of alien devaluing normative systems. In understanding individual coping powers it is thus necesseary to examine interpersonal and group-level strategies.

5   Interpersonal coping strategies

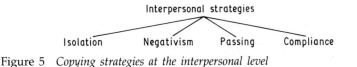

Figure 5   *Copying strategies at the interpersonal level*

Interpersonal coping strategies rely on changing relationships with others in order to cope with threat. Where intra-psychic coping strategies focus upon cognition, emotion and values, interpersonal coping strategies concentrate upon action which involves negotiation with others and their manipulation. There are a number of identifiable interpersonal action strategies (summarized in Figure 5) used when faced with threats to identity. They all have limited value.

Isolation

This is more of an inaction strategy than an action strategy. The individual occupying the threatening position seeks to minimize its impact by isolating himself or herself from other people. Where the threat constitutes an attack on self-esteem via the social stigmatization of the position occupied, the rationale behind self-isolation is easy to fathom. Isolated, the individual does not have to confront the rejection, pity or aggression appended to the stigma. Isolation of this sort can aid and abet denial tactics because it reduces the chance of realism interfering with the reconstituted 'facts'.

Self-isolation is a favoured option amongst the unemployed. Bunker and Dewsberry (1983) and Trew and Kirkpatrick (1984) found, in England and Northern Ireland respectively, that the unemployed in the main stay behind closed doors in their homes, reduce social contacts outside the family, and limit severely any leisure activities involving contact with other people. This containment within the house is fiercest amongst people in the 25-55-year-old age bracket. Those older start to fit into the pattern of activities associated with the retired; those younger are more likely to persist in pursuits common in adolescents at school. For the bulk of those unemployed at the prime of their working life, the experience is one of house-bound solitude, boredom, and disruption of familial life-style.

Part of the withdrawal from outside activities is explained in terms of the financial turmoil common after job loss but not all. Even activities which are free or inexpensive (e.g. visits to libraries or parks) are shunned; even those unemployed who have considerable material resources become isolated. The incentive driving the unemployed towards isolation is not purely monetary; in part, it is the desire to avoid social shaming, or well-meant but heart-rending pity, or simply answering personal questions. Isolation is an attempt to evade the social consequences of occupying a threatening position.

There is considerable irony associated with the attempt to use isolation as a method for coping with threats to identity since all the evidence accumulated seems to indicate that it is the worst possible thing to do when faced with any sort of stress. People experiencing stress, whether physical or psychological, are more likely to cope effectively if they have a large network of social contacts. For instance, size of social network is inversely correlated with attempted suicides, divorce and psychiatric breakdown. It is positively related to success in overcoming bereavement, post-operative pain, psychosomatic problems such as asthma, and arthritic inflammation of the joints in the elderly (Politser, 1980, reviews this data). Many psychologists and counsellors have argued that the provision of effective social-support networks is the answer to virtually all psychological and psychosomatic ills. This is admittedly a rather grand claim, particularly when one considers that what is meant by a social-support network is little more than the possibility of regular contacts with other people who often provide nothing more than company.

There is no adequate explanation of why social networks of this sort should be so efficacious in insulating people from psychological decline. The most attractive type of explanation focuses upon the opportunities within such a network for self-disclosure. Self-disclosure entails telling the other person about your most private and intimate thoughts and feelings. Such self-disclosure within what is considered to be a caring relationship, offers individuals a chance to gain positive feedback about themselves and, in that way, to validate the most central aspects of their self-concept.

Kelvin (1977) argues that self-disclosure has to be carefully timed because it opens the individual to emotional and material exploitation. Normally, it involves a graduated process: shifting from unimportant confessions about the self to those which are deeper and darker, with grave potential for misuse; only if the early disclosures are reciprocated and treated in confidence will the shift to more salient material normally occur. The emphasis upon reciprocation, mutuality of self-disclosure, is important. People do not like to make the immense investment signified by self-disclosure without getting something similar in return. Exchanges in disclosure cement a relationship, keeping the balance of power equitable. Total self-disclosure can involve considerable stress and can only be justified as long as there is total faith in the other person. Total self-disclosure can also alleviate considerable stress: anxieties shrink when they can be discussed; attitudes can be confirmed; beliefs can be validated; information can be gathered which will banish fear or doubt; and so on.

The larger the social-support network, the more opportunities for such self-disclosure and a wider range of feedback. The person with a large social network is not putting all of those metaphorical eggs in one basket: self-disclosure can be selective and diverse. Moreover, it can be repetitive without the risk of alienating the audience as one might with a single recipient. This may be why a sizeable social network acts as a buffer against the ravages of trauma and stress. In fact, no doubt the potential for self-disclosure is only one component in the efficacy of the social network. The practical aid from the network in material terms may be equally important.

Isolationist tactics remove the threatened individual from the sustenance of the social-support network. As a technique for coping with threat, therefore, it clearly has considerable disadvantages. In many cases, it is totally impracticable. For instance, the woman in sexually atypical employment cannot isolate herself from her social contacts. It is only possible in a limited number of situations. For instance, the physically disabled and elderly can do it. In some situations it is possible but still inadvisable. The unemployed can manage to isolate themselves but to do so is to work against their own interests. Not only are they depriving themselves of various psychological advantages of social contacts, they are also ignoring a vital source of information about new work. Most people hear about job vacancies not through the official agencies of the Job Centre or Careers Office or even the newspaper adverts but through word-of-mouth (Labour Studies Group, 1985). People with a large network of contacts have a better unofficial listening post on the job market.

Isolation as a coping strategy can also have massively deleterious consequences for the families of those who use it. Self-isolation tends to be accompanied by the desire to restrict the movements and friendships of others in the household. Some unemployed men interviewed as part of the study of young unemployed (Breakwell, 1985b) prevented their children from bringing friends home because they would then know about them being at home all day and they could not face that. In some cases, where a man was unemployed and his wife had work, her movements were carefully monitored and she was required to return home immediately after work. Any deviation in her timetable was subject to inquisition and rebuke. Extended isolation seems to be associated with a sort of social paranoia. People who have friendships outside of the home are believed to be traitors, plotting against the isolated.

Isolation tactics do not, in general, bring relief to the threatened individual. Those unemployed who become isolated do not find it easier to deal with the stigma of their position. By and large, they come to feel their self-induced isolation as a further badge of their stigma (Bunker and Dewsberry, 1983). Similarly, those who suffer gross physical deformities, perhaps after industrial accidents or car crashes, often withdraw from social contact and, yet, its loss merely emphasizes the psychological loneliness they feel. The unemployed talk about being abandoned, thrown on the rubbish heap to die. The physically deformed also decry society's callous disregard for any who are not pristine and fully functioning, useful or productive. In their tactic of self-isolation they are actually colluding with the society which would hide them from sight. This is a pity since the tactic seems to offer little return for all it costs.

Isolation may be used, no matter how ineffectively, to immure oneself against threat by avoiding many of the social consequences of threat because it minimizes social contacts. The assumption, should isolation prove effective, would be that it acts as a resistance against the fact of occupying a threatening position either by blocking assimilation of the new identity structure or by refusing to express publicly what has been assimilated. Either way, the impact of the threat would be assuaged. The social contacts which rub salt into the wounds of the threat are eliminated or much reduced.

Negativism

Negativism entails the opposite tactic: it involves outright conflict with anyone who would challenge the identity structure. Faced with a position which attacks continuity, distinctiveness or self-esteem, negativism would involve attacking the attackes. Negativism does not involve the avoidance of social contacts or the social consequences; instead it requires that they be bearded and confronted directly.

Apter (1982) provides the most complete description of negativism since it is at the base of his 'theory of reversals'. Apter (1983, p. 79) states: negativism is 'the state of mind which one is in when one feels a desire or a compulsion to act *against* the requirements or pressures from some external source. This may mean refusing to do what others wish or even doing the opposite of what is required or expected in a given situation.' The familiar expressions used to describe negativism include 'bloody-mindedness', 'trouble-seeking', 'cantankerous', 'pig-headed', 'cussedness', and so on. At its simplest, negativism is simply saying no. This has led Apter to suggest that we come to know who we are and what we are by saying 'no' to what we are not. Knowing is no-ing, to use Apter's phrase. Negativism, Apter asserts, is known to characterize all of life's great psychological transitions. Between the ages of 18 months and 3½ years, children show their growing psychological independence through increasing disobedience. Through negativism the child acquires a sense of will-power. At adolescence, the development of abstract thinking capacities, which permit a grasp of more of what it is possible to refuse, encourage renewed negativism, manifested in the search for social and sexual independence. Negativism is notable in old age. Then, the loss of autonomy, which physical decline and the financial constraints of retirement impose, generates renewed negativism that can represent a hedge against despair and the debilitation which institutionalization instigates.

Though most evident in these periods of major developmental transition, negativism is a perpetual possibility. It is an important foundation for continuity, distinctiveness and self-esteem. Continuity requires the ability to refuse to change despite attempts to impose change; this basically entails negativism. Distinctiveness can only be achieved by being willing to reject standard expectations and orthodoxies in the interests of creativity and uniqueness; this fundamentally entails negativism. Self-esteem is founded upon the ability to deny some evaluations which others would impose; this revolves around negativism. Negativism is a coping strategy which acts as a balance to all three identity principles, protecting the identity structure from collapse.

Negativism, like all powerful processes, is double-sided: it has both positive and detrimental effects. The detrimental effects normally arise in three ways. Firstly, where continuity needs clash with distinctiveness needs, negativism in the interests of one can attack the other. For instance, in the pursuit of continuity the individual may reject the potential membership of a group which should have been accepted if distinctiveness was to be achieved. This sort of problem with negativism is normally relatively easy to solve: the individual prioritizes the identity principles, saying which matters most, and negativism is unleashed to protect it. As long as negativism is then controlled, the strategy can be effective in coping.

In some cases, control is dissipated and gives rise to the second type of problem. Some people suffer from what Apter has labelled hypernegativism. Their rejections, resistance and refusals are just too generalized and too vicious; they lose the distinction between productive and counter-productive negativism. Psychopaths are commonly supposed to be characterized by this tendency.

The third dysfunction was labelled by Apter 'self-negativism'. This occurs when the external source of threat proves overwhelming and anger, or whatever emotion is generated, is turned inwards, against oneself. Self-negativism is an aberrant variant of the coping strategy which is manifested in masochism, asceticism, self-sacrifice, and self-damage ranging in severity from nail-biting to suicide.

Despite its potential aberrations, negativism can be a valuable tool. Hemmed in by pressures to conform, where conformity means sacrificing the identity principles, the resilience afforded by negativism should not be ignored or underestimated. Yet, given the proclivity which most people have towards conformity, it would also be inappropriate to over-emphasize the ease with which they can adopt negativism. Outside of the great points of transition in the life-span, people find it difficult to utilize negativism in a discriminating and productive way. The effort to resist conformity pressures is itself stressful. Some social-skills training courses now encourage the development of selective negativism for those experiencing stress (Wilkinson and Canter, 1982). They suggest the use of practice sessions or role play to enable the novice to learn the relief which is contingent upon the successful exercise of resistance. Practice is graded in order of difficulty: easy acts of negativism first, which meet with immediate payoffs which are later superseded by more difficult contexts for resistance with only long-term rewards. Small achievements in exerting wilful negativism build confidence and symbolize to the rest of the world that the person is no cipher that can be manipulated or used indiscriminately.

Negativism which is not universal but is used with discriminating forethought can be a powerful coping strategy. It has the greatest force because it alters the impression which others gain of its user. The impression may be critical, they may consider the person rude, anti-social, and stubborn; but they will not think of that person as flexible, putty to be moulded and modified at the whim of social pressure. The individual will become aware that this is the image which others have and will begin to assimilate this into the structure of identity. Success-ful negativism reinforces itself. It also reduces the likelihood that anyone will attempt to impose a change from outside: they will be too well aware of the reception which awaits them. Negativism can prepare a cocoon for the threatened person, a place of hibernation and safety. Yet it is unlikely to be one from which he or she emerges metamorphosed. Negativism, in the main, militates against any change in the content of identity. It relies upon the remorseless protection of the status quo causing the entrenchment of the existing content and value dimensions.

Passing

The best answer to a threat may be to remove oneself from the threatening position; what Tajfel (1978) calls the exit option. In reality, actual exit may be impossible. In that case, one alternative at the intra-psychic level is self-misidentification which was described in the last chapter. There is some sort of mobility involved in this unrealistic, non-conforming reconstrual of the self, but it is hardly something which could be called social mobility; it is truly a form of psychological mobility. However, the efficacy of such a strategy for personal change is dubious. What use is it for the coloured South African to believe himself white? Every day in every way, he would normally be faced with disconfirmations of his self-image. Perhaps this is why 'self-misidentification' is primarily the preserve of children under the age of 11. Self-delusion is practicable only when its perpetrators are so powerless that their actions are not given credence and thus not challenged: children and the 'insane' can be as psychologically mobile as they wish.

Where legitimate social mobility is impossible and psychological mobility possible but valueless, illegitimate social mobility may be both possible and effective. Illegitimate social mobility entails gaining exit from the threatening position through deceit. A new interpersonal network or group is entered on false pretences: the phenomenon known as 'passing'. Of course, certain sorts of threat admit of this option more easily than others because some signs of threat are more easily hidden than others. To put it mildly, an accent can be erased more easily than skin pigmentation. Passing normally refers to the process of gaining access to a group or social category (sexual, racial, political, economic or religious) by camouflaging one's group origins.

In his book *Passing for White*, Watson (1970) describes the techniques employed by South African Coloureds at that time to gain reclassification as 'White'. 'Pass-Whites', as he calls them, gain acceptance by an incremental process. Their income and occupation must be appropriate to the White status, they must gain housing in a White area, belong to a White church, and send their children to a White school. They must obtain recognition as White in diverse settings. Gaining recognition as White is a process of accretion which involves contact with Whites in a series of different roles which demand that the Whites make *ad hoc* decisions about whether the Coloured person is White or not. The Whites involved may be such people as a school principal, a church minister, the registrar of a hospital, or an employer. The 'pass' involves using relatively ambiguous and otherwise unimportant occasions and activities where such authority figures have to make on-the-spot attributions of status, immediate evidence of Coloured status is not available (either in skin tone, physiognomy or previously apparent history), the 'passer' claims to be White and, since there is no reason to call for proof of this claim, he is accepted as such. The tactic only works when the attribution of status is not considered momentous by the Whites making it and is not subject to review. However, according to Watson, 'When *ad hoc* decisions cumulatively favour upward mobility of the aspirant they constitute a process which enables some Coloured persons to change their status to that of White persons.' The whole process of gaining the status of White is self-consciously one which annihilates any allegiance to or militancy for the erstwhile group membership. To be accepted, you have to deny your origins and become as reactionary as or more reactionary than the legitimate Whites in terms of expressed norms, ideology and commitment. The leopard must not simply change its spots, it must also prey upon any of its own kind without this chameleon propensity.

Watson was describing how to 'pass' in an essentially institutional setting: how to get social support for claims to membership of the White group and thus get a White identity card which, at the time

Watson wrote, was insurance of membership. Such passing is not exactly hidden. In fact, it occurred through institutionalized channels, the technique was an acknowledged and overprescribed route to a change in personal status prior to legislative revisions. The individual had to be covert about using the technique but the technique itself was no secret.

Other forms of passing are prevalent and involve no formal or semi-formal route to acceptance. In these cases, passing is totally covert and normally occurs where the characteristics which identify the threatening position are easily hidden or erased. The 'pass' of the homosexual who feigns heterosexuality or the atheist who professes a religious vocation fall into this category. These claims to membership could be validated but validation can be evaded because the criteria of membership cannot be measured on any easy objective index. As long as no one tries to gain objective evidence of their sexual behaviour or of their religious beliefs, the fraudulent claims cannot be discovered. Passing represents movement between groups not in fact but in fraud.

The person who deals with the threat to identity by passing will experience a number of problems as a consequence. The pass may gain the person social approval and social status, and in that way may contribute positively to self-esteem. However, the consequences of enactment of the fraud cannot be underestimated. The person who passes must live a lie. This has psychological implications. The most obvious signs are in attitudinal changes. Passing results in hyperaffiliation to the group joined by deceit. Prejudices against the group from which the person escapes are vehement (Breakwell, 1979). Vilification of previous friends and compatriots can be psychologically stressful, especially when this is done in the full knowledge that one is no different from them in reality. Furthermore, the 'passer' lives with the continual fear of discovery and exposure. In this respect, passing can represent a threat to continuity in its own right.

Goffman (1976), in his discussion of the effects of stigmatization, distinguishes between *discredited* and *discreditable* identities. Being stigmatized leads to a loss of social approval; any attribute, physical, psychological or social, can become a stigma by being associated with a disparaging stereotype (Page, 1984). Having only one leg, having been a psychiatric patient, and having been a Fascist can all be stigmata. Stigmata vary in visibility. Disfigurement is normally more visible than a history of incarceration in mental hospitals. Goffman suggests that visible stigmata lead to the identity being immediately discredited whenever the person meets someone. When the stigma is not apparent, the identity is not discredited but potentially discreditable.

Only when identity is discredited does Goffman consider it to be 'spoiled'.

Goffman has a very static and fragmented model of identity under-pinning his assertions about the effects of stigmatization, founded upon his dramaturgical theory of role performance. Nevertheless, the notion of discreditable identities remains interesting since it might be said to apply to the individual who passes. Passing does not expunge the stigma, it merely gets hidden but hangs around fraught with the ability to discredit. For this reason, passing may only serve to heighten the threat to identity. The person lives with the possibility of exposure and not simply the repercussions of the stigma itself but also the loss of everything which has been built upon the lie.

Garfinkel (1967), in his discussion of transsexualism, has argued that passing should not be viewed as a status passage which is a permanent shift of category membership. As Kando (1977) indicated, sociologists have generally treated passing as a 'one-shot affair': from one life stage to another (Erikson, 1954), from one ethnic status to another (Myrdal, 1962) or from one organizational or occupational position to another (Strauss, 1959). Yet both Kando and Garfinkel suggest that such passages are not discrete biographical occurrences. Passing is 'a continuing process' (Kando, p. 152). So the transsexual has not passed at the time of the sex-change operation; she is, at any given time, 'ongoing passing' (Garfinkel, 1967). The notion underlying this is that the transsexual retains *both* male and female components of identity because some people will know of her history as a man and treat her accordingly, others will know only her new incarnation and behave appropriately to that. The transsexual has to negotiate presentations of self to both types of audience unless she can 'hermetically segregate those who know from those who do not'. Kando found that many transsexuals do seek to compartmentalize associates, particularly family versus friends. Where they cannot do so, they suffer conflicting feelings about themselves consequent upon the differing demands of these often incompatible audiences.

As a coping strategy for threat, passing requires strong resolve and is the option chosen only when the consequences of socially acknowl-edging the threatening position are more severe than those concomit-ant upon the fraud itself. For instance, homosexuals who pass as heterosexuals often argue that the disruption of 'coming out' would be too great a cost to bear; hurting too many close friends and relatives and not just themselves. Lesbians who leave the closet face a particular risk. As Stephens (1982, p. 91) pointed out, 'because of prejudice in the law involving custody of children, lesbian mothers are finding that the risk involved losing their children'. Passing for these women may realistically represent the only way to protect their children. When the family bonds which rationalize 'passing' decay, for instance when parents die or divorce or children grow up and leave home, Ginsberg (1977) showed that homosexual men are more likely to 'come out'.

The rationale for passing which revolves around saving others from the consequences of the truth is popular. It occurs equally often in the explanations given by young people engaging in substance abuse (glue-sniffing, alcoholism, drug addiction) for their refusal to admit their addiction (Eiser, 1982). It seems that, even though passing may not eradicate the internal or subjective experience of threat to the identity, it can minimize the social consternation to which public acknowledgement of it would give rise.

It is worth briefly pointing out that the study of the effects of passing is troublesome; not least because the successful pass should not be discoverable. People who pass are invisible to the social telescope. Evidence either comes from those who try to pass but fail, or those who decide to drop the charade having succeeded, or those who are placed in artificial settings where attempts at passing are visible without the knowledge of the culprit. All three sources of information confirm that passing may have social benefits and psychological costs when used as the exclusive strategy for coping with threat.

Some of the psychological costs of passing can be overcome where it is combined with other intra-psychic coping strategies. People who have been successful in efforts to pass, particularly over long periods, subsequently report how they come to be persuaded by their own act. Clearly, this is less likely where their private actions contradict their public face, in the cases, perhaps, of drug users and homosexuals, but is highly likely in cases where there is no secret existence to ignore, in the case of the Coloured person who lives completely in the White world. In the latter example, tactics of denial and reconstrual are bolstering the social impact of passing.

Passing produces a peculiar difficulty for the process of assimilation-accommodation. Passing may be used to maintain membership of a social category which should be rescinded. The young woman who gradually recognizes herself to be a lesbian may retain a heterosexual public image. In one sense, passing protects the continuity of identity for her. However, it creates a disparity between the subjective and the social experience of self. What is more, the gap between the two is likely to be expanded by subsequent social experiences which will be predicated upon the public image. Relationships and group memberships will be founded upon her apparent heterosexuality; her treatment by others will be that of a heterosexual woman. The process of assimilation-accommodation will be called into play to modify identity in a manner appropriate to these experiences and yet they will be incompatible with the subjective experience of self. The process is effectively being called upon to integrate new elements of value and content into an identity structure which is quite different from that expected. A schism between the identity structure prior to passing and that after it begins is likely.

The chances of schism are greater where the pass is not designed to maintain continuity of identity but is a definite step into a new social position which is expected to improve distinctiveness and self-esteem. Where racial or religious marginals pass, they risk creating a genuine chasm between pre-passing identity and post-passing identity. Of course, the depth and breadth of the chasm is related to how central the area of deceit is to the identity structure and how far its ramifications permeate large realms of social action. Everyone passes in minor ways to protect self-esteem. Lies about achievements, pretences about acquaintanceships, exaggerations of knowledge, and so on, are common facts of life. They are designed to manipulate the self-image, to ingratiate and to secure status. As far as passing goes, they are small fry; even though they do often underlie machinations to shift from one social group to another, one set of friends to the next. These minor passes do not create chasms in the identity structure; they are the life-blood of creative reconstruction of identity. Only passes involving large-scale and widespread revisions in the central or salient content and value dimensions generate chasms in the structure of identity. Where such a chasm or disjuncture does occur, the process of assimilation can initially appear to be building the new self-image upon thin air and not accommodating it in the prior structure.

There is a certain irony in this whole process. Passing is initiated to protect an identity structure from the consequences of occupying a threatening position. It does this by consigning that identity structure to a cold-storage oblivion where it is deprived of social expression. A new social face is imposed and the process of assimilation busily composes the requisite identity structure, incompatible in many respects with its founder. It seems that passing may not act as a coping strategy preserving the identity from threat but rather as a fairly radical force for self-revision. The role it has depends upon the precise nature of the threat and the centrality of the value and content elements to which it attaches. It also depends upon whether it encompasses both private and public domains or only the latter. If passing is mainly a public affair with private actions which contradict its import, self-revision is less feasible; there are too many experiences which will hamper accommodation to the new self-conceptualizations. This may mean that content elements which are incompatible exist in tandem in identity. The threat to the identity principles is maintained and even heightened where this occurs and, again, intra-psychic coping strategies (e.g. re-evaluation or re-definition) may be called upon to save the day.

Compliance

Compliance may be an interpersonal strategy which is used after others fail or it may be the strategy of first choice where its user has known others to use alternative strategies which have failed. People in threatening positions emulate anyone who has found a successful strategy and are quick to learn from the mistakes of others. So compliance may be the rational strategy for a number of reasons.

Compliance, as a strategy for dealing with threat, entails what Goffman (1976) called 'playing the role'. It means accepting the behavioural prescriptions associated with the threatening position; living up to expectations. It can mean that the threatened person gains social approval as a consequence. If social stereotypes are fulfilled, the threatened person is more easily accepted because conformity to expectations arouses no disruption of status and power hierarchies.

There is now a considerable amount of evidence that stigmatized people act out the expected role. Braginski, Braginski and Ring (1969) showed that schiozphrenics in psychiatric hospitals play out complex impression management performances to project the images of incompetence which were expected of them. Their payoff was simple: by fulfilling expectations they forfend changes in the regime pertaining to themselves and their treatment becomes predictable. Patients who failed to comply with the role allocated were deemed troublemakers, more highly disturbed, and treated accordingly.

Compliance is not restricted to institutional settings. Farina *et al.* (1971) exemplified the power of expectations, both actual and perceived. They took a group of ex-psychiatric patients and asked them to talk to a stranger. Half were told that the stranger knew nothing of their medical history; the other half were led to believe that he knew everything. Actually, the stranger was not told about the person's psychiatric background. When interviewed after the conversation with the stranger, those who believed that he knew of their previous illness felt less appreciated, found the task more difficult and felt they had performed worse than those who thought that the stranger was ignorant of their past. Perhaps more significantly, observers of the interaction, who knew nothing of their psychiatric record or of the experimental conditions, reported that those who had been led to understand that the stranger knew their record were more tense, anxious and poorly adjusted than the others.

The experiment, despite its dubious ethical status, is instructive. It shows that simply believing that the stranger knew of their history changed both self-perception and actual behaviour. The stranger did not elicit this change of perception or action directly, he knew nothing about the patient and could not have been transmitting anything about expectations through subtle cues since there were no prior expectations to transmit. It seems that it is the ex-psychiatric patient who carries a set of beliefs about what others expect of someone with a record of mental illness and when these are triggered they initiate changes in self-perception and behaviour. Whether the beliefs about others' expectations are accurate or not is a moot point. Since they are developed through interaction with others, they are likely to bear some resemblance to the actual expectations, though they may become caricatured through the influence of fear and selective perception of feedback from others.

It could be argued that evidence of compliance from psychiatric patients in an institutional setting and from ex-patients in an artificial experimental context is limited. The question then becomes: do people with other stigmata who suffer threats to identity as a consequence also use compliance? The answer is most certainly 'yes'. Examples of the physically handicapped acting out the role are numerous; so, too, are stories of the elderly. Both tend to be associated with the notion of *learned helplessness*.

In some threatening positions, compliance and learned helplessness go hand-in-hand because the role expectations attached to that position designate dependency. This is the case for the elderly and the physically handicapped. The phenomenon of learned helplessness was first mapped by Seligman (1975). The phrase describes what happens to people who are prevented from doing things for themselves; over time, because other people do them for them, they learn to be incapable of doing them for themselves. Old people might arrive at a home, lively, even truculent, capable of running their own lives. But the regime in the home proceeds to limit their range of decision-making and refuses opportunities to use prior skills; they come to feel redundant not just to society, but also to themselves. When you lose the freedom of choice and everything is pre-planned for you and everything requiring effort is done for you, you soon lose the knack of making decisions, planning, and executing goal-directed action. Dependency reigns supreme and you have learned to be helpless. Learned helplessness is really all about being swamped with other people's help and feeling unable to control events. The physically disabled report similar experiences. The blind and the lame describe how people will try their utmost to offer assistance, to the point of being actually offended if help is superfluous. The handicapped person who can cope is inundated often with redundant help; it is an easy option to forget how to cope.

Helplessness can become a career. Others foster and encourage mute acceptance of help. In institutions, passive inmates are easier to handle, they are malleable in the interests of the bureaucracy (Taylor, 1979). Taylor suggests that in hospitals there are 'good-patient' and 'bad-patient' roles. While 'good-patient' behaviour (i.e. compliance, passivity, co-operation, and acceptance of loss of control) may be good for the staff, it may not be good for the patient. Tagliacozza and Manksch (1972) pointed out that patients acting out the 'good-patient' role are generally not calm, accepting, co-operative and happy. In fact, they found them to be in conflict, usually between the desire for information about their condition, with the concomitant ability to make decisions about treatment, and the desire to gain staff attention and help. Such patients are encouraged to feel dependent in the interests of the efficiency of the hospital and in pursuance of the authority of staff. However, the outcome for the patients is learned helplessness (Raps *et al.*, 1982) and a potential decline in the effort to help themselves. The patient may even withdraw from active attempts to regain good health (Schulz, 1976).

Outside institutions the rationale is less prosaic. People like to feel they have helped. Helpfulness is addictive, the ideal palliative for much guilt. The 'helpless' person who rejects help is denying the helper the daily fix and that will not be rewarded. Learned helplessness is consequently reinforced for various reasons but one thing is certain: the compliance strategy in this area serves to de-skill and strikes at the heart of independence.

Compliance can obviously have other serious drawbacks. Living up to what you perceive to be the expectations of other people can be an arduous business. This is particularly so when part of the stereotype attached to the threatening position leads to treatment as a non-person; someone to be ignored, avoided or regarded as an object without pride or privacy. People often treat those who are stigmatized as if they had no power to control access to themselves. This is especially tempting

with the physically handicapped who can be manhandled 'legitimately'. But it extends to others, too. The access demanded need not
be physical but may be psychological; involving inquisition and prying.
The disfigured can be quizzed about the reasons for their problem and
it can be done publicly, by strangers. Personal questions are seen as
symptomatic of sympathy, concern, or interest by the inquisitor; they
tend to be seen as invasions of privacy by the disfigured. The
threatened tend to resort to one of two ways of dealing with this
righteous onslaught: withdrawal or bravado. Actual withdrawal may
be impossible, in which case, psychological withdrawal may cut in,
being manifested in anger or disdain. Bravado may buttress psychological withdrawal. Normally involving extravagant overstatements of
the problem or generating black humour directed against the source of
threat and playing upon the audience's sense of pity or guilt, bravado
can simultaneously castigate others and manipulate them.

Compliance can be used as a coping strategy by other types of
powerless people when they occupy a threatening position. It is not
necessary to be old or ill to have recourse to compliance. Compliance
can be a self-conscious tactic designed to gain social acceptance from
within the threatening position. For instance, Breakwell and Weinberger (1985a, 1985b) showed that young women in sexually atypical
employment will engage in selective compliance to gain credibility and
favour. They studied young women training to be technicians in the
engineering industry. These young women were interviewed in depth
twice, with an interval of six months between the interviews, during
their second year of training. At the inception of the study only 2 per
cent of all engineering technicians in Britain were female; the young
women studied could, therefore, be legitimately considered to occupy
a position which was unusual. They also could be said to be breaching
traditional expectations; engineering is still seen stereotypically as the
archetypal masculine industry: dirty, heavy and hard. The young
women interviewed were 17–19 years of age and very sensitive to their
own transgression of gender role expectations. They knew that they
were entering an unusual job for a woman and expected problems.
Most had been subjected to criticism or ridicule at some time for their
ambition to do a 'man's job'. For the majority, this reinforced their
determination to do the job better than male counterparts. This placed
them under considerable pressure. Yet, when asked to compare themselves with the typical male trainee, they claimed that they were more
conscientious, neat, responsible, punctual, interested, reliable, patient,
safety conscious, logical and tactful. They admitted only that the boys
tended to have greater leadership skills, more confidence and superior
technical abilities.

This self-characterization, through comparison, is interesting when juxtaposed with the descriptions which their supervisors gave of the girls. In comparison with the boys, the supervisors rated the girls higher on dedication, on interest in the work and in respect to motivation. Boys were considered more adaptable and capable of leadership and possessed of greater technical skill. There is a striking parallel between the self-descriptions and supervisor's ratings.

From this data it would be impossible to say whether the supervisor's image of the female technician was leading the girls to think of themselves and describe themselves in particular ways or whether the supervisors came to their impressions from watching the girls in action. However, there is other evidence which supports the conclusion that these young women are complying with what they perceive to be appropriate behaviour for a female engineer. Firstly, supervisors, all of whom were interviewed once and the majority twice, have two very different images of what would be ideal for a male technician and a female technician. According to them, the ideal girl can tolerate boredom, stick to monotonous repetitive tasks, and accept discipline without becoming resentful or aggressive. The ideal boy is quick on the uptake of new ideas, something of a rapscallion, but capable of stoic unemotionality. Even those supervisors who had no experience of training women before held these strangely dichotomized criteria for appropriate performances from the two sexes.

Two other preoccupations of both training managers and supervisors emerged during interviews: one was with 'sexy' types and the other with 'aggressive-feminist' types. Women were deemed generally ignorant of how they should relate to men when working with them in non-traditional jobs and men did not know how to deal with them. This, they thought, could create problems for all concerned but especially where the women were young and 'sexy' or aggressive and feminist. One confessed that he would not employ a woman who looked 'sexy': 'Good-looking is a recipe for disaster because the girl gets spoiled by the men.' Another pointed out that: 'All this talk of women being equal is rubbish. But the pendulum swung too far and is now swinging back again. Women are putting their bras back on, and a good thing too.' He went on to add that women who became engineers just to make a political point or to be different were no good. The dislike of feminism as a motive was paralleled by a dislike of any hint of aggression in the girls.

Most of the girls had a very clear understanding of what was expected of them within weeks of joining a firm and this solidified over the six-month interval between the initial interviews and the second. They knew that they were expected to show considerable dedication and not be too sexy or too aggressive. Aggression in this context included any explicit competition in social activities considered male preserves, like dinnertime football. They also knew that they were not expected to be overtly feminine or emotional at work. In fact, they had a fine balancing act to perform: being non-aggressive without apparently 'feminine' passivity; being un-sexy without encroaching upon domains where masculinity was to be expressed. The girls could articulate the demands which were made of them in terms of self-presentation with clarity and, on occasion, mirth. It does seem then that the self-characterization is produced in compliance with a pre-existent set of social beliefs held by those with power and authority (in this case, the supervisors).

It was also evident that some girls self-consciously decide to act out the role: not too assertive, overbearing or ambitious but equally not too placid, shy or feminine. Others reject the role and persist in some idiosyncratic presentation of the self. This decision appears to be of considerable importance. Those girls who performed the complex juggling act with self-image appeared to be more successful in the workplace not just socially but technically too. They were rated higher in engineering skills by supervisors and reported less difficulty in getting on with workmates. They had seemingly recognized that the key to success lay in two directions: mastery of the technical skills but also, and perhaps more importantly, mastery of the social skills necessary to deal with others from a threatened position. Compliance, acting out the role, can be seen to be a successful coping strategy in this context.

It is questionable whether compliance will inevitably engender changes in identity structure. It will not do so unless the assimilation-accommodation process actually integrates the implications that compliance with role requirements has for the content and value dimensions. Such integration may not occur if the role-enactment is construed as irrelevant to the real self or in some way an illegitimate reflection of the self, perhaps because it is produced with cynical and Machiavellian intent.

There seems to be no doubt that the majority of those female technicians who complied with their supervisor's demands for the ideal woman trainee did so with malice aforethought and recognized that they were manipulating the situation to their own ends. Yet, when asked simply to describe the features primarily distinguishing them, their self-descriptions tended to be permeated by the characteristics demanded in the role. One young woman, having previously described how she put on a show of non-aggression and docile thoroughness for her supervisor, went on to describe herself: 'not really assertive. I'm a bit of a perfectionist. I like getting things right first time. Suppose I'm conscientious really. Really don't like confrontation. Not much of a show-off, not really.' The irony of the number of 'really's' in the description of the true self which so echoes the supervisors' stereotype of the 'good' female trainee is not lost. It seems that even manipulative compliance may sometimes change the actual identity structure. Successful compliance, which breeds social approval, is especially likely to accelerate changes in the identity structure. After all, compliance which is rewarded is likely to be perpetuated and the longer the compliance continues, the greater will be its power to shape experience and, consequently, the material available for assimilation into the identity structure.

It is no simple matter to predict under what circumstances compliance will prove successful, not least because solid criteria of success are not easy to establish. Compliance undoubtedly can carry rewards in that it can incite social approval and initiate the relief of anxiety which is normally associated with conformity to social pressure. Compliance can even have payoffs by establishing the clearly defined social status of the threatened person; eradicating ambiguities which are anxiety-arousing. The problems arise when compliance serves none of these functions, when it does not enhance identity and instead militates against continuity, distinctiveness, or self-esteem. Then the threatened person can be caught in the classic double-bind situation: non-compliance generates social rejection but so does compliance. The member of a powerless, stigmatized ethnic minority who conforms to a dominant negative social stereotype of members of her group will not solve the threat to her identity, but neither will her male counterpart who rebels against the stereotype in his way of life.

The double-bind inherent in compliance points to the inadequacy of interpersonal coping strategies. All of them require the game to be played by a set of rules over which the threatened person has no control or absolutely minimal control. Isolation, negativism, passing and compliance, all entail the individual attempting to cope within the existing ideological and social structure amidst the restrictions of dominant social representations, attributions and moral codes. An alternative approach to coping is to seek to modify the rules of the game. This requires more than individual effort; it requires strategies of social change which are dependent upon the production of pressure groups and intergroup dynamics.

6 Intergroup coping strategies

Group dynamics are the most frequent source of threats to identity. These threats need not be personalized: they are directed at the individual as a group member, a cipher in a social category, not as a personality. So, for instance, the imperatives of intergroup conflict often result in the destruction or fragmentation of the lives of members. War can tear apart an identity; demanding actions which contradict all previous beliefs and, possibly, reducing to rubble all previous family and friendship networks. Of course, alternatively, threats generated by group dynamics can be very personalized. The threat may arise because the individual is ascribed to membership of a group which is stigmatized, powerless and subordinated and this attacks self-esteem. It can be because the individual loses a valued group membership after forced eviction. It may even be that membership is never adequately secured, as in the case of marginality.

Given that group dynamics are a prime source of threat, it is hardly surprising that they should provide a fertile breeding ground for coping strategies. Intergroup coping strategies can operate at a series of levels (Figure 6 represents them) and the structure of the groups concerned vary.

Multiple group memberships

Everyone belongs to a number of different groups simultaneously which combine to determine their position in the social matrix. A carefully blended mixture of multiple group memberships can operate

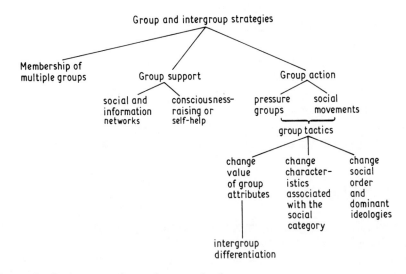

Figure 6 *Coping strategies at the group level*

to nullify or ameliorate the threat derived from any single membership. This can happen because the stigma attached to a group membership can be modified or eradicated by other memberships held. The attitudes of others towards the stigmatized person can be radically altered by knowledge of other memberships held. For instance, discriminatory attitudes towards blacks are moderated by information on their educational or occupational standing. If the respondent shares that standing, such attitudes are particularly affected. Minard (1952), in a well-known study of the Pocahontas coal mines, showed that discrimination by white miners against black miners was not manifested while they were at work and their shared occupational standing was emphasized, but it reasserted itself above ground. Harding and Hogrefe (1952) showed a similar phenomenon in large department stores in the USA where white workers showed no prejudice against blacks who had equivalent occupational status but continued to discriminate against other blacks. Doise (1978) refers to this as the result of 'crossed categorization': where people share one social categorization but not another, the positivity of the shared membership seems to override the intergroup differentiation which would normally be associated with the other membership. In terms of coping with threat, this means that the disadvantages associated with one membership may be assuaged by gaining other, more accepted, memberships.

The value of multiple group memberships does, however, seem limited. It depends on whether the deprecating actions and attitudes of others can be permanently altered; if the respite is transient (for instance, only while you are at work mining coal), the advantages may seem minimal. It also depends on the costs involved in joining the new group. A cost-benefit analysis in terms of outcomes for identity seems essential before embarking upon this sort of coping strategy. Of course, if the new membership has the power to enhance the identity structure quite apart from its capacity to mitigate the threatening effects of other memberships it should be grabbed. It may then reduce the salience of the threat on the content or value dimensions.

Group support

Individuals experiencing threat can come together with others who share their predicament or who are sympathetic to their cause to create a new group. Such groups can work on one or both of two bases.

As social and informational networks

Isolation is the natural bedfellow of threat to identity. The formation of a group of people sharing the same type of threat can be the cure of isolation. It can also ensure that information relevant to coping with the threat is made available more effectively to all concerned. The creation of these groups is now commonplace in western industrialized societies.

Women in sexually atypical employment, regardless of the actual nature of their work, report isolation and feel the absence of female peers particularly acutely. Organization has been used to overcome the problem. For instance, in 1978, a small group of women working in the City of London, who wanted to find a way in which women in senior managerial positions, often lacking peers in their own companies, could share common interests and solve mutual problems, created the City Women's Network. The Network represents a variety of professions and industries but mainly traditional city institutions like banking and the law. It aims to encourage women to seek executive, managerial and professional positions but it is not a pressure group in the accepted sense: it does not militate for political or legislative changes with regard to the employment of women. Instead, it functions as an informal network of contacts; a nascent old girls' network.

Grass-roots growth of an organization for women with similar occupational aspirations may be a more effective way of dealing with the problems of sexually atypical employment than training schemes and short courses superimposed by the government. The Network imposes no ideological framework and makes only limited personal demands upon members; it is ideal for the individualist who happens also to dislike isolation and being starved of information. The other advantage of such an organization is that it is in the control of its users. It can provide support without interference and advice without dogma. Stripped of bureaucratic hierarchies and sensitive to the immediate needs of members, such grass-roots support groups can radically alter the impact of threat to the identity structure.

As consciousness-raising or self-help groups
It may be arbitrary to distinguish between social and information networks on the one hand and consciousness-raising or self-help groups on the other. In her study of the women's liberation movement in the United States, Freeman (1975) argues that they blend into each other. Yet they do differ subtly. Information networks are concerned with transmitting facts efficiently, to the advantage of members. Consciousness-raising groups are explicitly designed to change the members' understanding of facts that they may already possess. The precise structures of consciousness-raising groups vary wildly: with numbers participating; with the length of time it exists; with the political and ideological orientation of members; and so on (Freeman, 1975).

The label 'consciousness-raising' is largely associated with the women's liberation movement, though many of the groups which grew up within that tradition would not have called themselves consciousness-raising. As Gill Philpott (1982, p. 585), writing in the magazine *Spare Rib*, said: 'In the early days of the women's liberation movement, groups *were* consciousness-raising groups, though they didn't always call themselves them. Small groups of women met regularly to talk about their personal experiences as well as to take other forms of action.' This sharing of experience with others facing similar problems, social or personal, is at the heart of the philosophy underlying consciousness-raising. It permits the externalizing of feelings and, in an atmosphere which is supportive, the discovery that these feelings are normal and shared by others. Where the feelings entail self-doubt, guilt, or self-blame, the revelation that others do and feel the same can be cathartic.

In her women's group, Philpott reports that they were continually surprised and encouraged by 'the similarity of our experiences, and as this sharing went on many of us found the confidence to do things that really mattered to us'. They made changes to their lives and in their self-image. Such involvement can bind the participants together but not just as individuals. The women involved in consciousness-raising groups report feelings of greater concern for and amity with all women, bringing awareness of the political as well as the personal contexts of their problems as women trying to break out of traditional gender roles.

Consciousness-raising groups are by no means restricted to the women's movement. They have been used by the disabled, by religious minorities, and by ethnic minorities. The features of the groups differ administratively but the underlying psychodynamics are similar: there is the norm of self-disclosure, the pressure to conform to reconceptualizations of the social position of individuals and the tireless push for tight group cohesiveness, the virtual sublimation of the individual by the group.

With the threatened, consciousness-raising normally takes the form of teaching them a way of understanding their own behaviour and feelings, the social structures and ideologies which determine their position and the history which produced it. The teaching is not formal, it works through mutual sharing of experience. Consciousness-raising also usually revises the value connotations of the social position. Consciousness-raising groups are typically part of the armaments of social movements designed to bring about social change. They are a powerful means of changing attitudes and remoulding beliefs because the individual is subject to intense conformity pressures within the group.

For the threatened, the process of persuasion can be a positive relief. Personal responsibility for making decisions about how to respond to the threat is relinquished, the group offers pre-packaged solutions in accordance with the particular philosophy it adduces. The orthodoxies differ across groups. Some laud independence, others community. They share the superordinate concern that members should accept their orthodoxy, their ideology, whatever it includes. Consciousness-raising groups, by and large, give members a new social awareness, a new way of explaining why they are threatened, and a recipe for dealing with it. They rarely offer choice. But, for the threatened, choice may appear a rather superfluous luxury anyway. The consciousness-raising group which succeeds in enabling them to reconceptualize the threatening position, in such a way that its capacity to attack self-esteem is reduced, will be deemed worthy of the sacrifice of some autonomy. For example, one woman manager in the textile industry had joined a women's group on the insistence of her daughter. She went without believing that the sort of problems she was experiencing at work could be helped by a 'chat over wine and cheese'. However, she found her problems were similar to those of others in the group, they too had difficulty in getting men working in jobs subordinate to their own to do what they were asking; they too found they were being teased for being too serious and single-minded; and they too went through periods of virtual self-hatred and perpetual self-doubt.

Discovering the experiences which threatened the woman's self-evaluation were commonplace had two effects: it minimized their overall importance and it implied that they were actually not specifically tied to her faults or failures. Group members advised on rituals of interaction which could be used at work to improve matters: tried and tested techniques they knew to be effective because they had used them. The woman said: 'After six months, I began to realize what parts of my predicament I was responsible for and could change and which parts were dictated by the history of male-female relations and the economic institutions of the country.'

Consciousness-raising groups are essentially in the business of revising the social representations of a social position which the individual may have learnt previously. They replace one set of values, beliefs and explanations with another; not in any formal tutorial manner but through providing the opportunity to share experiences and batter out some new basis for understanding. Where the group is a clear offshoot of a definable social movement, with a coherent ideology, the origin of the replacement social representation is evident and it can be imposed upon the rest by key figures in the group. If the group stands independent of existing social movements, and its social representation has no identifiable social roots, it has to be a product of the process of communication within the group itself. When this happens, individual members have a much greater part to play in reconstructing their own social representation of their position. They carry into the group idiosyncratic renderings of pre-existent social representations and the group processes themselves generate a new communal representation which, again, individuals will imperfectly reflect. Of course, even in this more fluid situation, not all individuals will carry equal weight in the process of reconstruction.

It is worth adding that groups do not have to be called consciousness-raising groups to serve the same function. Some training courses, therapy groups, and self-help groups have the same effect of revising the individual's understanding of their position and its social roots. For instance, Breakwell (1984a) showed that young people, involved in training at a college of further education as part of their Youth Opportunities Programme scheme, assimilated during their course the social representation of the causes of unemployment promulgated by their tutors. At the start of the course, these young people, who had previously been unemployed, regarded the reasons for unemployment to lie with the laziness, lack of experience, and lack of qualifications of the unemployed. They effectively blamed the unemployed for their unemployment. By the end of the course, they argued that unemployment was a product of worldwide economic recession and the monetarist policy of the British government; this was the view of their tutors from the start.

These young people may have been particularly amenable to the modification of their social representation of unemployment because they were being influenced by figures who had considerable authority and power over them. They are also likely to have adopted the revision because it cushioned them against future threat to identity from unemployment. They had been unemployed before and stood little chance of gaining employment in the future after their training finished. Acceptance of the tutors' explanation for unemployment meant that they would not have to blame themselves for their unemployment subsequently; it would have less power to damage self-esteem. That, in theory at least, would represent one barrier against the threat unemployment creates for identity. In fact, these young people were traced after leaving training. Many became unemployed and over a number of weeks on the dole were re-educated into their earlier social representation. They came to blame themselves again. This serves to point to the fact that groups which offer the threatened new ways of understanding their position can have little long-term impact if the wider society persistently derides and denies their message. But, as part of a broader effort to change societal norms and values, they clearly have a role to play.

Self-help groups also may act as consciousness-raising arenas, but more frequently they are a practical vehicle for the exchange of services and support. In this respect, they echo the information networks like the City Women's Network. However, they tend to offer more direct help, rather than merely information, and often trade in emotional sustenance. Probably the most obvious self-help groups are those which evolve around physical or mental illnesses. Cancer victims, particularly those who have undergone surgery, commonly create self-help groups. These provide a sympathetic group of people who have similar experiences where doubts and fears can be voiced and faced, and answers may be found by listening to how others have tackled the problems. Simply knowing that others have faced the threat and survived can be enough to instil optimism and persistence. Comparison with others suffering the same illness can also provide valuable information where medical or expert information is not available (Molleman *et al.* 1986). Use of such self-help groups may be temporary or long term; they can be dependency-forming but not necessarily.

Self-help groups are not all tied to illness by any means. Any individual problem which can be better tackled by two or more can initiate such a group. For instance, single-parent families can be organized into Gingerbread groups. These are essentially local self-help groups which are loosely found together within a national umbrella organization. Their object is to enable single-parents to pool their resources with others. This can be in terms of arrangements for swaps in baby-minding, the exchange of information about financial or social security benefits, and the less concrete provision of mutual emotional support. The Gingerbread organization is interesting because it has developed from a straight system of self-help groups working for the benefit of participants within the restraints of the existing social norms and legal regulations towards a national pressure group working simultaneously to influence legislation and alter attitudes.

It is easy to see that support groups sit on the border between efforts to induce personal change in the threatened and social change in their society. They modify the impact of the threat to identity by revising the social representation of the threatening position, thereby reconstituting the implications it has for the identity structure. They influence the emotional reserves the individual has for dealing with the threat by creating new interpersonal support networks where acceptance and approval are forthcoming. They provide new arenas for achievement and personal commitment. They offer valuable information likely to change both personal goals and action strategies. All of this is likely to generate personal change which will be in accordance with the principles of continuity, distinctiveness and self-esteem. Membership of the support group thus reduces the overall destructive impact of a threat. In addition, they can become vehicles for the representation of the threatened to the outside world. The group can become a focus for changing public attitudes by putting the case of the threatened cogently. Often it is enough simply to make their situation known more widely. However, as soon as support groups start to seek to exercise social influence, a whole new set of coping strategies comes into play.

Group action

Thus far, the coping strategies considered have been lodged at the level of the individual. They have involved the individual engaging in thought or action which sought to alleviate the threat; even joining a support group is at the individual level. However, the individual may need to rely upon group action in the intergroup context to initiate changes which will actually either eradicate the threat or minimize it. This is not to deny that groups are comprised of individuals acting in concert but it emphasizes that the strategies available to groups are different in quality and quantity to those open to the single individual.

Group action in favour of the threatened occurs within two broad types of group: the pressure group and the social movement. These differ primarily in the form of their organization. *Pressure groups* operate within the existing social and legal order, using methods largely accepted by mass society as legitimate. They may represent a large constituency of threatened people but tend to be highly centralized, bureaucratized, expert organizations. They are often managed by people who are not threatened but who have sympathy with their cause and some relevant expertise – what Goffman calls 'courtesy' members.

An example of a highly influential pressure group working on behalf of archetypically threatened people would be MIND, the National Association for Mental Illness, whose self-appointed role it is to protect the interests of the mentally ill. MIND has been intimately involved in all recent legislation in Britain appertaining to the mentally ill. It has also been instrumental in campaigns to revise the public image of mental illness. Success in rebuilding the social representation of mental illness has been imperative as the first step in dissolving the stigma attached to it and modifying the methods of treatment offered those threatened by mental illness. MIND has been a powerful source for the shift towards community care for those with psychiatric problems over the last twenty years. In the mid-1980s, it is now becoming a forceful advocate of the increasing need for adequate funding for community psychiatric services within regional health and social service provision. It can be seen to have become a pressure group operating not only within the medical community but also upon the stage of national politics; having a voice within policy-making governmental committees.

Social movements are typically deemed to be less institutionalized. Toch (1966) argued that a 'social movement represents an effort by a large number of people to solve collectively a problem that they feel they have in common'. It is essentially an effort to bring about change in the social order. It is not restricted to using methods considered legitimate within that social order. Where the pressure group machinates for incremental change from within the system, the social movement acts to bring about radical change from without. Initially, at least, it has little formal organization, arising spontaneously from the simultaneous consciousness across a range of people that they share a common grievance. Since it is not organized around an internal administration and because it does not seek formal or lasting channels of communication with the representatives of the dominant social order, the social movement is less likely to engage in negotiation and reasoned argument than in direct acts of violence to rectify the grievance. But such spontaneous violence tends to be short-lived and superseded by the development of a leadership hierarchy which marshals the aggression into symbolic protests: marches, sit-ins, occupation of property, and so on. Even at this point, the tactics of the social movement will rarely sit comfortably within the law. The protest too easily subsides into violent clashes with the police or other agents of the social order (Breakwell, 1984b).

Violence can either be directed outwards at opponents (in riots, terrorism, assassinations or outright warfare) or inwards at members of the movement (examples of self-mortification for the sake of the cause are common enough: hunger strikes, suicide squads, and self-incineration). To maximize the efficacy of violence it needs a veneer of justification (Turner and Killian, 1972). Explanation which legitimates it is what converts 'mindless violence' into protest. The meaning of an act can be transformed by a patina of rhetoric. Often the propagandists may fail to legitimate the violence in the eyes of outsiders but they have just as important an audience within the movement, whose members avidly wish their actions to be morally justified. Of course, anarchist terrorists use violence without justification deliberately. The fact that they can strike at random, without reason, optimizes the disruption, fear and despair which they can cause. Fear because everyone becomes a target. Despair because there is no chance of negotiation to end the hostilities. In such cases, violence is not a means to an end but an end in itself. Fortunately, for most social movements, violence is an often unpremeditated means to a non-violent end. To the extent that it may be incidental rather than intentional, violence may also be created by any pressure group which organizes mass protests which get out of control.

Pressure groups and social movements may differ in the degree of their centralization and institutionalization and in the immediate methods they employ, particularly in relation to violence, but they share common underlying objectives. They exist to promote the interests of the people that they represent and all their objectives are subordinated to this end. Fundamentally, they all entail wresting more power for themselves. Power, in this context, is defined in terms of capacity for self-determination. The greater the social influence and the greater the independence, the more power they possess. It is assumed that they exist to shift a conglomerate of people from a position of little power to a position of greater power. They will, therefore, pursue a series of objectives with this overall end in view:

(i) They will seek *a change in the value attributed to the qualities deemed characteristic of the people represented.* The change will be designed to make the group appear more positive, acceptable and worthy. In his theory of intergroup behaviour, Tajfel (1978) emphasizes that groups in subordinate positions will try to revise the social worth of those attributes which define the group's inferiority whenever it is impossible to eradicate those attributes. The classic example of this tactic is found in the driving sentiment of the negritude movement. Stokely Carmichael (1962) typified it: 'We must see ourselves as beautiful people.... We've got to understand that we have thick lips and flat noses and curly hair and we're black and beautiful.' This sort of re-evaluation of the salient characteristics of a subordinated social category in order to enhance self-esteem and counter stigmatization is not uncommon. Various feminist groups have argued that the emotionality and supposed intuitive illogicality of women should be lauded not despised (Glennon, 1979). It is obvious that this sort of campaign to influence the value of existing characteristics can help the threatened. If the threat is directed at self-esteem and emanates from the inescapable membership of the stigmatized social category, any move which serves to alleviate the stigma will also reduce the threat.

The process of changing the social value attached to a group characteristic never occurs in a vacuum. Firstly, all of the group's characteristics adhere to form a system. Changing one means concomitant changes in the others. Indeed, the re-evaluation of one may be dependent upon a shift in the relative salience of others in the public image of the group. This happens where what has been a minor attribute, peripheral to the image, is called into the centre stage and invested with much importance. Other, previously more focal, attributes diminish in import; this is especially important where these carried social disapproval. Effectively, the process involves the re-structuring of the identity of the group or social category. Secondly, the value of a group characteristic is never absolute or objective, it comes about through comparisons across groups. The value of a characteristic is always relative; influenced by how commonly it is found across groups. A characteristic which fails to differentiate between groups has no social value. Only those which differentiate have the potential to be invested with social value as a consequence of group action. Tajfel (1978, 1981a, 1982, 1984) has argued that a group seeks to maximize the apparent differentials between itself and others upon those dimensions of comparison where kudos can be achieved. The process of re-evaluating a characteristic which will differentiate between one's own group and others is to assure that it will contribute kudos and will have the power to enhance self-esteem. In effect, the group is manipulating the social value of its characteristics to ensure an improvement in its position relative to other groups and thus to inflate the self-esteem of its members.

(ii) They will seek *to change the characteristics associated with the social category.* Group action may revolve around attempts to add new characteristics to the public image of the social category or to excise some it already contains. Again, this is a component of the predictions made by Tajfel in his theory of intergroup relations. The task basically constitutes an exercise in redefinition of the essential parameters of the group. These may involve the values, norms or ideology of the group but may also be centred on types of activity undertaken by the group or on the intellectual and personality traits reified at the level of the group. The characteristics imported are normally ones already invested with social value. So, for instance, various feminist groups have argued that women have just as much mathematical and scientific ability as men. The characteristics excluded are those normally negatively valued. For example, feminists, paradoxically, have vociferously contended that women are neither passive nor voluble.

It is occasionally possible to introduce a new characteristic, not borrowed from elsewhere, and militate for it to have immediate social value. The introduction of the concept of androgyny by some feminists fits this model: the androgynous person is said to possess qualities which unite the best of masculine and feminine gender types and much evidence is evinced to prove that this leads to better mental health and social adjustment (Bem, 1977; Williams, 1979). Women can now claim to be androgynous, which symbolizes a system of traits invested with social value, and this is another route out of social subordination. The 'discovery' of psychological androgyny is interesting because it does not simply offer women the chance to claim for themselves characteristics previously regarded as the preserve of men; it also tends to create a new grouping. This group could comprise both men and women sharing a single gender identity: androgyny. If this were to be given serious consideration, it would perhaps not satisfy those women who wish to grasp new defining properties for their own female gender identity. The exercise may only serve to divide women into those who can and those who cannot claim the new gender identity. In a sense, the scientific 'discovery' of psychological androgyny has provided the possibility for some women to exit, as Tajfel would put it, from a subordinate group not physically but psychologically. This is an interesting variant of the psychological mobility entered into by children engaging in ethnic misidentification. Here the self-misidentification has been legitimated by the scientific establishment.

Again, the potential advantages for the threatened individual are clear: the excision of characteristics which attack self-esteem and the implantation of ones which enhance it. Of course, there may be some disruption of continuity as a consequence. However, where the changes encompass greater social value, they are unlikely to be resisted by the assimilation process.

Nevertheless, it is worth bearing in mind that the group action has two audiences: those outside the social category it defends and those inside. It is possible that the two audiences may respond differently. The group action may persuade the *broader external audience* but fail to convince its own membership. This may be particularly so where the group action is undertaken by a minority of those experiencing the threat supposedly on behalf of the rest but without their explicit consent or support. For instance, it is clear that neither the Black Power nor the Women's Movements carried the active involvement of more than a small proportion of their potential constituency. It is notable that they have failed to gather support in the older age groups and, in the case of the Women's Movement particularly, the lower socioeconomic classes. This may be because the structure of the rhetoric used was inappropriate for these subsections of the threatened; offering them too little, too late. It may also be that these are the threatened who have evolved other types of coping strategies and have no need of social movements to achieve salvation. Either way, this would result in resistance to the assimilation into the identity structure of the proposed new characteristics or the removal of the old. In the longer term, resistance might be fruitless. Assuming group action revised the social stereotype of the category, members would come to be treated differently and there would be new patterns of experience and reinforcement for identity.

As long as group action is effective in the social arena, the impact on the threatened themselves may be delayed but cannot be prevented. In the case of the position of women and ethnic minorities, pressure groups have, for instance, been instrumental in changing legislation which, over time, will alter the objective circumstances of both categories.

Sometimes the audience effects are reversed: *the threatened are persuaded* but not the wider society. Where this occurs there is scope for the development of a new subculture, with its own distinctive ideology, which may co-exist beside the dominant culture but has limited influence over it. Hall and Jefferson (1983) collected together a series of descriptions of how youth subcultures in post-war Britain have acted as alternative constructions of reality for their participants, providing new systems of belief, different moral and value codes, and alternative criteria against which to measure success.

The reverberations of these subcultures are perceptible in mass culture through the inroads made into fashion and popular music but their impact upon power structures is virtually non-existent. At most, they cause a minor flurry of concern where the media or popular imagination conjures around them what Cohen (1973) called a 'folk devil'. 'Folk devils' are groups which are believed to threaten the social order. Having identified one, mass society feels justified in what Cohen called a 'moral panic', questioning how the wickedness can be contained and how it could be bred of such a good society. Football hooligans are currently a folk devil, so are teenage drug addicts. Once a subculture harbours a folk devil, it gains prominence but only because it is scheduled for control. Thus, it influences mass society but not in any way it can direct.

Subcultures may not modify the social order but they can still help the threatened. Because they erect a different system of beliefs and values, they provide a social matrix nested within the social order. Within this matrix, the threatened can regain self-esteem, generate positive distinctiveness and promote continuity. The subculture distances the messages from the mass society which would wreck the reconstituted identity structure. For the threatened, the subculture can be an oasis in a social desert. For instance, Marsh *et al.* (1978) argued that football hooligans have a set of rules which govern their disorder and a role system which permits a lad to embark upon a career of hooliganism in which promotions and greater status can be earned. Marsh asserts that the lads involved are people who have no other realm of activity where they can gain praise or achieve status. A career in hooliganism is a substitute for an occupational career. It fosters self-esteem and distinctiveness through gaining the accolades of peers in a system of action expectations and value judgements not understood by the outside world. The very fact that it is misunderstood by outsiders simply exaggerates its significance for identity.

It would, however, be unwise to overemphasize the insulation properties of a subculture. Youth subcultures in particular are transient manifestations. At least, their form changes even if the function remains the same. More importantly, their membership changes. People grow older and cannot remain like Peter Pan in Never Never Land. The life within the subculture is a temporary answer to threats to identity. It may, of course, be enough if the threat is also tied to the vagaries of adolescence.

There are other types of subculture not predicated upon age but upon class, educational background, or geographical region which do not have a similar inbuilt redundancy. It might be expected that these would possess longer-term powers to insulate from threat. Yet, in fact, it seems to depend very greatly upon the form of the threat and the degree to which the subculture can maintain autonomy. For instance, it has been suggested that the unemployed in communities where unemployment is rife are more able to cope with the threat it represents because they are part of a subculture within which unemployment, since it is common, has ceased to stigmatize. Yet, studies of the unemployed in areas of high and stable unemployment, where as many as three generations in the same family are on the dole, have discovered no mitigation of its traumatic effects (Sixsmith, 1986). Sharing this particular threat to identity does not reduce its demands. Moreover, the subculture does not insulate the individual. It can provide no equivalent substitute for work as a source of self-esteem. It is too soaked in the expectations and values of mass society, too permeated by the mass media, and too financially dependent upon the welfare system to claim any real autonomy.

(iii) To be valuate in the longer term, group action must change the social order: *revising the relative power of groups and devising new ideological systems*. It would be useful to know what sort of group action is most likely to be effective in bringing about such change. Moscovici (1976) suggested that minorities acquire influence if they represent a view steadfastly and with unanimity (what he labels respectively diachronic and synchronic consistency). Success depends upon creating a social conflict in which the position represented by the minority becomes one sort of solution, one alternative route for social change. Mugny (1982) proposed an intergroup framework for the mechanism of minority influence. He distinguished three social agents operative in the context of social change: the power, a dominant group or pre-eminent norm exercising control; the population, the public which is the target for influence attempts; and the minority, which rejects the power. The relationships between the three social agents clearly differ. Between the population and the power, there is a dominance relationship. Between the power and the minority, there is an antagonistic relationship. Between the population and the minority, there is a relationship of social influence. To be effective in controlling social change, the minority must manipulate these relationships. In its antagonism with the power, the minority must be firm, stable, self-confident and autonomous. The minority must break off relationships with the power, refusing to negotiate with it and upsetting the established norms and rules of communication so as to create an imbalance in the smooth functioning of the social system. This faces both the power and the population, which will have to some extent accepted the ideology of the power, with conflict. In order to influence the population, Mugny argues, the minority has to show some flexibility as well as acting as a consistent opponent of the power. This requires the implementation of different styles of negotiation: rigidity towards the power; flexibility towards the population.

Mugny *et al.* (1984) have postulated that where a minority is perceived as rigid it is deemed to exclude all positions other than its own. In relation to the population, this is counterproductive; effectively excluding them from membership in advance and justifying discriminations in retaliation. Rigidity which is overstated will prevent the population from identifying communalities they share with the minority which will, in turn, lead them to bar its influence. Differentiating oneself from the minority in terms of characteristics and beliefs minimizes the potential for it to have an influence because succumbing to its influence would challenge identity. Flexibility on the part of the minority offers the potential for perceived communalities and consequent identification with it which will increase the likelihood of its influence.

Identification with the minority assumes the assimilation of its beliefs or values and also accommodation in identity of salient characteristics associated with its membership. This may, in part, explain why minorities in the real world, rather than in the social psychology laboratory, have relatively little influence. The characteristics appended to them by the power's ideology are negative, hardly likely to encourage identification. Dominant ideologies virtually always interpret the actions of minorities as deviant. Minority innovations, aimed at establishing some dimension of superiority or control, are not seen as expressions of social originality (Lemaine, 1974) but as the idiosyncratic behaviours of a few individuals who can be labelled criminal, insane, or malcontents. The frame of attribution about minority actions inherent in the dominant ideology serves two functions: it makes the minority unattractive to the population and it legitimates its legal constraint.

It may be inappropriate to dismiss the potential of minorities to induce social change just because members of the population may be disinclined to join them. Minority influence is often more latent than manifest. Latent effects occur, according to Mugny *et al.*, when the conflict induced is powerful and the time allowed to elapse considerable. A minority which generates deep conflict of value or belief cannot expect immediate effects. The change grows gradually as the implications of the conflict cannot be silenced by derogatory or criminalizing attributions to the minority. The minority's intervention then adjusts the social matrix within which identities are moulded; its impact upon the identities of the population is indirect but none the less for that.

Mugny *et al.* are interested in the structural properties of a minority's actions and how these correlate with efficacy. So they concentrate upon rigidity and flexibility in negotiation style. They do not consider the form of the rhetoric, propaganda or polemic which is the immediate instrument of attempts at influence. There is an extensive literature on the factors which affect the process of persuasion when it is directed at the individual (see any social psychology text, e.g. Wrightsman and Deaux, 1981). These include the characteristics of the source of influence (attractiveness, power, etc.); the medium, content and organization of the persuasive message; the content within which it takes place (for instance, how many distractions there are); and the attributes of the target for persuasion (intelligence, authoritarianism, locus of control, level of self-esteem, etc.).

There is no comparable information about how groups employ propaganda and what affects its influence. There was, of course, the early work of the Institute for Propaganda Analysis during the 1930s which aptly outlined the little techniques of propaganda in an impressionistic form. Doob (1948) summarized the techniques which they had discovered: name calling, glittering generalities, testimonials, 'plain folks' appeals, identification and transfer, 'card stacking', and band-wagonning. This work did not examine the relation between propaganda and social change; it was very largely aimed at the level of the individual response. The minutiae of propaganda are less interesting than the way groups in conflict tailor their efforts at influence to suit the exigencies of the moment. Of particular interest is the role which ideologies play in dictating rhetoric.

Breakwell and Rowett (1982) and Breakwell (1983a) report a study of the rhetoric used by the groups involved in an industrial conflict. It was shown that the rhetoric of the dominant group was designed to attack the identity of the group on strike which was already seriously weakened by internal divisions and fragmentation. The employers did not seek to persuade anyone that they were in the right, morally or economically, they launched instead into a swingeing critique of the immorality of the strikers, pummelling their internal divisions, challenging dimensions central to their self-definition. The strikers failed to evolve a self-defensive rhetoric and the identity of members was directly threatened by the management attack. The strike failed and the post-strike self-descriptions by the strikers emphasize their loss of self-esteem and the dissipation of cohesiveness within the group. The study showed that the employers' rhetoric was purely oppor-tunistic, taking advantage of the identity weakness of the opponent group; it had nothing to do with a broader ideology.

In a subsequent study, Breakwell (1983b) explored the conditions under which group ideology would regulate rhetoric. It was hypothe-sized that ideology has its greatest effects where a group is in conflict but has little or no knowledge of the opposition's strengths and weak-nesses. If a group knows of its opponent's identity weaknesses, it was argued, it would focus on them even if this meant ignoring its own idelogy.

In the experiment, participants were given a description of a conflict involving two sides: a council and a community. The drama entailed the council destroying a playground. The ideology of the council was clearly outlined; it centred on urban renewal and equality of housing. Their next target was a street of old, occupied houses which residents wished to retain. Participants were simply asked to describe the argu-ments used by the council representatives and the community repre-sentatives to justify and persuade. They were divided into two conditions according to the degree of information which they were given about the residents in the area. In Condition 1, no information was given on their demographic characteristics, attitudes, etc. In Condition 2, information was given on an array of subfactions and internal conflicts to provide the ammunition for an evaluation of the strengths and weaknesses of the residents as a group. It was found that, in Condition 1, council ideology regarding urban renewal and progress is used to justify their actions and the community representative is attributed the photo-negative set of beliefs and values. In Condition 2, the respondents expected the council representative to concentrate on emphasizing the disagreements and conflicts of interests amongst community residents. There is no mention of the council ideology. Moreover, the community representative was not expected to be able to articulate an integrated argument. There was thus no dominant ideology at play for the residents' representative to counter.

The study shows that people *expect* ideology to take a backseat in generating the structure of rhetoric where the source can capitalize upon organizational or other weaknesses in the opponent group. Matthews (1983) in a study of an actual council-community conflict, parallel to the hypothetical scenario in Breakwell's study, found that this expectation was correct. Rhetoric was controlled by a focus on group weaknesses. Also, she discovered that groups weakened by an onslaught against their cohesiveness could not generate self-defensive propaganda. It seems that people are good at predicting the techniques of manipulation used in intergroup conflict.

From the point of view of the threatened individual, the prognostication is not good. The power of a minority to effect social change is dependent upon its power to use propaganda or rhetoric to influence the attitudes, beliefs and actions of other groups and individuals. A minority which is fragmented or weakened by internal conflict is open to an attack designed to further denude the identity and value of the minority and its affiliates. A minority so attacked seems unlikely to be able to generate rhetorics of self-defence, let alone be able to introduce social changes beneficial to the threatened individual. Yet minorities composed of threatened individuals are most likely to find themselves subject to such attacks because they contain individuals who are already stigmatized and socially demeaned. The only hope in that case is to maintain cohesiveness, despite the social and moral scorn poured on the group. As long as cohesiveness is maintained, the worst effects of the onslaught on the individual identities of members can be turned aside. There is also the continued hope that the minority's ideology will then foster an effective rhetoric which is both defensive and offensive.

It can be appreciated, even from this brief review of the effects of multiple group memberships, support groups and group action, that coping strategies involving intergroup dynamics are not within the control of the individual. The individual has a simple basic choice: to be involved with the group or not and sometimes even this freedom is withdrawn. Once the decision is made or imposed, the rest is determined by group processes.

7 Limits to coping

Failure of coping strategies

Failure of the coping strategies means revision of the identity structure which is beyond the control of the individual. The coping strategy may, itself, have entailed much change but if it fails to banish the threat, the individual may no longer be able to direct or limit the change. At one level, control is always maintained because the individual can simply shut down the identity system, becoming totally unresponsive to all outside stimuli, as in the case of some psychiatric complaints. This is, of course, not so much control as withdrawal. In reality, as long as contact is maintained with the outside world, the change imposed by the threatening position may be inescapable. Even if it is, it would be inappropriate to consider, as Goffman (1976) suggests, that identity is 'spoiled' or 'failed'. The identity structure is changed in a way which abrogates the identity principles but this is part of its longer-term evolution. It continues to change and the identity principles will be reinstituted to direct future developments. Even when the threat continues across time, the identity will continue to be revised.

The discussion in the previous three chapters sets out the range of logically possible coping strategies available to the individual experiencing threat. It provides discrete examples of how each might be used but it does not explore what determines the choice of coping strategy; nor how strategies may be used in combinations by the same individual facing the same threat across time; nor, indeed, why a person moves from one to the next. In addition, it deals only cursorily with the potential inadequacies of coping strategies. The object of this chapter, in rectifying these omissions, is to assess the actual strategies adopted and their weaknesses. What proves most interesting is that people do not use the full range of strategies available and the ones they do choose are often manifestly doomed to failure.

Determinants of coping strategy choice

Figure 7 schematically represents a series of factors which interact to determine the choice of coping strategy:
   (i) type of threat
   (ii) social context
   (iii) identity structure
   (iv) cognitive resources.

Type of threat
In Chapter 3 it was argued that the response to a threat to identity would depend upon the personal and social meaning of that threat determined by dominant ideologies and internalized value and belief systems. However, having said that, it is also possible to categorize different types of threat which are likely to evoke the use of quite disparate coping strategies. Threats vary along at least three dimensions.

(a) *Internal v. external origin.* Some arise predominantly from a conflict between the three principles organizing identity processes; others arise from demands initiated by the social positions occupied which contravene the operation of one or more of the three identity principles.

(b) *Long-term v. short-term.* Some threats, even without remedial action by the individual, have a brief existence; for instance, where a threatening social position is occupied only for a short time because of a naturally high level in turnover of occupants. Other threats are clearly long-term, even where the individual may be actively involved in employing coping strategies against them; for instance, where the threatening social position occupied cannot be escaped, at least, objectively.

This distinction between long- and short-term threats is weakened somewhat by the fact that it is founded upon social rather than subjective time-scales. For the individual concerned even the briefest threat may appear long-lived. Also, frequently, at the onset of a threat it is difficult to gauge whether it will continue or will quickly

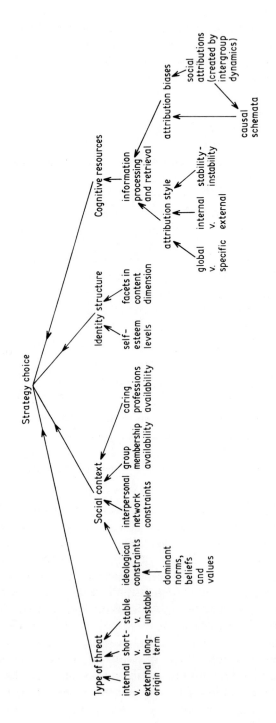

Figure 7 *Factors influencing choice of coping strategy*

evaporate. Furthermore, there is one other complication in this apparently simple distinction. The threat which objectively subsides rapidly, with removal from the threatening position, may continue to be relived and, even, exaggerated subjectively. For instance, the man who is made redundant and finds new work quickly may, nevertheless, have been so threatened by the experience of unemployment that the recollection of the event is sufficient to threaten subsequently. The father of one of the young unemployed studied by Breakwell (in press) was present during the interview and expressed this reaction in archetypical form. He said: 'I was made redundant two years ago, from a firm I'd been with for over fifteen years, no warning, just given my cards at 4 p.m. on Friday. Shocked I was. Terrible thing to do to a bloke. You know I still wake up in the middle of the night, sweating, and I can't think what I was dreaming but I know it has something to do with that afternoon. Doesn't make any sense. I got another job ever so quick. Reckon I still feel insecure. Disposable, that's me.'

Even the brief threat can so change identity content and value, especially the latter, that later experiences have quite different meanings for the identity: they are interpreted within a revised framework of semantics, value and affect.

(c) *Stable v. unstable.* The threat constituted by occupation of a particular social position can be stable or unstable in its content in the sense that the social representation and expectations of the occupant can be internally consistent and constant over time or not. Clearly, stability and instability are merely the poles of a continuum. Most threats fall in the middle; having some stable and some unstable components.

Each of these three dimensions along which a threat may be indexed have, in some sense, an *objective* existence. They can be measured independently of the threatened individual. However, it is also important to accept that they have a *subjective* existence too. The individual will actively interpret the extent of the externality, the longevity and the stability of the threat. This interpretation is unlikely to be a perfectly accurate reflection of the objective indices. Indeed, it may be grossly inaccurate once coping strategies involving redefinition and re-evaluation are introduced. No matter how inaccurate, *it will be this subjective interpretation which is one of the factors controlling the choice of coping strategy.*

Since the three dimensions vary independently of each other, there are eight potential permutations, each representing a differently structured threat. It is not possible to predict precisely the relationship between each permutation and the coping strategy chosen: there is too little empirical work on the issue and, in any case, the type of threat interacts with other factors in dictating strategy adopted. However, some general hypotheses might be suggested. For instance, threats which are internal in origin are more likely to be resolvable and to be tackled through re-conceptualization or re-evaluation of incoming information. Short-term threats, in the main, should result in fewer attempts at coping and the revision of the identity structure necessitated would be minimized. Unstable threats, since they allow for greater selectivity in the interpretation and acknowledgement of fluctuating information relevant to identity, would permit of maximal use of re-definition and re-evaluation tactics. Thus the prediction to be tested empirically would be that an internal, short-term, and unstable threat would result in an emphasis upon cognitive and affective strategies, whereas an external, long-term, and stable threat would push the individual towards social change strategies involving the creation or membership of a group whose object is to bring about change. Between these two extreme structural constellations, mixed strategies might be expected.

There is, of course, an alternative, or even parallel, system for categorizing type of threat in terms of the identity principle abrogated. So threats might be classified in relation to whether they breach continuity, distinctiveness or self-esteem. Certainly, it would be predictable that each might evoke somewhat different coping strategies. However, this sort of typology of threat has at least two weaknesses. Firstly, a threat may attack more than one principle at the same time. Secondly, such a taxonomy might predict the purpose for which a strategy is used rather than the sort of strategy itself, since the same strategy may be employed to reinstitute continuity or distinctiveness or self-esteem. Consequently, this form of categorization of threat is not used here.

Social context
The social context limits the choice of coping strategies in a number of ways.

(a) *Ideologically*. The ideological milieu characteristic of the social context establishes moral and value codes and systems of beliefs which control what types of action, and even affect, are possible for the individual.

(b) *Interpersonal network*. The size and structure of the interpersonal network open to the individual will limit the usage of various coping strategies. Reduced to its simplest, self-disclosure to a reassuring friend is impossible where the individual has no friend; for that individual, self-disclosure becomes an impossible strategy unless the social context can be so altered as to produce a social-support network.

(c) *Group memberships available.* Strategies which entail militancy for social change require the existence within the social matrix of pressure groups or social movements, or, at least, the potential for their creation. The individual opting for strategies involving group action or group membership is dependent upon them being available.

(d) *Availability of caring professionals.* Where members of the caring professions (psychologists, social workers, psychiatrists, counsellors, etc.) are available the range of coping strategies open may be extended since the professional may be able to facilitate the use of otherwise inaccessible strategies.

   Each of these four aspects of the social context controls the degree of freedom available to the individual in choosing a coping strategy.

Identity structure

Where the limitations imposed on coping by the social context revolve around the availability of social resources, *the restrictions generated by the identity structure concern psychic resources.* For instance, it might be predicted that individuals with a very high level of self-esteem prior to the threat, which may even be levelled at self-esteem, would be more resilient to change, more capable of evolving coping strategies whether at the cognitive reconstrual level or at the level of social action. In fact, there is a considerable body of experimental research which supports such an assertion (Wells and Marwell, 1976; Gergen, 1971). It is not unreasonable to assume then that *the actual content and value of the identity structure prior to threat will predispose the choice of coping strategy.* The problem lies in the fact that the prediction of the actual relationship between the two is hardly a precise science. There are scraps of evidence (e.g. Weinreich, 1983; Kitwood, 1980) which are sufficient to support the overall assertion but not enough to articulate the dynamics of the relationship, though Weinreich (1980) has been developing techniques for accessing information about these using personal construct theory.

   Gaining such evidence is fraught with methodological problems. Firstly, there is the problem of achieving non-reactive measures of the identity structure. This may be possible to a limited extent within an experimental paradigm but this would largely entail the exploration of the effects of experimentally induced threat which has to be trivial if it is to fall within the tolerance limits of experimental ethics. Secondly, in the non-experimental method, there is the problem of establishing, in advance, that a threat is likely, so that the identity structure can be monitored prior to the experience of threat. The second problem, at least, may be overcome by a selective case history approach. Individuals at high risk of threat would be examined longitudinally pre- and post-threat. For instance, it might be predicted that migration, even if transient, would be threatening. It would be possible to follow a number of businessmen chosen by their firms to represent them abroad both before and after emigration. There is an example of this approach in the literature on redundancy. Wedderburn (1964) was able to follow a group of workers from the period *before* redundancy into the time after their factory closed. Unfortunately, for present purposes, she was not examining identity dynamics but rather the sociological implications of redundancy. Also, her study would have some intrinsic problems for anyone examining the impact of threat since the workers were aware by the start of research that they were to be made redundant. Changes in coping strategies could have already begun by the time the study was rolling.

It is important, if coping strategy choice is the target for study, to ensure that the observations of the individual predate the institution of the threat. The *longitudinal* study of the individual, and his or her social context, is essential if the relationship between identity structures and coping strategies is to be explicated. It is certainly not good enough to examine the identity structure retrospectively after the experience of threat. Coping strategies evoked may already have revised the content or value dimensions by that stage.

Assuming that reasonably non-reactive measures of identity structure can be developed, the longitudinal approach will be the most productive. Yet, even this has weaknesses. Those longitudinal studies which have been done tend to relate to single types of threat. For instance, responses to unemployment, or surgery for serious illness, or ethnic minority status, and so on. Researchers of these disparate sources of threat have not drawn together the insights they have achieved about the relation of identity structure to coping strategy. It is hoped that the present model provides the sort of integrative framework within which these pieces of information can be lodged in order to produce a more comprehensive understanding.

Cognitive resources
It is possible to differentiate between the cognitive resources, the information processing and retrieval system, available to the individual

and the structure of that individual's identity. In essence, the identity structure is the product of these cognitive systems in interaction with the social context. Without the information-processing capacities of the system, identity could not be constructed. However, human information-processing systems are subject to a vast range of constraints and consequent biases (Neisser, 1976; Kahneman *et al.* 1982; Nisbett and Ross, 1980). These biases intervene to limit the choice of coping strategies where threat is experienced.

One set of biases which has been exhaustively studied concerns attributional style. Attribution is the process whereby the individual elaborates explanations for events; it entails assigning causes to occurrences. Abramson, Seligman and Teasdale (1978) have been concerned with how people make attributions about bad events, particularly where they attempt to do something but fail. Their interest stems from their desire to pinpoint under what circumstances a person comes to feel helpless and depressed. Seligman (1975) argues that there is a marked parallel between the experience of helplessness and the phenomenology of depression. He comments that the symptoms of both are 'passivity, cognitive deficits, lowered self-esteem, sadness, anxiety, hostility but simultaneous loss of overt aggression, and norepinephrine depletion'. It appears that people can learn to be helpless if they recognize that their actions fail to control outcomes. The depressed have a generalized belief that responding will be ineffective. Learned helplessness and depression both seem to be associated with a particular constellation of attributions which some people generate when they face bad life events and failure. Rosenhan and Seligman (1984) summarize the structure of these attributions claiming that they have three dimensions.

(a) *The internal-external dimension.* The reason for the bad event or failure can be located internally or externally. Internal attributions would lay the responsibility for the failure with the person experiencing it. It could be an explanation in terms of personality or intellectual characteristics, or in terms of inappropriate or accidental activity. External attributions explain the failure in relation to the environmental, both social and physical, constraints or circumstances. Abramson (1978) showed that when a person fails at an important task and makes internal attributions for that failure, passivity ensues and is followed by a marked decline in self-esteem; whereas, when an external attribution is made self-esteem remains high even where passivity still occurs.

(b) *The stability-instability dimension.* The cause of the bad event or failure can be considered permanent or transient. Where the cause of failure is deemed stable and is thus expected to persist into the future, there is a marked tendency for self-perceived persistent helplessness to arise. Consequently, according to the attributional model of learned helplessness, stable attributions lead to permanent deficits in coping and unstable attributions engender transient deficits.

(c) *The global-specific dimension.* The cause of the bad event or failure can be considered global or specific. A global factor will produce failure in a wide variety of circumstances; a specific factor only in similar circumstances. The attributional model of helplessness holds that when individuals make global attributions for their failure, helplessness deficits will occur in a wide variety of situations.

In relation to these three dimensions there is a particular syndrome commonly associated with learned helplessness and depression. Depressed psychiatric patients tend to believe bad events are caused by internal factors (their own fault), by stable factors (they will last for ever), and by global factors (they will undermine everything they try to do). More importantly, individuals who have this attributional style but are not depressed, become depressed when they later encounter bad events (Peterson and Seligman, 1984).

The relevance of these findings for the prediction of how people cope with threats to identity is clear. There is a direct parallel between the response to a bad event and a threat, which is after all an archetypical example of a bad event. Moreover, should one attempt at coping with the threat fail, or be perceived as a failure, the individual will also be making attributions about that failure. Attributional style is clearly a determinant of coping strategy choice. People with internal, stable and global biases in attribution will be less likely to try a series of strategies) they are more likely to become passive in response to threat. It would be predicted on the basis of the attributional model that the individual making external attributions would tend to engage in interpersonal and group coping strategies which intervene in the steady state of the environment to elicit change. Unstable attributions would lead to greater flexibility in coping strategies, with greater optimism about the spontaneous remission of the threat which might preclude any very speedy response to it. Highly specific attributions would lead to a focusing of coping strategy upon a narrow band of targets for change. Obviously, it would be possible to develop much more elaborate hypotheses about the relation of attributional style to coping strategies. However, they would be, as yet, purely speculative, logical inferences from the work on depression and helplessness.

One thing can be said with some certainty, nevertheless. Individuals with internal, stable and global attributional biases will not cope well with threat. Seligman (following Beck *et al.* 1979) has suggested that, in their cases, the appropriate therapeutic intervention is designed to change attributions by showing how anticipated bad events may be avoided and effective responses developed. The object of therapy is, basically, to replace one system of beliefs about adequacy with another.

There are undoubtedly other cognitive resource biases which will influence choice of coping strategy. For instance, limitations in memory or knowledge and in problem-solving or intellectual capacities may be influential. Such limits are extensively documented but not specifically in relation to coping with identity threats.

Before proceeding, there is one word of warning concerning attributional styles worthy of mention. Although depressives and those who respond to traumatic life events by becoming depressed possess clearly defined attributional styles, not everyone in the population is subject to attributional biases. Some people have no *consistent* attributional style bias. They may be subject to bias occasionally but this is inconsistent and transient. For these, there will be no predictable habitual coping style precipitated by attributional factors. Of course, it is still possible that the particular choice of a coping strategy for a specific threat may be influenced by the specific attribution made to it.

It is worth remembering here that attributions are not determined purely by individual cognitive restrictions. Jaspars and Hewstone (1985, p. 27) comment that: 'Causal explanations in everyday life originate not just as a consequence of individual information processing but through social interaction and hence become shared or collective beliefs of an explanatory kind.' The individual attribution will be influenced by these collective explanatory beliefs or social attributions. Certainly, what Kelley (1967) called their 'causal schemata' (ready-made sets of explanations) will be largely pre-determined by such social attributions. Social attributions relevant to the origin of threat or to the social context of coping will shape personal attributions and, through influencing information processing, evaluation and retrieval, will help to control the choice of coping strategy. Since social attributions are engendered through interpersonal interaction and are heavily dependent upon intergroup dynamics, it seems reasonable to suppose that they will be linked to the actual ideological milieu surrounding the individual. This means that intergroup influences have a series of routes through to affecting the ultimate choice of coping strategy.

To summarize this section on the determinants of coping strategy, it is suggested that the four factors which interact to produce the chosen response to threat are the type of threat, the social context, the prior identity structure, and available cognitive resources. It is possible to suggest how each might independently influence the strategy used; however, it is important to recognize that the effect of each will be modified by the operation of the others. Indeed, there is every reason to suppose that they do not vary independently. Type of threat will almost certainly derive in some way from the social context. Prior identity structure will be a function of the cognitive capacities of the person concerned. Since there is the potential for many levels of inter-action between the four factors, the prospect of early predictability of coping-strategy choice is negligible. The description of these four factors is required for analytic clarity but much more empirical work is needed before any cast-iron assertions can be made about their inter-action to determine actual strategy usage.

Phases in coping

A threat may elicit more than one coping strategy. A whole chain of strategies may be employed one after another in a patterned response to threat. It is then possible to talk in terms of phases in coping. Where a threat is long-lived and initial coping strategies, by definition, fail to eliminate it either subjectively or objectively, it is feasible to examine the successive phases in coping which ensue. In relation to specific threats, these phases in coping can be described. They are interesting and valuable to the therapist, for instance, because, in so far as there are communalities across individuals, knowing the phases in coping allows for greater accuracy in prediction of response to threat. The identification of phases in coping may also point to why some strategies work and others do not; perhaps because the effective ones are used only after the ground has been cleared by apparently ineffective ones. When a chain of strategies is unfurled, they cannot be assessed for efficacy independently.

An example of phases in coping: unemployment

In the research on unemployment, there has been a great deal of attention paid to the way its psychological effects vary according to the duration of joblessness. It is possible, therefore, to examine phases in coping with long-term unemployment as a concrete example of the way strategies are successively used and discarded. Eisenberg and

Lazarsfeld (1938) argued that there is a three-stage response to unemployment.

The first stage has two sub-phases: initially shock, disbelief and numbness but this disorientation very quickly gives way to denial and optimism. The bulk of this first stage, once the shock of losing the job is passed – and job-loss does tend to come as a shock even where redundancies have been predictable – is taken up with active job-search and is pervaded by the sense that being without work is temporary and an opportunity for catching up on household chores or even for having a holiday. With successive failures to find a job, there is a growth of pessimism and doubt.

The individual then passes into the second stage in response, which is characterized by anxiety and distress. People perceive changes in their relationships in the family; becoming more moody and irritable, and looking longingly at the past, they incite serious arguments with those who are close to them.

The passage into the next stage is gradual and initially imperceptible. Active distress gives way to fatalism, inertia and 'acceptance of jobless-ness as a way of life' (Briar, 1977). Some of the depression characteristic of the second stage lifts, the individual and family settle down to a new set of standards and expectations. By the third stage, the forced and meaningless leisure has been institutionalized, job-seeking is haphazard and hopeless, and chunks of the day are spent day-dreaming or fitfully asleep. The days glide indistinguishably together. There is a tendency to withdraw from family life and social activities. Television-watching, nowadays, becomes a central time-occupier; the passage of weeks being marked by the recurrent cycle of soap operas and serials.

Although Eisenberg and Lazarsfeld were writing in the 1930s, their assertions about the sequence of responses to unemployment are deemed by many to have contemporary relevance. Harrison (1976), reviewing studies conducted in the early 1970s, concluded that the stage-structure was operative and suggested that a concomitant of stage two pessimism is a drastic reduction in self-esteem and psychiatric stability. Bakke (1933, 1960) had already suggested that this psycho-logical decline is not markedly redressed with the onset of fatalism and with the resignation and adjustment of expectations which accompany it. Hill (1978) argued that the cycle has a recognizable time-scale, though it is subject to individual variations. Stage one takes about two months; stage two, typified by the progressive social and occupational de-skilling of the individual may take up to nine months; it is only then that habituation and apathy descend.

This represents what has come to be the 'conventional wisdom' about the phases of response to unemployment. It is appealing since it fits what is known about the pattern of reactions to other situations of loss or threat which are long-lived. For instance, Parkes (1972), in describing what he calls 'psycho-social transitions', which are basically events that radically alter a person's life-style, changing expectations and planned activities, suggests that most are followed by a similar sequence of adjustments. For example, bereavement, imprisonment, demotion, divorce, and retirement, even simply falling out of love (Stroebe and Stroebe, 1984), all are supposed to share with unemployment the same pattern of reaction: shock and denial, but optimism; followed by anxiety and a longing for the past; and, finally, resignation and adjustment.

The evidence for the conventional wisdom about unemployment is somewhat suspect, however, as it is open to methodological criticism. Most of the studies from which it was derived were cross-sectional rather than longitudinal. Drawing causal inferences from such data is notoriously fraught with problems: if differences are apparent between the short-term and long-term unemployed in pattern of adjustment, it is impossible, on the basis of cross-sectional data, to determine whether the longer period without work generated the psychological decline or whether the length of time without work was determined by a pre-existent psychological deficit or, indeed, whether both are predisposed by some third factor.

Sampling, in these studies, was also problematic: most of the research was concerned solely with middle-aged men who were made redundant. There is a dearth of information, even now, upon young people, women and those who become unemployed voluntarily or without ever having had a job. These studies are also weak with respect to the measures of changes in psychological functioning which they used which were often either purely subjective or unvalidated.

Perhaps more important than the methodological criticisms, is the fact that successive recent studies offer no support for the conventional wisdom. Kasl (1979) reports a longitudinal study of fifteen middle-aged men who had been continuously unemployed for up to six months, and claims that there was no significant deterioration during that time on indices of mental health and physiological processes. From a cross-sectional study of 171 men, Goodchilds and Smith (1963) concluded that there was no effect of length of unemployment (over five months) upon self-esteem and self-confidence. Using a single item measure of depressive affect, Feather and Davenport (1981) report no significant relationship between negative emotion and length of unemployment.

Warr *et al.* (1982), in a study of 420 school-leavers interviewed over two years, argued that neither self-esteem nor psychological distress are correlated in young men with length of unemployment. For the women in their sample, no relationships were discovered between self-esteem and duration of unemployment, but in one cohort longer unemployment was associated with reduced psychological distress. This was shown to be due to the fact that these young women had actually withdrawn from the labour market to have children and presumably no longer considered themselves unemployed. Only Hepworth (1980), whose sample of seventy-eight men included eighteen who had been unemployed for over twelve months, reports small but significant correlations of duration of unemployment with minor psychiatric morbidity risks and with general dissatisfaction with life.

Clearly, there is considerable evidence which is dissonant with the conventional wisdom, the import of which suggests that unemployment triggers a *saltatory* decline in self-esteem and psychological well-being rather than a gradual or sequential pattern of surrender to fate. In addition, there is some evidence to support the notion that any accentuation of the psychological difficulties is tied quite closely to specific incidents during the period of unemployment. For instance, Breakwell *et al.* (1984b) in a cross-sectional study of seventy-two 16-19-year-olds, found duration of unemployment, over a period of up to twenty-five weeks, unrelated to self-esteem, psychological health or life satisfaction, but found that those young people facing anxiety over the possibility of gaining a place on sought-after government training schemes showed much greater psychological deficits and uncertain self-esteem.

These sorts of findings militate against the assumption that there is a consistent pattern of temporally structured response to unemployment. It does not seem to be merely a matter of length of unemployment which determines the psychological response. It is much more a matter of what happens during that period. This is evidenced by the very varied responses to unemployment from people who reside in different life contexts. Responses differ according to age (Warr and Lovatt, 1977; Little, 1976) and occupational group, which is a reflection of socio-economic class (Hartley, 1978; Thomas and Madigan, 1974).

Hesitancy about rejecting the conventional wisdom on the basis of these studies may, however, be justified. These studies largely depend upon psychometric indices of functioning, they do not entail a comprehensive investigation of the individual's activities and thought. They give snapshots, of great definition and clarity but of very limited areas of the individual's total pattern of response. The few recent studies involving in-depth extensive interviews or ethnographic observation tend to be more supportive of the conventional wisdom. For instance, Fagin and Little (1984) studied twenty-two families, interviewing twice over a period of six months, and reported a pattern of adaptation not dissimilar to the conventional wisdom in a large proportion of their sample, at least, in relation to stages one and two. However, they proposed a much more differentiated model to predict the occurrence of physical and psychological illness resulting from unemployment. They suggest that jobs loss becomes a stress precipitating psychological or physical symptoms when it is associated with marital conflict or familial tension, poverty, increased alcohol and cigarette consumption, and a history of previous ill health. The slide into illness is accelerated, they argue, where social attitudes towards the unemployed are negative. Under those circumstances adoption of the 'sick role' is seen to be an escape route from the social stigma of unemployment. Since so many of their sample succumbed to the 'sick role', it was difficult to say whether the third stage actually occurred or not. Illness, and acting out the sickness role, confounded the information on habituation to unemployment. Sickness so changed the familial lifestyle that other modifications in expectations and standards contingent upon unemployment *per se* indistinguishable.

The conventional wisdom suggests that there are discrete phases of coping with unemployment with a different strategy implemented in each. The first revolves around *denial*, the refusal to acknowledge the reality of the change in status. Studies reliant upon psychometric tools (e.g. Likert-scaled self-report indexes of well-being, and attitudes) tend not to report this phase. This is likely to be a direct consequence of the fact that the instruments are not designed to tap denial. Moreover, this phase is fleeting, perhaps lasting only twenty-four hours, offering a transient time-out before facing the truth. Most studies would not detect denial because they interview the unemployed person after it has been superseded. It is rare for a researcher to be able to interview someone on the day that they become unemployed. In any case, it is doubtful whether the denial would be maintained in the face of investigation. However; respondents, in retrospect, are able to describe the experience of denial.

The second phase in coping involves active attempts to remove oneself from the threatening position: a *concerted effort to regain employment* is the common characteristic of the second half of stage one. It is only where this strategy fails that the individual comes to feel helpless and becomes *anxious and depressed*. Passivity ensues and engenders *social isolation.* This gives way to *actual changes in identity structure* in the third phase of coping, when many adopt a new element into the identity by enacting *the sickness role.* This new component to the identity structure defends against the attack on self-esteem and distinctiveness arising from unemployment.

It is interesting to note that each phase of coping is dependent for its development upon its predecessors. People do not jump straight into passivity when they become redundant, even if they have had prior experience of unemployment and know what to expect. People work towards being passive. In a rather paradoxical sense, this implies that even passivity is a purposive strategy adopted in order to cope; even withdrawal and isolation are an intentional phase in coping. Whether any of these strategies actually succeed in defending the identity structure against the threat is questionable. Certainly, the initial structure does not remain intact if all of the strategies are used because the ultimate one described relies upon a modification in self-definition, either through the sickness role or through revised expectations.

While the coping strategies used, and the order of their usage, is illuminating, it is equally interesting to examine what type of strategy is not used. The unemployed are notable for their absence from the traditional political arena. Their strategies are lodged at the intra-psychic and interpersonal levels. They do not seek to change their position or the opprobrium attached to it through corporate action via joining or creating groups. Marsh, Fraser and Jobling (1985), reviewing the relatively small number of studies in the United States and Europe which have explored the political responses of the unemployed, summarized the findings which apply regardless of geographical area: the unemployed express more critical and/or radical political attitudes than the employed but are less likely to register as voters or to vote at elections; if they vote, they do so for parties which are pledged to raise public expenditure but they are less likely to be active participants in unions or other politically relevant organizations; and, they are less likely to engage in other protest movements.

These generalizations were based largely on studies in the USA and none dealt with the political reactions of young people who are unemployed. However, Breakwell (in press) reports from a study of young unemployed in Britain a somewhat similar picture. These young people acknowledged their willingness to act to bring about a change in their position through violence (for example, through riots) but simultaneously would have nothing to do with conventional political parties or organized social movements. It implies that, at least in the case of the young unemployed, traditional forms of political activity may not be preferred but this does not mean that they are passive or even politically naïve. Of course, violent talk cannot be equated with violent action. Some of the young people claimed to be willing to support attempts to bring about change through violence but whether they would actually do so is quite another matter. Nevertheless, while involvement in standard political channels does not seem to attract the unemployed, less traditional forms of protest might be expected from them.

This might constitute a spasmodic corporate coping strategy but its probability of bringing about any substantive change in the social position of the unemployed is minimal. Unlike manipulations through traditional political channels, such spontaneous and uncoordinated protests are too easily labelled illegitimate and ignored. When used by the unemployed, they are particularly susceptible to derogatory rhetoric because the unemployed have no existence as an organized group with an elaborated ideology which offers recipes for self-defence. So, when a riot occurs and a mob makes statements about grievances about housing or employment prospects, there is no central corps of people representing their grievance.

Because they are unorganized, the unemployed are treated as individuals; they are segregated and individuated and deprived of the power which comes with unity. Grievances are deemed idiosyncratic; explanations for unemployment are pinned at the level of individual inadequacies and weaknesses. Lacking cohesiveness, failing to create a corporate entity, the unemployed cannot achieve an effective voice through spontaneous, highly transient protests. Of course, it is easy to see that the type of coping strategy which results in passivity at the individual level will be echoed in quiescence at the political level; this is simply bolstered by the rhetoric and polemic used against those who become involved in protests.

In Chapter 3, it was stated that the unemployed tend to blame themselves for their own unemployment. In fact, they make internal attributions for it: they feel that they fail to find work because they are unqualified, unskilled, inexperienced or lacking in sufficient determination. The origin of this attributional bias may lie in the general social representation of the unemployed, which traditionally castigates and blames them, and which the unemployed simply learn. Irrespective of its origin, their explanation of their unemployment in terms of personal inadequacies may partially account for their political inactivity. Believing themselves to be the source of their own misfortune, political remedies are seen as irrelevancies. Of course, it is forgivable to believe that there are no viable political answers to structural unemployment in any case. Anyone who listens to government statements would recognize that many of the messages are in the form: 'unemployment is terrible but . . . there is nothing that we can do about it . . . it is an inevitable product of the worldwide economic climate'. Thus, even those unemployed who do not wallow in self-blame but attribute their position to external economic processes may conclude politics is sterile: the politicians in power so regularly voice their powerlessness against inexorable economic processes; only politicians out of power claim to have the ultimate solution and their credibility is tarnished by their need to get into power. Whether internal or external attributions are made for unemployment, political answers may appear untenable.

The internal attributional bias is tied to another coping deficit. Breakwell (1985b) examined how young people who are unemployed claim that they responded when insulted or attacked for failing to get a job. Most of the seventy-two in the sample had experienced some incident where they had been condemned as scroungers or lazy or parasites. The majority blamed their own inadequacy for their unemployment and when reviled for being without work did not regard the abuse as unjust. They accepted that people had a right to criticize them. They only evolved two lines of mitigating self-defence (as was mentioned earlier): firstly, pleading powerlessness or helplessness to get work despite strenuous efforts to do so; secondly, begging for the attacker to try to imagine what it would feel like to change places. The first line is redolent with fatalism; the second simply seeks empathy to forfend further assaults. These young people accept that they are in one sense responsible for their unemployment, because they lack the salient personal qualities which would, they assume, make them marketable, but know that nothing they can do will remove their inadequacies, so in another sense they are not responsible.

Fatalism, and its siblings hopelessness and passivity, can be seen as a reconceptualization which takes the sting out of self-blame. At one level, fatalism is a coping strategy, taking the pressure off self-esteem. However, it opens the way for other threats, especially those arising from direct interpersonal attacks. The unemployed studied had no real barrier of self-defensive rhetoric, no way of excusing or rationalizing themselves.

It is evident that the coping strategies used by the unemployed focus upon survival inside the status quo rather than militancy to change their position as a social category. Even as individuals they are rarely willing to engage in offensive rhetoric in the interests of self-defence. It is ironic that the strategies favoured are not particularly effective in protecting mental or physical health, let alone self-esteem.

Why persist with suboptimal coping strategies?

The majority of the unemployed adopt, and persist with, strategies which do not optimize their chances of effective coping. They are by no means exceptional in this. People facing threats often fail to employ the optimal strategy or persist with a strategy to the point where it becomes suboptimal. There are four elements in the explanation for this.

(i) *It is no simple matter to anticipate what will be the optimal strategy.* Predicting its power to protect identity against the threat or its capacity to eradicate the source of the threat may be impossible since they will be contingent upon factors in the social context beyond the control, and probably knowledge, of the individual. Arriving at the optimal strategy may rely upon trial and error. However, that sort of successive sampling of strategies is most often impossible because the individual does not have total freedom of choice; the choice is shaped, which leads to the second explanatory element.

(ii) *The choice of coping strategy is dictated by an interaction of the type of threat, the social context, the prior identity structure and the available cognitive resources*: rationality and logic have little part to play and there is nothing in these interactants to suggest that choice would be inevitably designed to maximize efficacy in any absolute sense. The individual is hemmed about with constraints on choice: the best *available* strategy may be taken but it need not be the best *conceivable*. The individual may be able to envisage the optimal strategy but also recognize that it would be impractical to execute given the circumstantial constraints. Alternatively, it is possible that the individual may never perceive the potentially optimal strategy. For instance, cognitive resource bias would make some strategies inconceivable.

(iii) *The constraints which precipitate the usage of suboptimal strategies may perpetuate them.* Unless the pattern of interaction between the four determinants of choice changes, it is difficult to modify the strategy used. For example, the attributional bias, which initiates the chain of self-blame, helplessness and depressive-anxiety, also maintains it against encroachment because the cognitive style itself persists.

(iv) *Usage of a strategy may trap the user into its continued use.* The strategy may have effects which bolster it, creating changes in circumstances conducive to its own survival. Take, for example, the common strategy of self-isolation in unemployment. This results in the dissolution of previous interpersonal networks which are then no longer available should the individual wish to switch to strategies which require social support. Passivity and helplessness self-characterizations have the same self-sustaining capacity, perpetuating themselves by making anything else seem impossible: the helpless define themselves as powerless to become helpful to themselves.

Given pressure from these four sources, it is hardly surprising that suboptimal strategies are used and are used persistently.

Consistency and coping

If one were to accept traditional formulations within social psychology, one might predict that consistency drives would both initiate coping strategies and dictate their form. At least since the specification of the cognitive consistency theories of attitude change, it has been forcibly argued that people find inconsistency aversive. They dislike holding mutually exclusive attitudes or attitudes which contradict behaviour or, indeed, engaging in separate sets of activities that are inconsistent with each other. The consistency theories (balance, Heider, 1946; congruity, Osgood and Tannenbaum, 1955; and dissonance, Festinger, 1957) all, in their various forms, predicted and provided evidence that people would do everything in their power to eradicate the aversive inconsistencies. If extended to the present model of identity, this would mean that any new input to the content or value dimensions which was incompatible with the prior structure would result in some manipulation to annihilate the inconsistency, by changing the old, the new or both. This bears some resemblance to the argument that continuity is a prime directive for the identity processes. Yet *consistency and continuity are not synonymous:* consistency requires that elements be non-contradictory, continuity merely requires their persistence over time. In fact, there could quite easily be continuity in inconsistency: elements which are incompatible co-existing across time. So, although it is possible that the desire for consistency might motivate coping, it is quite distinct from the demands made by continuity requirements. Besides initiating coping, consistency might be expected to circumscribe the range of coping options used in conjunction, or sequentially, since they would have to be perceived as compatible with each other.

However, this may be a naïve and rather premature conclusion. There is now considerable evidence that people do find it tenable to hold inconsistent attitudes and behave inconsistently without being motivated to change (Billig, 1982 and 1984; Cochrane, 1985). Either people do not make the same rational comparisons between components of what they do and think as psychologists do or they have good techniques for absolving themselves for the inconsistencies which they do monitor. Billig (1985) points out that theories emphasizing the need for consistency fail to recognize the importance of argumentation, contradiction and flexibility in the cognitive structure. He suggests that consistency is socially emphasized because it increases people's accountability for their actions and rhetoric uses calls to consistency to enforce social norms. Consistency is seen by society as a good thing, making people more predictable and consequently more controllable. This does not, however, mean that they are actually consistent. Consistency may be the social ideal, but it is not the psychological reality: people are not tidy mental book-keepers. In addition, Jaspars and Hewstone (1985) argue that inconsistency may be buttressed by sharing. Indeed, some inconsistencies become institutionalized: produced and reproduced by dominant social institutions. For instance, it may be the norm to be both racist and egalitarian at one time. This type of fundamental inconsistency may be underwritten by powerful social institutions like the Church which may preach equality but practise pragmatic inactivity. In some cases, then, individual inconsistencies will be a consequence of the individual's compliance with societal strictures.

Since the evidence for consistency as a motivating force is equivocal, it is not feasible to make predictions about its impact upon coping or about its power to threaten. It certainly seems unlikely that people will feel bound to use only coping strategies which are logically consistent with each other. It also seems unlikely that the perception of an inconsistency, either in the identity structure or in the relation of identity to action, will drive people immediately to ameliorative strategies.

Of course, it is possible that inconsistencies may come into existence as by-products of coping techniques. Strategies whcih compartmentalize experiences, keeping their implications for identity segregated, may reify inconsistencies because there is no facility for comparing them and notifying the existence of contradictions. The compartmentalization strategy is tailored to prevent the acknowledgement of incongruity or imbalance; inconsistencies are therefore established and allowed to flourish by the very technique designed to cope with them. The essential point is that the compartmentalization strategy defends the identity structure from any change which might be required by the existence of inconsistency. It does not eradicate the inconsistency – it simply allows it to be discounted.

Coping and the processes of social comparison

Festinger first published the fully formulated version of social-comparison theory in 1954. The fundamental basis for the series of hypotheses which comprise it was the assertion that *there exists in human beings a drive to evaluate their opinions and abilities which operates because it has survival value.* Accuracy in self-evaluation minimizes the risk of inappropriate action. Ideally, the appraisal is made relative to objective, non-social criteria but when this is not possible people will evaluate themselves through comparison with the opinions and abilities of others. Where neither objective nor social comparison is feasible, Festinger predicted that self-knowledge becomes unstable and behaviour erratic.

Festinger sought not only to establish the importance of social comparison but also to predict who would be chosen as the comparitor. He argued that someone else close to the individual's own opinion or ability would be chosen, comparisons with dissimilar others are not considered to tell one very much about oneself because gross differences would then overwhelm precise distinctions. A corollary of this is that people seek out situations where they can find similar others so as to provide a ready pool of comparitors. Where completely similar people are unavailable, comparisons are made with those who are moderately similar and the individual tends to change so as to minimize the differences or attempts to induce the comparitors to change. Either way, the object is greater uniformity and, through it, stable and precise self-appraisal.

The drive towards self-evaluation is stronger, according to Festinger, when the ability or opinion to be assessed is important, relevant to immediate behaviour or to one's attractiveness to others, or important to the comparison group. Under such circumstances, uniformity is most likely to result.

Festinger hypothesized that opinions and abilities needed to be treated separately because in the case of abilities there is a uni-directional drive towards perceived improvement not operative in relation to opinions. In terms of their abilities, people wish to be ever better than the next person, though this may be modified by the conformity pressures. This will result in efforts to be just slightly but consistently better in terms of abilities than any comparitor. In contrast, opinions can become highly uniform since there is no drive to outdo the comparitor. This will result in conformity with the attitudes and beliefs of individuals chosen as comparitors.

It is implicit in this hypothesis that comparison serves not only to inform about opinions and abilities, it also engenders an estimate of the relative social value of the individual. Latane (1966), in describing this, which has come to be known as the *ego- or self-enhancement function of social comparison,* noted that it may mean that we seek out comparisons with those who are slightly inferior on the relevant dimension and thereby gain enhancement. Clearly, tailoring the choice of comparitor to serve self-enhancement may be costly because it may result in the loss of more relevant information which could be gained from comparisons with true peers.

Festinger extended the notion of social comparison to predict some-thing of inter-group dynamics. Segmentation into groups, he argued, allows people to ignore the differences between themselves and members of other groups for the purposes of self-evaluation. They compare themselves primarily with members of their own group, where similarities are greatest. Nevertheless, perfect incomparability across groups is rare, so some intergroup comparisons are inevitable. These are clearly most hazardous for members of groups with low status or little power because on intergroup comparisons they can expect little self-enhancement. Festinger suggested that members of powerless groups would consequently have less secure self-evaluations and would resort to extensive intragroup comparisons to retrieve stability, resulting in strong pressures for uniformity and little tolerance of differences in ability or opinions within the group.

Festinger did not predict how people would use social comparison where their abilities or opinions were under direct attack, as they often are when the identity is threatened. It would, however, be consistent with his model to suspect that they would seek to barricade both through seeking potentially enhancing comparisons. For instance, it is entirely predictable that the individual suffering an onslaught on self-esteem might try to retrieve it through an appropriate set of comparisons that would produce kudos. Selective social comparisons might operate as an effective coping strategy. However, there is some evidence (Brickman and Bulman, 1977) that social comparison will cease if a person's self-esteem is so lowered that all available compari-sons would result in a reaffirmation of inferiority.

In order to examine the role of social comparison for a group with low self-esteem, Breakwell (1986) studied thirty-two young women who were involved in a government scheme to train otherwise unemployed young people to become unskilled engineering operators. They were 16-17 years old, mostly unqualified and inexperienced, and had spent considerable time out of work before joining the scheme. They were all from working-class homes, and one-third were members of ethnic minorities. Residing in a run-down inner city area, with little prospect of employment after the scheme finished, these girls can be considered to be multiply disadvantaged. Since all regarded work as of central importance in their lives and considered themselves to be hard-working, it could be argued that their position in the labour market was likely to be experienced as threatening. Certainly, the core constituent of their identity represented by their working life hardly made for self-esteem, continuity or positive distinctiveness. The question posed in the research was simple: what happens to social comparison processes and to self-description under these circumstances?

Festinger's model would predict that they would withdraw from comparisons with others outside the training scheme, concentrate upon comparison within it and seek to achieve uniformity across participants in the scheme of both perceived abilities and opinions. Predictions based on the self-enhancement extension of the theory would be slightly different; suggesting that they would choose outsiders who were in a worse condition than themselves for comparisons (for instance, young women who were still unemployed and not benefiting from training) or that they would seek to differentiate themselves from other trainees on minor dimensions of comparison where some added positivity could be scavenged.

The first target was to get some idea of the core dimensions of the trainees' self-concepts. The 'I am . . .' sentence completion method was used. The girls simply had to complete the sentence in whatever way they chose. Normally, people find self-description easy, even fascinating; this was not true for these young women. Over a third could offer no self-description whatsover. The others offered a single physical characteristic (for instance, I am tall) or said that they were 'girls'. This chasm in self-description was not some product of deliberate sabotage of the research by the respondents. At least, that is unlikely, since their interviewer spent eight weeks in participant observation of their workshop and became a confidante of many of the young women. They simply had enormous difficulty talking objectively about themselves.

It was thought that asking them to describe themselves on a series of pre-determined bipolar semantic differential scales might prove more fruitful in revealing something of their self-concept. Despite individual administration of the scales, with infinite care to explain everything, they had the utmost difficulty in using them. One girl pinpointed the trouble: 'It's not natural, is it? I don't go around thinking of meself as a little bit more of this than that. I got no great brain. There's just not that much to me. You do it ... you ... rank ... me on them descriptions.' Interpretation of the ratings are consequently problematic; however, one thing is evident and this is that the girls held remarkably similar self-images. They had a consensual picture of themselves: quite satisfied with themselves, socially accepted, friendly, reasonably competent and able to stand up for themselves, secure, hard-working and interesting. They also concurred that they were inferior and powerless.

The homogeneity of self-image is intriguing in relation to the question of how social comparison is used. It implies that uniformity had been evolved through intragroup comparisons. Yet if social comparison were operative, one would expect people to be able to identify ways in which they are similar or dissimilar to others. After all, this is the foundation for choice of comparitors. Therefore the trainees were asked to say in what ways they were similar to the other girls on the scheme. One-third said that they were the same, that is identical in all respects, but could not name even one of these dimensions of similarity. Another third said they were not similar in any way but they too failed to describe any dimension of comparison. The others claimed not to know whether they were similar or not. The obverse question was also put to them: how were they different from other girls on the scheme. Two-thirds said they were not different in any way. As one girl said: 'We're all the same, ask any of them. Nothing different about any one of us.'

It seems that the data, while offering limited support for Festinger's contentions about uniformity, do not support the self-enhancement predictions of the reformulated theory. These girls were not seeking individuation or uniqueness or even a modicum of positive distinctiveness – at least, not through intragroup comparisons. Their inability to specify dimensions of comparison implies that it is possible that these young women were not consciously aware of the processes of social comparison and may even not have engaged in them.

There is a possibility, of course, that while these young women were unable to articulate the dimensions of comparison formally, they would operate a system of comparison at the behavioural level. Put crudely, it is feasible that they could do it without being able to talk about it. The participant observations provided an opportunity to map any signs of it which might occur. For instance, a girl might seek self-enhancement behaviourally by acting either closely in accordance with or in contra-distinction to a group norm controlling activity, achieving individuality and distinctiveness as an outcome. Activities in the workshop were monitored for symptoms of attempts to establish some unique value. In fact, the group had two strong norms: one concerned food, the other sex. Food should be shared. The norm regarding sex was more complex: explicit references to sexual inter-course or sexuality were not permitted but general discussion of boy-friends was accepted. Such talk was, however, far from romanticized or idealistic. Typically, it involved debate of how much warning a lad should be given before he was abandoned if he chose to date someone else; how much money or how many presents he should provide; whether he could be expected to be physically violent; and the improb-ability of a successful marriage. In these discussions, the girls were manifestly developing attitudes and opinions through comparison. To that extent, they complied with Festinger's prediction on the validation of opinions. Yet they showed no signs of using these discussions to prove themselves individually superior in relation to either norm. The norms did not serve as pivots for individuation for self-enhancement.

It was thought possible that the trainees might engage in spontaneous overt comparisons in relation to highly concrete activities (like work-rate, fashion-sense, time-keeping, etc.). Again, activities and utterances were monitored for examples of such social comparisons or attempts at self-enhancement. Very, very few occurred in the entire eight-week period of the study. The girls simply did not appear to be engaged in evaluative struggles that depended on social comparisons.

Within their group, the girls were not engaging in social comparison or differentiation in the manner expected in order to gain self-enhancement. This is vital. Comparison with relatively similar others is supposed to provide the most valid evaluations of self, attitudes and abilities. If they were comparing themselves with others outside the group (though there was no direct evidence that they were doing so), they would be making less useful comparisons on informational criteria and for self-enhancement since their group hardly occupied a strong position relative to others in the labour market.

The absence of any good evidence that these young women were making appropriate or salient social comparisons is important in the light of the fact that they also appeared to be unable to articulate any clear abstract self-definition. Moreover, most had very little idea of their own future goals or purposes; the notion of an identity project pursued through time would have been meaningless to them. If social comparison is a main artery into the heart of self-conceptualization, then, in its absence, one might expect to find exactly such uncertainty about the content of identity.

It is possible that these young women had withdrawn from the process of social comparison as a means of self-defence. Where all comparisons are negative and derogating, persistence amounts to masochism. It may be that the threats to identity posed by their labour market experiences, in collaboration with their other disadvantages, initiated a coping strategy that required a moratorium upon direct comparisons. But the spin-off of such a strategy is doubt about the precise nature of one's current opinions and abilities. These girls were left genuinely uncertain of who or what they were and where they could go next.

The fact that the trainees were still adolescents should not be overlooked. It may be that adolescent identity crises in the Eriksonian mould (Erikson, 1968) really do result in a form of psychosocial moratorium. If they do, this could be expected to wreak havoc with the ordered operation of social comparison processes since the adolescent temporarily calls a halt to the assimilation of information through the identification with others. The process of identification, as envisaged by many self theorists, is extraordinarily similar in outcome to the process of social comparison (Berger, 1977).

Adolescents have greater opportunity to use the abandonment of social comparison as a strategy in the face of threat to their identities. Society licenses adolescence as a recognized time for experimentation with identity forms. The normal restrictions on the conduct of building an identity are slackened. To this extent, the social context becomes less of a determinant in choice of coping strategy. Thus, an adolescent can choose not to engage in the most appropriate social comparisons, and can apparently resist all comparisons, without being heaped with the social outrage reserved for adults and fully fledged members of society.

This view may, however, underestimate the importance of social comparison processes during adolescence. Palmonari *et al.* (1984) have, in fact, argued that Erikson generally fails to locate the concept of identity 'within the framework of the social relationships and the social climate in which the subject lives' (p. 115). His assumption that the psychosocial moratorium will follow an identity crisis fits the trend of this omission. He ignores how social relationships might be actively used in, or comprise passive restraints to, various responses to crisis. In contrast, Sherif and Sherif (1964, 1965, and 1969), who were explicitly examining the problems facing the adolescent identity, focus upon the vital role of group membership and peer influence.

The Sherifs use the term 'self-system' when referring to the properties of identity. The 'self-system' is a constellation of 'categorical structures' (Sherif, 1980, p. 15) formed through interaction with the physical and social environments which detail the connections between significant objects (animate or not) in the individual's experience and the notions of 'me', 'I', and 'mine'. Some of these categorical structures are of personal relevance and define the self. All are arranged hierarchically in accordance with rank (i.e. importance) and direction of affectivity (the emotional valence attached to them). The interacting components of the 'self-system' are said to provide anchorage for perception and evaluation of any experience. In a sense, the self-system is a network of rules or guidelines which direct action. During adolescence, changes in physiology and social status throw up discontinuities, ambiguities and uncertainties, disturbing the constellation of the 'self-system'. The guidelines it comprises in terms of values and relationships become redundant as the child makes the transition to adulthood. At this juncture, according to the Sherifs, the adolescent's peers take on a new significance, being recognized as contemporaries in experience and a new source of significant relationships which change the categorical structures of the 'self-system'. Coevals become more vital as persons of reference to be emulated and used as models for behaviour (Rosenberg, 1967).

In sum, the Sherifs envisage the self-system as undergoing radical transformations during adolescence and these will be heavily influenced by the reference position held by the individual's contemporaries. This implies that the adolescent is highly subject to the social-comparison imperative. It requires that the adolescent be aware of peer characteristics and beliefs or values since otherwise there would be no potential for modelling. However, it does not require that the adolescent strive for distinctiveness through social comparison as the self-enhancement proposition suggests. The answer to adolescent uncertainty, in the light of the Sherif's argument, lies in group cohesiveness and the loss of individuality within the peer reference group, not in efforts to achieve independence through the psychological moratoria or through attempts to gain individual kudos through social comparison. The indulgence in social comparison, if it occurs, happens to ensure similarity. Hence the fact that the young women studied presented such similar self-images and declined to use tactics of differentiation.

Thus, both the psychoanalytic approach of Erikson and the social psychological approach of the Sherifs could explain some components of the findings from the young women described. Neither can explain all of the findings. Certainly, the Sherifs would find the absence of any clearly defined self-system problematic and Erikson would find the immersion within the group difficult. The actual operation of social comparison in this sort of arena requires a theory of identity which traverses the psychodynamic and sociological domains. As Palmonari *et al.* (1984, p. 117) pointed out, neither Erikson nor the Sherifs have produced this.

For the girls in the study, not engaging in social comparison may have been just as valid a route through to the recovery of some smidgeon of self-esteem as extensive searches to find a comparitor against whom self-enhancement would be possible. Despite the fact that they were not doing 'identity work' to repair the damage done by the omnipresent threat of unemployment and poverty in the manner prescribed by social comparison theory, it may be premature to suggest that they had given up the unequal struggle to resurface identity. Most of these girls were multiply disadvantaged: unqualified, uneducated, unskilled, inexperienced (in terms of work), from broken homes, some with a history of trouble with the police, living in an inner city slum, and a fair proportion suffered the incipient effects of institutionalized racism due to their ethnic origin. Given that backdrop, they may have learnt that social comparisons bring nothing but grief. Comparisons with people dissimilar to themselves might only serve the same function. Even if they were superior in some way to similar others, they would know it to be an illusory status: all fo them are still at the bottom of the social pile. In the Kingdom of the Blind, the one-eyed man may be God, but what good is that if the kingdom is surrounded by hordes with 20/20 vision and its frontiers are undefended? Under such circumstances, blindness can be bliss. Not making comparisons is a type of self-imposed myopia.

It would be valuable to know how social comparisons are more generally used by those facing threats to identity. The reason for describing the findings of the study above in such depth, quite apart from their intrinsic interest, is to illustrate that it may be hazardous to assume either that social comparisons are made continually or that, in their absence, an abstract self-awareness can always be articulated.

Ceasing to cope

Where an individual suffers chronic and sequential threats to identity over a long time, it might be expected that attempts at coping would decline and, at some point, cease. If threats are chronic and sequential as soon as one strategy was deployed, and an adjustment in the content or value of identity made or some social change initiated, another, potentially contradictory one, would be demanded. If the individual continued to respond to such demands for re-working self-definition and evaluation, identity would degenerate into a permanent state of flux. The assimilation-accommodation process could not function in a principled manner and stability would be lost. Achieving some semblance of equilibrium may be dependent upon abandoning work on the identity when faced with sequential threats, particularly if no control over the source of the threats can ever hope to be attained. Instead of responding, the sufferer builds an impenetrable vacuum about identity. It becomes the small invertebrate imprisoned in amber.

Cessation of coping is tied to withdrawal at one or any of four levels.

(i) *Psychologically*: the person can sever all conscious links with the world outside. This is characteristic of some forms of schizophrenia, for instance, catatonic stupor in which the victim becomes completely apathetic and immobile, though there is reason to suppose that during these periods of apparent inactivity hallucinatory or delusional experiences occur (Davis, 1984).

(ii) *Socially*: the person can reject all dominant social norms and values, becoming alienated or what Hammond (1985) prefers to call estranged: accepting no extant ideological system and consequently having no fixed frame against which identity can be evaluated and found lacking.

(iii) *Temporally*: the person can cut the links with the past by forgetting the previous content and value of identity. Amnesia may dispose of many threats to identity. Psychogenic amnesia, which may follow severe psychological trauma such as the death of a child or the collapse of a career, is often accompanied by a fugue state, a flight from the previous environment (Rosenhan and Seligman, 1984). The amnesia prevents the recognition of the threats to identity and obviates the need for coping through adjustment. Amnesia can be generalized, and then the entire identity is forgotten, but it can be more localized, blocking only knowledge of the traumatic information or of its consequences. The flight during the fugue state may provide a new social context where the threat is absent and presents an opportunity to start a new identity, as if the old worn-out structure could be put in a bodybag and sent back home for a decent burial without anyone ever looking inside. Such amnesia is rarely long-term so the respite from threat may be only temporary but while it lasts the individual has achieved some control over history, withdrawing from time through the vagaries of memory.

(iv) *Physically*: the person can withdraw totally; suicide or attempted suicide are not uncommon. The studies of suicide suggest that it may be a rational decision for some involved. Certainly, not all are psychiatrically ill. For example, novelist Arthur Koestler and his wife, Cynthia, were found dead in their London home. He was terminally ill and chose to die rather than to live in great pain for the short time left to him. His wife refused to live on without him. Their decision can be considered rational in the circumstances. However, most suicides, or attempted suicides, appear less rational. Suicides tend to be very unhappy and often clinically depressed, suffering all of the symptoms of helplessness characteristic of depression. Depressed patients ultimately commit suicide at a rate at least twenty-five times as high as control populations (Robins and Guze, 1972). The helplessness and sense of lost autonomy may explain why so many execute their suicide as a type of gamble: they risk being discovered in time and saved, even in death they have no confidence in their own capacity to call the tune.

With psychological, social, temporal or physical withdrawal, the individual is no longer seeking actively to cope with the threats to identity. The coping strategies have been overloaded and swamped: the limits to coping have been reached. An interesting theoretical advance will be made when it is known under what conglomeration of circumstances individuals actually reach their coping limits. At the moment, it is possible to say what alternatives might happen once the limits are reached but not when they will be reached. Even then, it is impossible to say which of the alternatives will be chosen in any individual case.

Summary

This chapter firstly surveys four central factors influencing the choice of coping strategy used to defend a threatened identity. These are: the type of threat (its origin, longevity and stability); the social context of its occurrence (ideologically, and in terms of the available interpersonal networks, group memberships, and caring professions); the pre-extant identity structure (which differs in self-esteem and in actual defining properties); and the cognitive resources at work (influenced by biases in both personal and social attribution processes). It is argued that these factors interact to produce the choice of coping strategy and, since the patterns of their interaction are large in number, predictions of the strategy to be chosen become difficult.

Secondly, the phases involved in coping are considered. Threats will elicit a sequence of strategies. Evidence of responses to unemployment is presented to exemplify the changing impact of a single threat and the communalities in the temporal pattern of coping it evokes. Such evidence makes it apparent that ineffective and sometimes dangerous strategies are employed. Consequently, the next section of this chapter explores the rationality implicit in the use of sub-optimal coping strategies.

Thirdly, having examined the factors influencing the choice of strategy and the limitations evident in coping evinced, the chapter turns to two processes traditionally supposed in social psychology to influence the functioning of identity: cognitive consistency drives and social-comparison processes. Consistency drives have been seen virtually as structural limitations to the cognitive system, motivating biases in information processing and action. Social comparison is, in contrast, a function performed by the cognitive system: it is not a motivating force, it is a technique for coming to conclusions about the value of information self-generated or otherwise.

The notion of consistency is distinguished from continuity in the discussion and it is suggested that there is empirical support for the idea that people do not invariably seek consistency as a priority. Consistency drives are, therefore, not treated as prime determinants of coping strategies.

The evidence concerning social comparison is more ambivalent. Social-comparison processes are an inherent part of self-evaluation and upon occasion may be the channel mediating between an objectively threatening position and conscious awareness of it. They may also be used to garner self-enhancement and thus retrieve self-esteem which may have been attacked by a threat. However, the process is by no means inevitably used. Threat to identity that is sufficiently great can place the person in a position where all social comparisons would be foolhardy since none would result in any increment in self-esteem. Findings which support this hypothesis are presented. In their own manner, both consistency drives and social-comparison processes can operate as limits to coping.

Any discussion of the limits to coping must consider what happens when people cease to strive with threat. The final section of the chapter examines how ceasing to cope is tied to withdrawal: psychologically, socially, temporally, and physically.

8 Central tenets of the model of identity, threat and coping

This chapter has two functions. The first is to examine the considerations necessary for the elaboration of the bald model of identity, threat and coping postulated thus far. The second is to summarize the resulting central tenets of the model.

Elaborating the framework

The purpose of this book was to describe an integrative theoretical framework within which threatened identities might be analysed. In pursuit of that end, it has sought to:

(i) specify a model of the structure and processes of identity

(ii) represent the structure and processes of the social matrix which contextualize identity

(iii) delineate the origins and dynamics of threats to identity

(iv) outline the range of coping strategies employed to deal with threat

(v) describe what factors influence the choice and efficacy of coping strategy.

As a synthesis of what is known about identity dynamics, especially under threat, the formulation offered has strengths and limitations. Some of the latter, upon reflection, turn out to be more imagined than real but it seems desirable to offer them an airing. In discussing some of the limitations of the framework, an attempt will be made to shown how they may prove to be the foundations for its extension and development.

Universals in process and structure

The recent upthrust in concern for a historical social psychology (Gergen and Gergen, 1984) has emphasized the need to build theories which take account of temporal transitions. A challenge has been thrown down to anyone who believes that psychological theories should identify relationships between processes which are supposedly atemporal and ahistorical. Gergen (1984b) argues that it is necessary to acknowledge that the processes so neatly outlined in social psychological theories to explain social behaviour are malleable. Social processes change over time, due to the infinitely complex and subterranean influence of material conditions upon social structures, and social rules or regulatory principles change as a consequence. These socially imposed rules permeate the function of psychological processes, modifying time in turn. The psychological processes are, it is argued, shaped and controlled by the social context in which they are embedded (Vygotsky, 1978). A theory which asserts processes are universal, atemporal or ahistorical, is consequently open to criticism.

However, the assertion that psychological processes are mutated by their social context is contentious. It is clearly debatable whether all psychological processes are mutable. It may not be the process which changes (for example, memory) so much as its rules of operation (for example, in the case of memory, permissable biases or mnemonics) or realms of operation (for example, again in the case of memory, a shift from public to personal details). If this were so, the argument that theories should not employ process universals would fall. A theory might assume a process to be universal but specify the social conditions affecting the rule and realm of its operation. It is also debatable, even assuming that a process is mutable, just how modifiable it will be. It is an empirical question just how far a process may be changed before it disappears for all intents and purposes. When it changes but maintains many of its old characteristics, is it then the same process or some new creature?

The argument that psychological processes are dependent upon their social and temporal context appears more tenable when used about the sort of processes typically located within social psychological theories than those proposed as explanatory concepts within other areas of the discipline. So, for instance, it has been suggested that the process of conformity is less common nowadays than forty years ago. This arises from the fact that some repetitions (Perrin and Spencer, 1981; Spencer and Perrin, 1981) of the classic experiments on conformity by Asch (1956) have, in recent years, failed to replicate his results or found them in an attenuated form (Nicholson *et al.*, 1985). Subjects will now, when making judgements about perceptual stimuli (like the length of lines presented on a screen), act independently of a unanimous majority view, expressed in their presence, which supports an erroneous judgement. Harris (1985) has said even Asch failed to prove conformity in such conditions. Several researchers have suggested that the reason for this failure to replicate might lie in fluctuations at various times in the overall societal value of the conformity process within the individual. It can be seen that such an argument is really based upon a misconception about what constitutes a process. Conformity is not a psychological process; it is an end state produced by processes of persuasion and so on. The prevalence of conformity will undoubtedly change as social rules and structures change because its value as an end-state is revised. Whether the processes of social influence, and their foundation in self-interest, are so flexible is another matter entirely.

This debate about universal processes is relevant to the proposed framework for threatened identities. The framework is founded upon the assumption that the statements about the structure and processes of identity are not temporally relative. In fact, there is only the slenderest possibility that the structure and processes postulated might be historically specific. Both are content-free. The structural assertion is simply that identity has a content and a value dimension. The process assertion is merely that identity is created by assimilation-accommodation and evaluation. Beyond that, the importance of social context is built-in as an intrinsic part of the framework and its historical transformations are explicitly considered in detailing the dynamics of social change. The *actual* content and *actual* value of identity are acknowledged to be a dynamic product of the interaction between the individual's cognitive resources and the social context. Thus, the specific content and value are historically relative; the fact of content and value is not.

However, there are the three principles which are said to guide the operation of the identity processes: continuity, distinctiveness, and self-esteem. These are obviously not content-free. It is quite possible that they are culturally and temporally specific. They can be regarded as the product of what society has dictated shall be considered an acceptable form for identity. They are a socially established set of criteria against which identity is measured. If they are socially constructed, they are open to change as social structures and processes change. It is feasible to imagine a culture, for instance, where distinctiveness is not valued and it would then lose its power to guide what elements are assimilated into identity and how they are evaluated. Something of this sort has actually already been described with reference to the young women who sought no personal distinctiveness in the previous chapter. In their case, there seemed to be a subcultural norm which militated against distinctiveness gaining salience as a guiding principle for work on identity. It is less easy to envisage a societal form or subculture where continuity and self-esteem were lost as organizing principles. Nevertheless, the remote possibility has to be acknowledged. It is also conceivable that other principles might be added to the triumvirate listed. Social processes might establish consistency more firmly as a guiding principle under some cultural configurations.

It seems then that the historical specificity of the three principles used in the integrative framework proposed represents a weakness. However, it may be an illusory weakness. The framework is sufficiently flexible to encompass either the removal or the addition of principles. The framework remains viable as long as the principles that are operative, whatever they happen to be, function in the manner predicted for those already described. As long as any subsequent principles, if abrogated, engender a threat to identity, the framework can be upheld. The main point is that in current industrialized capitalist cultures these three principles do seem to operate.

It is evident that only empirical work which is diachronic in structure will be able to tap any changes that occur in the actual principles operative. The framework presented here simply serves to focus the orientation of that research. For the time being, the three principles outlined seem to be dominant, though changes should be monitored.

It should also be possible as the flow of psychological information from China (Brown, 1981) and from the Soviet Union (Strickland, 1979; Lauterbach, 1984) increases to explore just how far these three principles operate in cultures based on fundamentally different social philosophies. From what little is already available it is feasible to suppose that distinctiveness at the personal level would hardly feature as a prime directive, though distinctiveness as part of a corporate entity might well do so.

Obviously any cross-cultural psychology is fraught with difficulty. Strickland (1979), in reporting on a conference where social psychologists from the east and west met in any number for the first time in over fifty years, described the immense conceptual barrier which existed between the two groups. Concepts basic to the western view of social psychology simply did not exist in the eastern analytical framework. Concepts founded upon notions of individualism and autonomy were not used in the Soviet theories; concepts based on collectivism and total interdependence were unavailable to the North American models. The ideologies dominant in each society had infiltrated theory-building. This is hardly surprising. Social psychologists are, after all, a product of their society and, no matter how hard they try, they can never be totally objective observers of it. The very forms of their discourse are trammelled by ideology (Billig, 1982).

In relation to models of identity, this means that there is a need for them to be carefully monitored for cultural myopia. It also means, however, that evidence emanating from one culture which seems to challenge a model originating in another should also be treated cautiously. The evidence can have been collected with alien 'stipulative' assumptions (Israel, 1972) in mind. Soviet social psychologists who fail to find distinctiveness operating as a prime guiding principle for the identity processes may do so because the level of analysis they employ is inappropriate, being founded upon stipulations that the collective or interdependent factors are the appropriate unit for analysis or interpretation. Cross-cultural data cannot be taken at face value. It, like all data, has to be analysed in terms of the preconceptions which motivated its collection and in relation to the pool of alternative information from which it is drawn.

Nevertheless, it would be interesting to examine what communalities may exist in the principles guiding identity processes. But it has to be said that the very concept of an individual identity may be a nonsense in certain cultures. All of the recent literature on the self-concept emanating from anthropologists asserts the cultural relativity of the concept. Marsella, DeVos and Hsu (1985), in a book of readings about the self, comparing the west with Indian and Chinese traditions, have argued that cultural understandings affect and, to a degree, determine its constitution and the manner in which it is experienced in different societies. Shweder and Bourne (1984) also emphasize that the concept of the person varies cross-culturally. They use anthropological examples of the way the person is perceived in Bali, New Guinea and India and conclude that in these cultures (if they can be considered each to possess a single homogeneous culture) a mode of social thought exists 'culminating in the view that specific situations determine the moral character of a particular action, the individual person *per se* is neither an object of importance nor inherently worthy of respect, that the individual as moral agent ought not to be distinguished from the social status s(he) occupies' (p. 158). Shweder and Bourne feel that, in these cultures, the individual is not acknowledged as an abstract ethical or normative category. Given such examples, it would be arrant nonsense to assume that the model of identity principles here applies to anything more than western industrialized countries.

Relative priorities of the identity principles

Quite apart from the question of whether the three principles mentioned in the framework represent an exhaustive list of those operative or whether they might be subject to historical revision or whether they are culturally relative, there is the issue of their relationship to each other. The relationship of the three principles is not explicitly specified in the framework. They are implicitly treated as three independent and equally important principles. In fact, this relies on analytic licence: theorists, like poets, need some arbitrarily created room for manoeuvre. In reality, there is likely to be a salience or priority hierarchy amongst the three principles.

The nature of this salience hierarchy is undetermined. It may be indeterminate. The problem is that it is, in all probability, situation-specific and is certainly likely to be temporally transient. Different situations, at different times, will make differential calls upon the distinctiveness, continuity and self-esteem principles. It is already fairly well-established that the expression in action of various components of the content dimension of identity is situation-specific. For example, a number of researchers (e.g. Okamura, 1981; Waddell and Cairns, 1986) have shown that people differ across contexts in the expression of their ethnicity; by and large, it becomes a more important determinant of feeling and action where inter-ethnic contacts are demanded. Moreover, it had been shown that the salience of the desire for intergroup differentiation and intra-group similarity is also dependent upon the specific network of relations between groups which pertains at any one time (Brown, 1984; Tajfel and Turner, 1979; Deschamps and Brown, 1983). It is hardly surprising then that the principles of distinctiveness, continuity and self-esteem should be seen to vary in relative, or, indeed, absolute salience according to context.

In conducting research to establish their hierarchy or changing salience it is important not to impose premature closure on the model of their relationship on the basis of too few contextual examples. The real objective should be to formulate a set of rules of transition which would specify under what circumstances the individual moves from applying one principle in operating identity processes to applying the next. Such rules of transition would be likely to be historically specific but, at least, they would say something about the relationship between the principles at one time. As long as the eras across which the hierarchies held and the transition rules operated were sufficiently long-lived to be encapsulated in research, there would be little problem.

There is another possibility. This is that rules of transition might not be available for formulation because the principles operate simultaneously or are used in very quick succession (which is the functional equivalent of simultaneity). If this is proven so, the issue of salience may be illusory. Of course, salience amongst the principles remains a problem where threat is concerned. The threat may be generated as a consequence of the conflict between the demands of two principles acting incompatibly. Equally, it may be ameliorated by movement from operation in accordance with one to operation in accordance with an alternative principle. In either case, priority again becomes important. But then, the question of priority arises for a different reason, pragmatic rather than theoretical. It is then necessary to have information on priority hierarchies in order to predict when threat will arise and what strategy will be most opportune. For this reason alone it may be valuable to promote research upon priority hierarchies among the principles and how they change according to context.

The substance of the identity processes
The identity processes have been delineated in terms of their functions. Assimilation entails the addition of new components to the identity structure; accommodation involves the reorganization of existing components to encompass the new. Evaluation is the process whereby value is allocated to identity components in accordance with social and personal criteria of worth. This type of definition does not describe the substantive systems underlying the functions that ensure that they are performed. Some considerations of the substantive system is required and the framework as it stands fails to provide it.

Assimilation-accommodation could be conceptualized as a memory system. Kihlstrom and Cantor (1984) discuss the way in which the self may be regarded as a memory system. As such, the self-concept is simply a mental representation of a particular person – oneself – and is therefore just a part of the individual's total knowledge of the social world. This social knowledge is a segment of the entire memory system. They argue that this memory is comprised, on the one hand, of declarative knowledge and procedural knowledge and, on the other, of episodic memory and semantic memory. Declarative knowledge consists of facts and information; procedural knowledge consists of the rules for manipulating those facts in a manner consistent with logic and socially established codes of judgement. Procedural knowledge includes strategies for acquiring, storing and retrieving memories and motor skills. Episodic memory comprises recollections of personal experiences within their spatial and temporal frame of reference. Semantic memory contains the person's mental lexicon, categorical information stored without reference to the context of its acquisition or its personal meaning. There is a suggestion that, in addition to this memory system in its quadruped form, there may also be what is called a metamemory: the awareness of what facts are available in the main-frame storage and what procedures may be used to access them. In their conceptualization, the components of identity would be a subset of declarative knowledge and the principles of identity an element in procedural knowledge. Memories about the self can, of course, fall into both episodic and semantic memories.

Kihlstrom and Cantor are basically treating the self-concept as the product of an information-processing system which can actively reconstruct and order inputs shaped by social experiences. This is essentially what the assimilation-accommodation process is said to do. There is no reason why the Kihlstrom and Cantor approach should not be fitted into the framework which has been proposed. While it is not essential to the logic of the framework to specify the substantive composition of the identity processes, yet the information processing-memory model dovetails with it so precisely it should not be overlooked.

The process of evaluation seems to lie outside the information-processing model domain. It may be that the evaluative process is largely founded upon a system of ordered comparisons in which identity components are compared against social and objective criteria to assess their worth. This would tie in with the theory of social comparison processes. It would, of course, be pinioned within a network of rules for drawing evaluative inferences which would ultimately rest within an information-processing system that will depend upon memory.

One suspects that, if the processes of identity are pushed to their fundamental roots, it is the biochemistry of memory which will be the target for exploration.

It is worth saying that, as a memory system, the self-concept has peculiarities: it has a larger store which can be accessed more speedily and more flexibly than most memory systems. Furthermore, there are extensive documented biases in the ways memories are encoded. Greenwald (1980) outlined three such biases.

(i) Memory is best for information highly relevant to the self; this is tied to the fact that recall of material learnt actively is better than that received passively.

(ii) People readily see themselves as responsible for positive outcomes of their action but deny responsibility for negative outcomes (beneffectance).

(iii) People seek information which accords with their existing self-
concept and autobiographical memories are retrospectively
revised to comply with the current self-concept.

These are fundamentally biases in the information-processing system
which evidently has self-interest rather than accuracy or inferential
logic as its prime directives. An adequate understanding of the rules of
bias is a precursor to the thorough description of the operation of both
the assimilation-accommodation process and the evaluation process. It
is illuminating that those biases Greenwald (1980) has already identified are ones which would be predicted if the processes of identity
were indeed functioning in accordance with the principles of
continuity, distinctiveness and self-esteem. It may, of course, be
possible that the constraints upon information processing actually
change when the identity seeks to cope with threat. The current model
would predict that they should not. The constraints are built into the
identity system and would dictate the form coping takes.

Self-awareness and cognitive development

The framework proposed is founded upon the assumption that people
are self-aware, possessing abstract self-knowledge which is reflexively
monitored. This in itself is uncontentious, at least at the theoretical
level. Philosophers have long accepted the notion (Shoemaker, 1984,
reviews their perspective). Thus identity is regarded as both a cognitive
system processing information and a cognitive product of that system.
No paradox is meant to be involved in seeing the self as both knower
and known; they are simply two facets of the same process. Moreover,
the origin of these two facets should not be confused. The self as a
cognitive information-processing system is the product of the interaction between capacities intrinsic to the biological organism and
influences embedded in the social structure. The self as a cognitive
product is constructed by the information-processing system in collaboration with inputs provided by the social context.

Examples of people who are incapable of articulating in abstract
self-description, like the young women engineering operators
described in an earlier chapter, are problematic for the framework.
They give rise to the awesome possibility that the system is not always
reflexively monitoring itself. Obviously, it is possible to claim that there
is a distinction between the real absence of self-awareness and the

absence of the ability to articulate it verbally or in abstract form. It is possible that the young women described simply could not do the latter. There is, however, just the vague chance that self-awareness is not highly developed in everyone. For some it may be retarded or allotted minimal importance. The interesting question then becomes: why should this be so? This may be significant when examining threat. It is difficult to envisage how anyone who was minimally self-aware could experience threat even if the position occupied was threatening. But it is also possible that chronic threat for which no coping strategy works may ultimately result in the suppression of self-awareness. This would be in some senses equivalent to the withdrawal phenomena (physical, temporal, social and psychological) which occur when people cease to cope. Abandoning or minimizing self-awareness could be a final attempt to elude the threat. It is not as extreme an answer as total amnesia but it has properties in common. The threat recedes because the self-awareness which makes it subjectively important has been muted. Assuming self-awareness remains depressed, subsequent threatening positions would have a much reduced power to generate the experience of threat.

This leads on to questions about the development of self-awareness. Since the cognitive system underlying identity is a product of the interaction of the maturing biological organism and evolving social processes (Serafica, 1982; Doise and Mugny, 1984; Higgins *et al.*, 1983) identity, too, should be subject to developmental changes. As it stands, the framework is not concerned with the pattern of developmental changes which may be manifested in the functioning of the identity processes. There is considerable evidence about developmental trends in the self-concept available. Flavell (1977), for instance, discusses the stages of cognitive development related to the self-concept. Descriptions of the self show age-related trends in increased richness, differentiation and complexity. Such evidence indicates that the self-concept is an active construction through learning and that the learning is controlled by the rate of the development of the cognitive information-processing system. The propensity to develop seems an innate characteristic of the biological organism. Such information about developmental trends either in the type of identity components or in the rules of their assimilation can be fitted into the integrative framework.

Without the developmental perspective, the framework cannot be regarded as an adequate model of personal evolution. It may even become misleading with regard to predictions of what will constitute threat because it is just possible that the principles guiding the identity processes are subject to developmental revision. This requires empirical exploration. What evidence there already is (for instance, that from Flavell, 1977; Flavell and Ross, 1981) seems to support the developmental constancy of the three principles, though their salience seems to vary across the lifespan (Savage *et al.*, 1977), but even this may be context-specific.

Propositions of the model

The model of identity, threat and coping proposed has a number of central propositions.

(1) The structure of identity is a dynamic social product of the inter-action of the capacities for memory, consciousness and organized construal which are characteristic of the biological organism with the physical and societal structures and influence processes which con-stitute the social context. The identity resides in psychological processes but is manifested through thought, action and affect. It can therefore be described at two levels, in terms of its structure and in terms of its processes.

(1a) People are normally self-aware: monitoring the status of identity.

(1b) Self-awareness levels may differ developmentally and across different cultures.

(2) The structure of identity has two planes: the content dimension and the value dimension.

(2a) The content dimension consists of the characteristics which define identity: the properties which, taken as a constellation, mark the individual as unique. It encompasses both those characteristics previously considered the domain of social identity (group member-ships, roles, social category labels, etc.) and of personal identity (values, attitudes, cognitive style, etc.). The distinction between social and personal identity is abandoned in this model. Seen across the biography, social identity is seen to become personal identity: the dichotomy is purely a temporal artefact.

(2b) The content dimension is organized. The organization can be characterized in terms of (i) the degree of centrality, (ii) the hierarchical arrangements of elements and (iii) the relative salience of components. The organization is not, however, static and is responsive to changes in inputs and demands from the social context.

(2c) Each element in the content dimension has a specific positive or negative value appended to it; taken together these values constitute the value dimension of identity.

(2d) The value dimension of identity is constantly subject to revision: the value of each element is open to reappraisal as a consequence of changes in social value systems and modifications in the individual's position in relation to such social value systems.

(3) The structure of identity is regulated by the dynamic processes of accommodation-assimilation and evaluation which are deemed to be universal psychological processes.

(3a) Assimilation and accommodation are components of the same process. Assimilation refers to the absorption of new components into the identity structure; accommodation refers to the adjustment which occurs in the existing structure in order to find a place for new elements.

(3b) Accommodation-assimilation can be conceptualized as a memory system (equivalent to an information-processing system) and subject to biases in retention and recall. These biases are determined by the identity principles.

(3c) The process of evaluation entails the allocation of meaning and value to identity contents, new and old.

(3d) The two processes interact to determine the changing content and value of identity over time; with changing patterns of assimilation requiring changes in evaluation and vice versa.

(4) The processes of identity are guided in their operation by principles which define desirable states for the structure of identity.

(4a) The actual end states considered desirable, and consequently the guidance principles, are temporally and culturally specific.

(4b) In western industrialized cultures the current prime guidance principles are: continuity, distinctiveness and self-esteem.

(4c) These three principles will vary in their relative and absolute salience over time and across situations.

(4d) Their salience also varies developmentally.

(5) The identity is created within a particular social context within a specific historical period.

(5a) The social context can be schematically represented along two dimensions concerning, in turn, structure and process. Structurally, the social context is comprised of interpersonal networks, group and social-category memberships, and intergroup relationships. The content of identity is assimilated from these structures which generate roles to be adopted and beliefs or values to be accepted. The second dimension consists of social influence processes which conspire to create the multifaceted ideological milieu for identity. Social influence processes (education, rhetoric, propaganda, polemic, persuasion, etc.) establish systems of value and beliefs, reified in social representations, social norms, and social attributions, which specify both the content and value of individual identities.

(5b) Identity is not totally determined by its social context. There are contradictions and conflicts within the ideological milieu, generated by intergroup power struggles, which permit the individual some freedom of choice in formulating the identity structure. Furthermore, the limitations of the cognitive system itself impose some constraints upon identity development. Changes in identity are therefore normally purposive. The person has agency in creating identity.

(5c) Social changes in the structure of processes of the social context will call forth changes in identity varying in extent according to: (i) their personal relevance; (ii) the immediacy of involvement in them; (iii) the amount of change demanded; and (iv) how negative the change is deemed to be.

(5d) Movement of the individual from one position in the social matrix to another will bring pressure to bear for a change in identity since this is likely to introduce a changed pattern of social influences and restrictions.

(6) A threat to identity occurs when the processes of assimilation-accommodation and evaluation are unable, for some reason, to comply with the principles of continuity, distinctiveness and self-esteem.

(6a) Origin of threat can be internal or external. It can be considered to originate internally where the individual seeks to alter his or her position in the social matrix in accordance with one principle only to discover that this contravenes one of the other principles. It can be said to originate externally when a change in the social context calls for identity changes incompatible with any of the three principles.

(6b) Threats are aversive and the individual will seek to reinstitute the principled operation of the identity processes.

(6c) For a threat to evoke action, it must gain access to consciousness. It is therefore possible to distinguish between occupying a threatening position and experiencing threat. If coping strategies are effective, occupancy of a threatening position may lose its power to threaten.

(7) Any activity, in thought or deed, which has as its goal the removal or modification of a threat to identity can be regarded as a coping strategy.

(7a) Coping strategies can be pitched at a number of different levels: the intra-psychic, interpersonal and group/intergroup.

(7b) Intra-psychic coping strategies rely upon:

(i) the process of assimilation-accommodation to either deflect or accept the implications of the threat for identity. Deflection tactics entail the refusal to modify either the value or content dimensions of identity. They include: denial, transient depersonalization, belief in the unreality of the self, fantasy, and reconstrual and reattribution. Acceptance strategies act to modify the identity structure in ways required by the threat. Acceptance is rarely wholesale capitulation to the threat. Mostly it reflects a compromise negotiated between the threat and the needs of identity. Acceptance tactics include anticipatory restructuring, compartmentalism, compromise changes, and, only after these, fundamental changes in identity. There is another type of strategy which involves the revision of the salience allotted the three principles guiding the identity processes. Rearranging their priority may shift the emphasis from the threatened to the unthreatened components of identity.

(ii) the process of evaluation revising the value placed upon either the existing or prospective content of identity to make the changes mooted more palatable.

(7c) Interpersonal coping strategies rely upon changing relationships with others in order to cope with the threat. There are a number of such strategies: isolationism, negativism, passing and compliance.

(7d) Group or intergroup coping strategies can operate at a series of levels and the structure of the groups concerned vary. Individuals can use multiple group memberships to insulate against threat. They can engender group support for their dilemma, using a group to provide a social and information network or as a context for consciousness-raising or self-help. Group action may be used to bring about changes in the social structure or in the ideological milieu. The object of the group action may be to alter the characteristics and value of the individual's social position. Such groups, evolved to aid the threatened, may develop ideologies and rhetoric of their own and can become a force for social change.

(8) The choice of coping strategy is determined by an interaction between the type of threat involved, the salient parameters of the social context, the prior identity structure and the cognitive capacities available to the individual.

(8a) As long as the constellation of factors which produced the choice of a suboptimal coping strategy is maintained, the individual will persist with that strategy.

(9) Coping strategies are influenced by the demands of cognitive consistency requirements and social-comparison processes.

(10) Where coping strategies fail, the structure of identity will change in ways incompatible with the constraints normally imposed by the principles guiding the processes of identity. The individual temporarily loses the power to limit or direct change. Failure of the coping strategies in the face of chronic threat may result ultimately in withdrawal, either psychologically, socially, temporally or physically, or in the suppression of self-awareness. It is dubious whether these extreme forms of withdrawal, such as amnesia or suicide, can be considered coping strategies in themselves.

In the past, there has been abundant work upon the effects of specific threats to identity. Countless examples of threat have been extensively studied, some of which have been described earlier in this volume: responses to ethnic or religious marginality, to membership of a powerless minority, to unemployment or occupations breaching gender-role expectations, to divorce, separation or bereavement, to serious or disabling physical or mental illness. These investigations have sometimes had valuable practical implications, influencing the help which can be offered to people facing such diverse problems and occasionally having impact upon legislation and government policy (for example, in relation to provision for the handicapped and the anti-discrimination laws). However, in the main, they have been fragmented and highly specialized pieces of research targeted at testing and evolving theoretical models of specific threats. The result has been a proliferation of theories, each aimed at explaining the origin and/or the outcomes of a particular threat.

In its own way, this is no bad thing. However, the absence of a comprehensive and systematic framework within which the diverse insights about specific threats can be located is problematic. It means that there has been repetition both in research and in theorizing: different researchers, focusing upon different types of threat, reaching the same conclusions about, for instance, the coping strategies used and their relative inadequacies. Of course, these researchers and aware of each other's work and there is much cross-fertilization of ideas. An exdample of this would be the way theorists of unemployment use the models of loss and grief evolved by those studying bereavement to predict phases in coping following job loss. However, there has been no previous attempt to establish a generalizable model of identity, threat and coping which can encompass the findings in a whole host of threat-inducing contexts. The advantages of doing so are considerable.

Such a model pinpoints the communalities across threats not just in subjective experience and in patterns of coping elicited but in the factors inducing threat. This then assists in the prediction of when and where threats will arise and of the phases in coping which might be expected. A thorough understanding of the range of coping strategies available to the threatened and a grasp of the factors determining which strategies are deployed is valuable to practitioners, like social workers or counsellors, seeking to help the threatened. In addition, the conceptual continuity, if not clarity, of an integrative framework, should point to where there are lacunae in the understanding of threat and would indicate what direction new research should take. Nevertheless, this sort of exercise in conceptual systematization is not meant to erect a straitjacket designed to constrain the development of work upon threatened identities. The framework, resting upon existing knowledge and drawing together previous theoretical formulations, should function as a sort of wardrobe. The wardrobe protects its contents, keeping them clean and well-ordered, but most things can be hung in it; the proportions of the structure impose the slenderest of limitations upon its subsequent contents.

References

Abramson, L.Y. (1978) 'Universal versus personal helplessness', unpublished dissertation, University of Pennsylvania.

Abramson, L.Y. Seligman, M.E.P. and Teasdale, J. (1978) 'Learned helplessness in humans: critique and reformulation', *Journal of Abnormal Psychology* 87, 32–48.

Ajzen, I. and Fishbein, M. (1980) *Understanding Attitudes and Predicting Social Behavior*, Englewood Cliffs, NJ, Prentice-Hall.

Allport, G.W. (1955) *Becoming: Basic Considerations for a Psychology of Personality*, New Haven, Conn., Yale University Press.

Almond, G.A. (1954) *The Appeals of Communism*, Princeton, Princeton University Press.

Althusser, L. (1985) 'Ideology and the ideological state apparatuses', in V. Beechey and J. Donald (eds) *Subjectivity and Social Relations*, Milton Keynes, Open University Press.

Antonovsky, A. (1956) 'Towards a refinement of the "marginal man" concept', *Social Forces* 35, 57–62.

Apter, M.J. (1982) *The Experience of Motivation: The Theory of Psychological Reversals*, London, Academic Press.

Apter, M.J. (1983) 'Negativism and the sense of identity', in G.M. Breakwell (ed.) *Threatened Identities*, Chichester, Wiley.

Archer, J. and Lloyd, B. (1982) *Sex and Gender*, Harmondsworth, Penguin.

Argyle, M. (1976) 'Personality and social behaviour', in R. Harré (ed.) *Personality*, Oxford, Blackwell.

Asch, S.E. (1956) 'Studies of independence and conformity: a minority of one against a unanimous majority', *Psychological Monographs* 70 (9, whole no. 416).

Ashton, D.N. (1986) *Unemployment Under Capitalism*, Brighton, Wheatsheaf Books.

Bakke, E. (1933) *The Unemployed Man*, New York, Nisbet.

Bakke, E. (1960) 'The cycle of adjustment to unemployment', in N.W. Bell and E.F. Vogel, (eds) *A Modern Introduction to the Family*, New York, Free Press.

Bandura, A. (1982) '"Self-efficacy mechanisms" in human agency', *American Psychologist* 37, 122–47.

Banks, M. and Jackson, P. (1982) 'Unemployment and risk of minor psychiatric disorder in young people: cross-sectional and longitudinal evidence', *Psychological Medicine* 12, 789–98.

Bavelas, J.B. (1978) *Personality: Current Theory and Research*, Monterey, Calif., Brooks/Cole.

Beck, A.T. Rush, A.J. Shaw, B.F. and Emery, G. (1979) *Cognitive Therapy of Depression*, New York, Guilford Press.

Bellack, A.S. and Hersen, M. (1984) (eds) *Research Methods in Clinical Psychology*, Oxford, Pergamon.

Bem, S.L. (1977) 'On the utility of alternative procedures for assessing psychological androgyny', *Journal of Consulting and Clinical Psychology* 45, 196–205.

Berger, P.L. and Luckmann, T. (1975) *The Social Construction of Reality*, Harmondsworth, Penguin.

Berger, P.L. et al. (1974) *The Homeless Mind*, Harmondsworth, Penguin.

Berger, S.M. (1977) 'Social comparison, modeling and perseverance', in J.M. Suls and R.L. Miller (eds) *Social Comparison Processes*, New York, Wiley.

Biddle, B.J. (1979) *Role Theory: Expectations, Identities and Behaviors*, New York, Academic Press.

Billig, M. (1976) *Social Psychology and Intergroup Relations*, London, Academic Press.

Billig, M. (1982) *Ideology and Social Psychology*, Oxford, Blackwell.

Billig, M. (1984) 'Political ideology: social psychological aspects', in H. Tajfel (ed.) *The Social Dimension*, vol. 2, Cambridge, Cambridge University Press.

Billig, M. (1985) 'Rhetoric', ESRC Conference on Social Beliefs, Cambridge, March.

Bion, W.R. (1959) *Experiences in Groups*, New York, Basic Books.

Blumer, H. (1962) 'Society as symbolic interaction', in A. Rose (ed.) *Human Behaviour and Social Processes*, London, Routledge.

Braginski, B. Braginski, D. and Ring, K. (1969) *Methods of Madness: The Mental Hospital as a Last Resort*, New York, Holt.

Breakwell, G.M. (1974) 'Ethnic stereotypes and person perception', unpublished M.Sc. dissertation, University of Strathclyde.

Breakwell, G.M. (1979) 'Illegitimate group membership and intergroup differentiation', *British Journal of Social and Clinical Psychology* 18, 141–9.

Breakwell, G.M. (1983a) (ed.) *Threatened Identities*, Chichester, Wiley.

Breakwell, G.M. (1983b) 'Propaganda and polemic in intergroup conflict', paper presented at the European Association of Experimental Social Psychology Conference on 'Groups in Conflict', Israel.

Breakwell, G.M. (1984a) 'Attitudes of the young unemployed towards YOP schemes', *Journal of Community Education* 3 (3), 12–23.

Breakwell, G.M. (1984b) *Social Movements and their Strategies*, Open University D307, Unit 22.

Breakwell, G.M. (1985a) *The Quiet Rebel*, London, Century Press.

Breakwell, G.M. (1985b) 'Abusing the unemployed: an invisible injustice', *Journal of Moral Education* 14, (1), 56–62.

Breakwell, G.M. (1986) 'Identities at work', In H. Beloff (ed.) *Getting into Life,* London, Methuen.

Breakwell, G.M. (in press), 'Political and attributional responses of the young short-term unemployed', *Political Psychology.*

Breakwell, G.M. and Carter, C. (in prep.) 'Children's conceptions of work: unemployment and gender roles'.

Breakwell, G.M. and Rowett, C. (1982) *Social Work: The Social Psychological Approach,* Wokingham, Van Nostrand Reinhold.

Breakwell, G.M. and Weinberger, B. (1983) *The Right Women for the Job,* Guildford, Surrey University Press/MSC.

Breakwell, G.M. and Weinberger, B. (1985a) *Young Women Engineering Technicians,* research report, Department of Employment.

Breakwell, G.M. and Weinberger, B. (1985b) 'Young women training to be engineering technicians', *Department of Employment Gazette,* April.

Breakwell, G.M. Collie, A., Harrison, B. and Propper, C. (1984a) 'Attitudes towards the unemployed: effects of threatened identity', *British Journal of Social Psychology* 23, 87–8.

Breakwell, G.M. Harrison, B. and Propper, C. (1984b) 'Explaining the psychological effects of unemployment for young people: the importance of specific situational factors, *British Journal of Guidance and Counselling* 12 (2), July, 132–40.

Brenner, M., Brown, J. and Canter, D. (1985) *The Research Interview: Uses and Approaches,* London, Academic Press.

Brenner, S., Brenner, O. and Bartell, R. (1983) 'Psychological impact of unemployment: a structural analysis of cross-sectional data', *Journal of Occupational Psychology* 56 (2), 129–37.

Briar, K. (1977) 'The effect of long-term unemployment on workers and their families', *Dissertation Abstracts International* 37, 19-A, 6062.

Brickman, P. and Bulman, R.J. (1977) 'Pleasure and pain in social comparison', in J.M. Suls and R.L. Miller (eds) *Social Comparison Processes,* New York, Wiley.

Brown, G.W. and Harris, T. (1978) *Social Origins of Depression,* London, Tavistock.

Brown, J. and Sime, J. (1981) 'A methodology for accounts', in M. Brenner (ed.) *Social Method and Social Life,* London, Academic Press.

Brown, L. (1981) *Psychology in Contemporary China,* Oxford, Pergamon Press.

Brown, R.J. (1984) 'The effects of intergroup similarity and cooperative vs competitive orientation on intergroup discrimination', *British Journal of Social Psychology* 23 (1), 21–34.

Bunker, N. and Dewsberry, C. (1983) 'Unemployment behind closed doors: staying in and staying invisible', *Journal of Community Education* 2 (4), 37–45.

Burman, S. (ed.) (1979) *Fit Work for Women,* London, Croom Helm.

Burns, R.B. (1979) *The Self Concept,* New York, Longman.

Butcher, J.N. (1972) *Objective Personality Assessment,* London, Academic Press.

Carmichael, S. (1962) 'Negritude', in V.S. Naipaul *The Middle Passage,* London, Andre Deutsch.

Carver, C.S. and Scheier, M.F. (1981) *Attention and Self-Regulation: A Control-Theory Approach to Human Behavior*, New York, Springer-Verlag.

Carver, C.S. and Scheier, M.F. (1984) 'Self-consciousness and the experience of the self', paper presented at the BPS Self and Identity Conference, University College, Cardiff, July.

Cattell, R.B. and Dreger, R.M. (1977) *Handbook of Modern Personality Theory*, New York, Halsted Press.

Cattell, R.B. and Kline, P. (1977) *The Scientific Analysis of Personality and Motivation*, London, Academic Press.

Central Statistical Office (1985) *Social Trends* 15, London, HMSO.

Cheek, J.M. and Briggs, S.R. (1982) 'Self-consciousness and aspects of identity', *Journal of Research in Personality* 16, 401–8.

Chetwynd, J. and Hartnett, O. (eds) (1978) *The Sex Role System: Psychological and Sociological Perspectives*, London, Routledge & Kegan Paul.

Chiplin, B. and Sloane, P.J. (1982) *Tackling Discrimination at the Workplace: An Analysis of Sex Discrimination in Britain*, Cambridge, Cambridge University Press.

Clark, K.B. and Clark, M.P. (1947) 'Racial identification and preference in Negro children', in T.M. Newcomb and E.L. Hartley (eds) *Readings in Social Psychology*, New York, Holt, Rinehart & Winston.

Cochrane, R. (1985) 'Political socialization', paper presented at ESRC Social Beliefs Conference, University of Cambridge.

Cochrane, R. and Billig, M. (1982) 'Extremism of the centre: the SDP's young followers', *New Society* 60, 291–2.

Cohen, S. (1973) *Folk Devils and Moral Panics*, London, Paladin.

Cohn, R.M. (1978) 'Effect of employment status change on self-attitudes', *Social Psychology* 41, 81–93.

Cook, E.P. (1985) *Psychological Androgyny*, Oxford, Pergamon.

Cooley, C.H. (1902) *Human Nature and the Social Order*, New York, Scribner's.

Cooper, C. and Davidson, M. (1982) *High Pressure: Working Lives of Women Managers*, London, Fontana.

Cox, M. (1978) *Structuring the Therapeutic Process*, Pergamon, Oxford.

Davey, A. (1983) *Learning to be Prejudiced*, London, Edward Arnold.

Davis, D.R. (1984) *An Introduction to Psychopathology*, 4th edn, Oxford, Oxford University Press.

Deconchy, J-P. (1984) 'Rationality and social control in orthodox systems', in H. Tajfel (ed.) *The Social Dimension*, Vol. 2, Cambridge, Cambridge University Press.

Deem, R. (1980) *Schooling for Women's Work*, London, Routledge & Kegan Paul.

Deschamps, J-C. and Brown, R. (1983) 'Superordinate goals and intergroup conflict', *British Journal of Social Psychology* 22 (3), 189–96.

de Waele, J.P. (1985) 'The significance of action psychology for personality research and assessment', in G.P. Ginsberg, M. Brenner and M. von Cranach (eds) *Discovery Strategies in the Psychology of Action*, London, Academic Press.

Di Giacomo, J-P. (1980) 'Intergroup alliances and rejections within a protest movement (analysis of the social representation)', *European Journal of Social*

Psychology 10, 329–44.

Doise, W. (1978) *Groups and Individuals: Explanations in Social Psychology*, Cambridge, Cambridge University Press.

Doise, W. and Mugny, G. (1984) *The Social Development of the Intellect*, Oxford, Pergamon Press.

Donald, J. and Hall, S. (1986) (eds) *Politics and Ideology*, Milton Keynes, Open University Press.

Donovan, A. and Oddy, M. (1982) 'Psychological aspects of unemployment: an investigation into the emotional and social adjustment of school leavers', *Journal of Adolescence* 5, 15–30.

Doob, L.W. (1948) *Public Opinion and Propaganda*, New York, Holt.

Eccleshall, R., Geoghegan, V., Jay, R. and Wilford, R. (1984) *Political Ideologies*, London, Hutchinson.

Edelman, M. (1977) *Political Language: Words that Succeed and Policies that Fail*, New York, Academic Press.

Eisenberg, P. and Lazarsfeld, P. (1938) 'The psychological effects of unemployment', *Psychological Bulletin* 35, 358–90.

Eiser, J.R. (1982) (ed.) *Social Psychology and Behavioural Medicine*, Chichester, Wiley.

Ericsson, K.A. and Simon H.A. (1984) *Protocol Analysis: Verbal Reports as Data*, Cambridge, Mass., MIT Press.

Erikson, E.H. (1954) 'Identity and totality: psychoanalytic observations on the problem of youth', *Human Development Bulletin*, University of Chicago 5th Annual Symposium on Human Development.

Erikson, E.H. (1968) *Identity: Youth and Crisis*, London, Faber & Faber.

Fagin, L.H. (1979) 'The impact of unemployment', *New Universities Quarterly* 34, 48–65.

Fagin, L.H. and Little, M. (1984) *The Forsaken Families: The Effects of Unemployment on Family Life*, Harmondsworth, Penguin.

Farina, A., Gliha, D., Boudreau, L., Allen, J. and Sherman, M. (1971) 'Mental illness and the impact of believing others know about it', *Journal of Abnormal Psychology* 77, 1–5.

Farr, R.M. and Moscovici, S. (1984) *Social Representations*, Cambridge, Cambridge University Press.

Feather, N.T. (1982) 'Unemployment and its psychological correlates', *Australian Journal of Psychology* 34, 309–23.

Feather, N.T. and Barber, J.G. (1983) 'Depressive reactions and unemployment', *Journal of Abnormal Psychology* 92, 185–95.

Feather, N.T. and Davenport, P. (1981) 'Unemployment and depressive affect: a motivational analysis', *Journal of Personality and Social Psychology* 41, 422–36.

Fenigstein, A., Scheier, M.F. and Buss, A.H. (1975) 'Public and private self-consciousness: assessment and theory', *Journal of Consulting and Clinical Psychology* 43, 522–7.

Festinger, L. (1954) 'A theory of social comparison', *Human Relations* 14, 48–64.

Festinger, L. (1957) *A Theory of Cognitive Dissonance*, Stanford, Calif., Standford University Press.

Fielding, G. and Evered, C. (1980) 'The influence of patients' speech upon doctors: the diagnostic interview', in R.N. St Clair and H. Giles (eds) *The Social and Psychological Contexts of Language*, Hillsdale, NJ, Lawrence Erlbaum Associates.

Fiske, S.T. and Taylor, S.E. (1984) *Social Cognition*, Reading, Mass. Addison-Wesley.

Flavell, J.H. (1977) *Cognitive Development*, Englewood Cliffs, NJ, Prentice-Hall.

Flavell, J.H. and Ross, L. (1981) *Social Cognitive Development: Frontiers and Possible Futures*, Cambridge, Cambridge University Press.

Forgas, J. (1979) *Social Episodes: The Study of Interaction Routines*, London, Academic Press.

Franks, D.D. and Marolla, J. (1976) 'Efficacious action and social approval as interacting dimensions of self-esteem: a tentative formulation through construct validation', *Sociometry* 39, 324–41.

Fransella, F. (1981) *Personality*, London, Methuen.

Freeman, J. (1975) *The Politics of Women's Liberation*, New York, Longman.

Friday, N. (1981) *My Secret Garden: Women's Sexual Fantasies*, London, Quartet Books.

Fromm, E. (1939) 'Selfishness and self love', *Psychiatry* 2, 507–23.

Furnham, A. (1982) 'The PWE and attitudes toward unemployment', *Journal of Occupational Psychology* 55, 277–86.

Furnham, A. (1984) 'The Protestant work ethic: a review of the psychological literature', *European Journal of Social Psychology* 14, 87–104.

Furnham, A. (1985) 'The determinants of attitudes towards social security recipients', *British Journal of Social Psychology* 24, 19–27.

Furnham, A. and Bland, K. (1983) 'The Protestant work ethic and conservatism', *Personality and Individual Differences* 4, 205–6.

Furnham, A. and Lewis, A. (1986) *The Economic Mind*, Brighton, Wheatsheaf.

Garfinkel, H. (1967) *Studies in Ethnomethodology*, Englewood Cliffs, NJ, Prentice-Hall.

Gecas, V. and Schwalbe, M.L. (1983) 'Beyond the looking-glass self: social structure and efficacy-based self-esteem', *Social Psychology Quarterly* 46 (2), 77–88.

Gergen, K.J. (1968) 'Personal consistency and the presentation of self', in C. Gordon and K.J. Gergen (eds) *The Self in Social Interaction*, vol. 1 New York, Wiley.

Gergen, K.J. (1971) *The Concept of Self*, New York, Holt, Rinehart & Winston.

Gergen, K.J. (1973) 'Social psychology as history', *Journal of Personality and Social Psychology* 26 (2), 309–20.

Gergen, K.J. (1982) 'From self to science: what is there to know?', in J. Suls (ed.) *Psychological Perspectives on the Self*, vol. 1, Hillsdale, NJ, Lawrence Erlbaum Associates.

Gergen, K.J. (1984a) 'The performative basis of mental claims', paper presented at the BPS Self and Identity Conference, University College, Cardiff, July.

Gergen, K.J. (1984b) 'Theory of the self: impasse and evolution', in L. Berkowitz (ed.) *Advances in Experimental Social Psychology*, vol. 17, New York, Academic Press.

Gergen, K.J. and Davis, K.E. (1985) *The Social Construction of the Person*, New York, Springer-Verlag.

Gergen, K.J. and Gergen, M.M. (1981) 'Causal attribution in the context of social explanation', in D. Gorlitz (ed.) *Perspectives on Attribution Research and Theory*, Cambridge, Mass., Ballinger.

Gergen, K.J. and Gergen, M.M. (1984) (eds) *Historical Social Psychology*, Hillsdale, NJ, Lawrence Erlbaum Associates.

Ginsberg, G.P. Brenner, M. and von Cranach, M. (1985) (eds) *Discovery Strategies in the Psychology of Action*, London, Academic Press.

Ginsberg, K.N. (1977) 'The "meat-rack": a study of male homosexual practices', in C.D. Bryant (ed.) *Sexual Deviancy in Social Context*, New York, New Viewpoints.

Glennon, L.M. (1979) *Women and Dualism*, New York, Longman.

Goffman, E. (1976) *Stigma: Notes on the Management of Spoiled Identity*, Harmondsworth, Penguin.

Goldberg, M.M. (1941) 'A qualification of the marginal man theory', *American Sociological Review* 6, 52–8.

Goodchilds, J. and Smith, E. (1963) 'The effects of unemployment as mediated by social status', *Sociometry* 26, 287–93.

Goodwin, D.W. and Guze, S.B. (1984) *Psychiatric Diagnosis*, 3rd edn, Oxford, Oxford University Press.

Gordon, C. and Gergen, K.J. (1968) (eds) *The Self in Social Interaction*, vol. 1, New York, Wiley.

Greenwald, A.G. (1980) 'The totalitarian ego: fabrication and revision of personal history', *American Psychologist* 35, 603–18.

Greenwald, H.J. and Oppenheim, D.B. (1968) 'Reported magnitude of self-misidentification among negro children – artifact?', *Journal of Personality and Social Psychology* 8, 49–52.

Hall, C.S. and Lindzey, G. (1978) *Theories of Personality*, New York, Wiley.

Hall, S. and Jefferson, T. (1983) *Resistance through Rituals: Youth Subcultures in Post-War Britain*, London, Hutchinson.

Hamilton, D.L. (1979) 'A cognitive-attributional analysis of stereotyping', *Advances in Experimental Social Psychology* 12, 53–84.

Hammersley, M. and Atkinson, P. (1983) *Ethnography: Principles in Practice*, London, Tavistock.

Hammond, S. (1985) 'Alienation and estrangement', ms, University of Surrey.

Harding, J. and Hogrefe, R. (1952) 'Attitudes of white department store employees towards negro co-workers', *Journal of Social Issues* 8, 18–28.

Harré, R. (1976) (ed.) *Personality*, Oxford, Blackwell.

Harré, R. (1979) *Social Being*, Oxford, Blackwell.

Harré, R. (1984) *Personal Being*, Oxford, Blackwell.

Harris, P.R. (1985) 'Asch's data and the "Asch Effect": a critical note', *British Journal of Social Psychology* 24, 229–30.

Harrison, R. (1976) 'The demoralizing experience of prolonged unemployment', *Department of Employment Gazette* 84, (4), 339–48.

Hartley, J. (1978) 'An investigation of the psychological aspects of managerial unemployment', PhD thesis, University of Manchester.

Hartnett, O. (1978) 'Sex-role stereotyping at work', in J. Chetwynd and O. Hartnett (eds) *The Sex Role System*, London, Routledge & Kegan Paul.

Hayes, J. and Nutman, P. (1981) *Understanding the Unemployed*, London, Tavistock.

Hegel, G.W.F. (1807) *Phenomenology of Spirit* (translated by A.V. Miller), Oxford, Clarendon Press, 1977.

Heider, F. (1946) 'Attitudes and cognitive organization', *Journal of Psychology* 21, 107–12.

Hepworth, S.J. (1980) 'Moderating factors of the psychological impact of unemployment', *Journal of Occupational Psychology* 53, 139–45.

Herzlich, C. (1973) *Health and Illness*, London, Academic Press.

Hewstone, M. (ed.) (1983) *Attribution Theory: Social and Functional Aspects*, Oxford, Blackwell.

Hewstone, M. (1985) 'On common-sense and social representations: a reply to Potter and Litton', *British Journal of Social Psychology* 24, 95–7.

Hewstone, M., Jaspars, J. and Lalljee, M. (1982) 'Social representations, social attribution and social identity', *European Journal of Social Psychology* 12, 241–71.

Higgins, E.T., Ruble, D.N. and Hartup, W.W. (1983) *Social Cognition and Social Development*, Cambridge, Cambridge University Press.

Higgins, E.T., Ruble, D.N. and Hartup, W.W. (1985) *Social Cognition and Sexual Development*, Cambridge, Cambridge University Press.

Hill, J. (1978) 'The psychological impact of unemployment', *New Society* 19, January, 118–20.

Hofman, J. (1983) 'Social identity and intergroup conflict', paper presented at the EAESP Conference on Conflict and Intergroup Relations, Shefayim, Israel, October.

Hoiberg, A. (ed.) (1982) *Women and The World of Work*, New York, Plenum.

Holland, R. (1977) *Self and Social Context*, London, Macmillan.

Hollis, M. (1977) *Models of Man*, Cambridge, Cambridge University Press.

Holy, S. and Stuchlik, M. (1983) *Actions, Norms and Representations*, Cambridge, Cambridge University Press.

Hraba, J. and Grant, G. (1970) 'Black is beautiful: a re-examination of racial preference and identification', *Journal of Personality and Social Psychology* 16 (3), 398–402.

Israel, J. (1972) 'Stipulations and constructions in the social sciences', in J. Israel and H. Tajfel (eds) *The Context of Social Psychology: A Critical Assessment*, London, Academic Press.

Jackson, P.R. and Warr, P.B. (1983) 'Age, length of unemployment, and other variables associated with men's ill-health during unemployment', MRC/SSRC SAPU Memo 585.

Jacques, E. (1955) 'Social systems as a defense against persecutory and depressive anxiety', in M. Klein, P. Heimann and R.E. Money-Kyrle (eds) *New Directions in Psychoanalysis*, New York, Basic Books.

Jahoda, G. Thompson, S. and Bhatt, S. (1972) 'Ethnic identity and preferences among Asian immigrant children in Glasgow: a replicated study', *European Journal of Social Psychology* 2 (1), 19–32.

Jahoda, M. (1979) 'The impact of unemployment in the 1930s and 1970s', *Bulletin of the British Psychological Society* 32, 309–14.

Jahoda, M. (1981) 'Work, employment and unemployment', *American Psychologist* 36, 184–91.

Jahoda, M. (1982) *Employment and Unemployment: A Social-Psychological Analysis*, Cambridge, Cambridge University Press.

James, W. (1890) *Principles of Psychology*, New York, Holt.

James, W. (1917) *The Varieties of Religious Experience*, New York, Longmans, Green & Co.

Jaspars, J. and Fraser, C. (1984) 'Attitudes and social representations', in R.M. Farr and S. Moscovici (eds) *Social Representations*, Cambridge, Cambridge University Press.

Jaspars, J. and Hewstone, M. (1985) 'Collective beliefs, social categorization and causal attribution', ESRC Conference on Social Beliefs, Cambridge, March.

Jaspars, J., Fincham, F. and Hewstone, M. (eds) (1983) *Attribution Theory and Research: Conceptual, Developmental and Social Dimensions*, London, Academic Press.

Kahneman, D., Slovic, P. and Tversky, A. (1982) *Judgement under Uncertainty: Heuristics and Biases*, New York, Cambridge University Press.

Kando, T. (1977) 'Passing and stigma management', in C.D. Bryant (ed.) *Sexual Deviancy in Social Context*, New York, New Viewpoints.

Kaplan, A.G. and Sedney, M.A. (1980) *Psychology and Sex Roles: An Androgynous Perspective*, Boston, Little, Brown & Co.

Kasl, S. (1979), 'Changes in mental health status associated with job loss and retirement', in R.M. Rose and G. Klerman (eds) *Stress and Mental Disorder*, New York, Raven Press.

Kellerman, H. (1979) *Group Psychotherapy and Personality: Intersecting Structures*, New York, Grune & Stratton.

Kelley, H. (1967) 'Attribution theory in social psychology', in D. Levine (ed.) *Nebraska Symposium on Motivation*, vol. 15, Lincoln, Neb., University of Nebraska Press.

Kelly, G.A. (1955) *The Psychology of Personal Constructs*, vols 1 and 2, New York, Norton.

Kelvin, P. (1977) 'Predictability, power and vulnerability in interpersonal attraction', in S. Duck (ed.) *Theory and Practice in Interpersonal Attraction*, London, Academic Press.

Kelvin, P. (1984) 'The historical dimension of social psychology: the case of unemployment', in H. Tajfel (ed.) *The Social Dimension*, vol. 2, Cambridge, Cambridge University Press.

Kelvin, P. and Jarrett, J.E. (1985) *Unemployment: Its social psychological effects*, Cambridge, Cambridge University Press.

Kihlstrom, J.F. and Cantor, N. (1984) 'Mental representations of the self', in L. Berkowitz (ed.) *Advances in Experimental Social Psychology*, vol. 17, New York, Academic Press.

Kitwood, T. (1980) *Disclosures to a Strangers*, London, Routledge & Kegan Paul.

Klapp, O.E. (1969) *Collective Search for Identity*, New York, Holt.

Kline, P. (1983) *Personality: Measurement and Theory*, London, Hutchinson.

Kratochwill, T.R., Mott, S.E. and Dodson, C.L. (1984), 'Case study and single-case research in clinical and applied research', in A.S. Bellack and M. Hersen (eds) *Research Methods in Clinical Psychology*, Oxford, Pergamon Press.

Labour Studies Group (1985) 'Economic, social and political factors in the operation of the labour market', in B. Roberts, R. Finnegan and D. Gallie (eds) *New Approaches to Economic Life*, Manchester, Manchester University Press.

Latane, B. (1966) 'Studies in social comparison – introduction and overview', *Journal of Experimental Social Psychology*, supplement 1, 1–5.

Lauterbach, W. (1984) *Soviet Psychotherapy*, Oxford, Pergamon Press.

Lazarus, R.S. and Alfert, E. (1964) 'Short-circuiting threat by experimentally altering cognitive appraisal', *Journal of Abnormal Social Psychology* 69, 195–205.

Lazarus, R.S. and Folkman, S. (1984) *Stress, Appraisal and Coping*, New York, Springer.

Lazarus, R.S. and Longo, N. (1953) 'The consistency of psychological defenses against threat', *Journal of Abnormal Social Psychology* 48, 495–9.

Leff, M.J., Roatch, J.F. and Bunney, W.E. (1970) 'Environmental factors preceding the onset of severe depressions', *Psychiatry* 33, 293–311.

Lemaine, G. (1974) 'Social differentiation and social originality', *European Journal of Social Psychology* 4(1), 17–52.

Leonard, P. (1984) *Personality and Ideology: Towards a Materialist Understanding of the Individual*, London, Macmillan.

Lerner, M.J., Miller, D.T. and Holmes, J.G. (1976) 'Deserving and the emergence of forms of justice', in L. Berkowitz (ed.) *Advances in Experimental Social Psychology*, vol. 9, 133–62, London, Academic Press.

Lewin, K. (1951) *Field Theory in Social Science*, New York, Harper.

Lewis, S. and Cooper, C.L. (1983) 'The stress of combining occupational and parental roles: a review of the literature', *Bulletin of the British Psychological Society* 36, 341–5.

Lickona, T. (1976) (ed.) *Moral Development and Behavior*, New York, Holt, Rinehart & Winston.

Liebkind, K. (1984) 'Minority identity and identification processes: a social psychological study', *Commentationes Scientiarum Socialium* 22.

Liem, R. and Atkinson, T. (1982) 'The work and unemployment project: personal and family effects of job loss', unpublished ms.

Little, C.B. (1976) 'Technical-professional unemployment: middle-class adaptability to personal crisis', *Sociological Quarterly* 17, 262–74.

Luckmann, T. (1983) 'Remarks on personal identity: inner, social and historical time', in A. Jacobson-Widding (ed.) *Identity: Personal and Socio-Cultural*, Uppsala, Uppsala University Press.

McCall, G.J. (1977) 'The social looking-glass: a sociological perspective on self-development', in T. Mischel (ed.) *The Self*, Oxford, Blackwell.

McCall, G.J. and Simmons, J.L. (1982) *Social Psychology: A Sociological Approach*, New York, Free Press.

Maccoby, E.E. and Jacklin, C.N. (1974) *The Psychology of Sex Differences,* Stanford, Calif., Stanford University Press.

Maher, B.A. (1970) *Principles of Psychopathology,* New York, McGraw-Hill.

Markova, I. (1984) 'Knowledge of the self through action', paper presented at the BPS Self and Identity Conference, University College, Cardiff, July.

Markus, H. and Nurius, P. (1984) 'Possible selves', paper presented at the BPS Self and Identity Conference, University College, Cardiff, July.

Marsella, A.J., De Vos, G. and Hsu, F. (1985) *Culture and Self,* London, Methuen.

Marsh, C., Fraser, C. and Jobling, R. (1985) 'Political responses to unemployment', in B. Roberts, R. Finnegan and D. Gallie (eds) *New Approaches to Economic Life: Economic Restructuring, Unemployment and the Social Division of Labour,* Manchester, Manchester University Press.

Marsh, P., Rosser, E. and Harré, R. (1978) *The Rules of Disorder,* London, Routledge & Kegan Paul.

Martin, J. and Roberts, C. (1984) *Women and Employment: A Lifetime Perspective,* London, HMSO.

Matthews, J. (1983) 'Environmental change and community identity', in G.M. Breakwell (ed.) *Threatened Identities,* Chichester, Wiley.

Mead, G.H. (1934) *Mind, Self and Society,* Chicago, Chicago University Press.

Milner, D. (1973) 'Racial identification and preference in "black" British children', *European Journal of Social Psychology* 3 (3), 281–95.

Milner, D. (1984) 'The development of ethnic attitudes', in H. Tajfel (ed.) *The Social Dimension,* vol. 1, Cambridge, Cambridge University Press.

Minard, R.D. (1952) 'Race relationships in the Pocahontas coalfield', *Journal of Social Issues* 8, 29–44.

Mischel, T. (1977) (ed.) *The Self,* Oxford, Blackwell.

Mischel, W. (1968) *Personality and Assessment,* New York, Wiley.

Molleman, E., Pruyn, J. and van Knippenberg, A. (1986) 'Social comparison processes among cancer patients', *British Journal of Social Psychology* 25, 1–13.

Morland, J.K. (1963) 'Racial self-identification: a study of nursery school children', *American Catholic Society Review* 24, 231–42.

Moscovici, S. (1976) *Social Influence and Social Change,* London, Academic Press.

Moscovici, S. (1981) 'On social representation', in J. Forges (ed.) *Social Cognition: Perspectives on Everyday Understanding,* London, Academic Press.

Moscovici, S. (1984) 'The phenomenon of social representations', in R.M. Farr and S. Moscovici (eds) *Social Representations,* Cambridge, Cambridge University Press.

Moscovici, S. (1985) 'Comment on Potter and Litton', *British Journal of Social Psychology* 24, 91–2.

Mugny, G. (1982) *The Power of Minorities,* London, Academic Press.

Mugny, G., Kaiser, C., Papastamou, S. and Perez, J.A. (1984) 'Intergroup relations, identification and social influence, *British Journal of Social Psychology* 23, 317–22.

Myrdal, G. (1962) *An American Dilemma,* New York, Harper & Row.

Neisser, U. (1976) *Cognition and Reality,* San Francisco, Freeman.

Nicholson, N., Cole, S.G. and Rocklin, T. (1985) 'Conformity in the Asch situation: a comparison between contemporary British and US university students', *British Journal of Social Psychology* 24, 59–63.

Nisbett, R. and Ross, L. (1980) *Human Inference: Strategies and Shortcomings of Social Judgement*, Englewood Cliffs, NJ, Prentice-Hall.

Okamura, J.Y. (1981) 'Situational ethnicity', *Journal of Ethnic and Racial Studies* 4, 452–65.

Osgood, C.E. and Tannenbaum, P.H. (1955) 'The principle of congruity in the prediction of attitude change', *Psychological Review* 62, 42–55.

Page, R. (1984) *Stigma*, London, Routledge & Kegan Paul.

Palmonari, A., Carugati, F., Ricci Bitti, P.E. and Sarchielli, G. (1984) 'Imperfect identities', in H. Tajfel (ed.) *The Social Dimension*, vol. 1, Cambridge, Cambridge University Press.

Parkes, C.M. (1972) *Bereavement*, London, Tavistock.

Paykell, E.S. (1973) 'Life events and acute depression', in J.P. Scott and E.C. Senay (eds) *Separation and Depression*, AAAS.

Payne, R.L., Warr, P.B. and Hartley, J. (1983) 'Social class and the experience of unemployment', MRC/SSRC SAPU Memo 549.

Perfetti, C.J. and Bingham, W.C. (1983) 'Unemployment and self-esteem in metal refinery workers', *Vocational Guidance Quarterly* 31 (3), 195–202.

Perrin, S. and Spencer, C. (1981) 'Independence and conformity in the Asch experiment as a reflection of cultural and situational factors', *British Journal of Social Psychology* 20, 205–9.

Peterson, C. and Seligman, M.E.P. (1984) 'Explanatory style and depression: theory and evidence', *Psychological Review*.

Philpott, G. (1982) 'Consciousness raising: back to basics', in *Spare Rib Reader*, Harmondsworth, Penguin.

Piaget, J. and Inhelder, B. (1966) *The Psychology of the Child*, London, Routledge & Kegan Paul.

Politser, P.E. (1980) 'Network analysis and the logic of social support', in R.H. Price and P.E. Politser (eds) *Evaluation and Action in the Social Environment*, New York, Academic Press.

Potter, J. and Litton, I. (1985) 'Some problems underlying the theory of social representations', *British Journal of Social Psychology* 24, 81–90.

Pushkin, I. and Veness, T. (1973) 'The development of racial awareness and prejudice in children', in P. Watson (ed.) *Psychology and Race*, Harmondsworth, Penguin.

Rabbitt, P. (1985) 'Psychology of Ageing', *The Times Higher Education Supplement*, January.

Raps, C.S., Peterson, C., Reinhard, K.E., Abramson, L.Y. and Seligman, M.E.P. (1982) 'Attributional style among depressed patients', *Journal of Abnormal Psychology* 91, 102–3.

Roberts, B., Finnegan, R. and Gallie, D. (1985) (eds) *New Approaches to Economic Life*, Manchester, Manchester University Press.

Robins, E. and Guze, S.B. (1972) 'Classification of affective disorders', in T.A. Williams, M.M. Katz and J.A. Shields (eds) *Recent Advances in the Psychobiology of the Depressive Illnesses*, Washington, DC, US Government Printing Office.

Rokeach, M. (1978) *Beliefs, Attitudes and Values*, San Francisco, Jossey-Bass.

Rosenberg, M. (1967) 'The dissonant context and the adolescent self-concept', in S.E. Dragastin and G.H. Elder (eds) *Adolescence in the Life Cycle*, New York, Harper & Row.

Rosenberg, M. (1984) 'Transient depersonalization: the loss of identity in adolescence', paper presented at the BPS Self and Identity Conference, University College, Cardiff, July.

Rosenhan, D.L. and Seligman, M.E.P. (1984) *Abnormal Psychology*, New York, Norton.

Rubin, Z. and Peplan, L.A. (1975) 'Who believes in a just world?', *Journal of Social Issues* 31, 65–88.

Ruddock, R. (1972) (ed.) *Six Approaches to the Person*, London, Routledge & Kegan Paul.

Russell, B. (1930) *The Conquest of Happiness*, London, Allen & Unwin.

Sartre, J-P. (1963) *Search for a Method*, New York, Vintage.

Savage, R.D., Gaber, L.B., Britton, P.G., Bolton, N. and Cooper, A. (1977) *Personality and Adjustment in the Aged*, London, Academic Press.

Sayers, J. (1982) *Biological Politics*, London, Tavistock.

Scheier, M.F. and Carver, C.S. (1983) 'Two sides of self: one for you and one for me', in J. Suls and A.G. Greenwald (eds) *Psychological Perspectives on the Self*, vol. 2, Hillsdale, NJ, Lawrence Erlbaum Associates.

Schulz, R.S. (1976) 'Effects of control and predictability on the physical and psychological well-being of institutionalized aged', *Journal of Personality and Social Psychology* 33, 563–73.

Seligman, M.E.P. (1975) *Helplessness: On Depression, Development, and Death*, San Francisco, Freeman.

Semin, G.R. (1985) 'The "phenomenon of social representations": a comment on Potter and Litton', *British Journal of Social Psychology* 24, 93–4.

Serafica, F.C. (1982) *Social-Cognitive Development in Context*, London, Methuen.

Sherif, C.W. (1980) 'Coordination of the sociological and psychological in adolescent interaction', unpublished ms.

Sherif, M. and Sherif, C.W. (1964) *Reference groups: Exploration into Conformity and Deviation of Adolescents*, New York, Harper & Row.

Sherif, M. and Sherif, C.W. (1965) *Problems of Youth: Transition into Adulthood in a Changing World*, Chicago, Aldine.

Sherif, M. and Sherif, C.W. (1969) 'Adolescent attitudes and behavior in their reference groups', in J.P. Hill (ed.) *Minnesota Symposia on Child Psychology*, vol. 3, Minneapolis, University of Minnesota Press.

Shoemaker, S. (1984) *Identity, Cause and Mind*, Cambridge, Cambridge University Press.

Shotter, J. (1985) *Social Accountability and Selfhood*, Oxford, Blackwell.

Shweder, R.A. and Bourne, E.J. (1984) 'Does the concept of the person vary cross-culturally?', in R.A. Shweder and R.A. LeVine (eds) *Culture Theory: Essays on Mind, Self and Society*, New York, Cambridge University Press.

Sixsmith, J. (1986) 'Dealing with sensitive situations', unpublished seminar paper, based on PhD work, University of Surrey.

Smith, A.D. (1973) *The Concept of Social Change*, London, Routledge & Kegan Paul.

Spencer, C. and Perrin, S. (1981) 'The Asch effect and cultural factors: further observations and evidence', *Bulletin of the British Psychological Society* 34, 385–6.

Stafford, E. (1982) 'The impact of the Youth Opportunities Programme on young people's employment prospects and psychological well-being', *British Journal of Guidance and Counselling* 10, 12–21.

Stafford, E.M., Jackson, P.R. and Banks, M. (1980) 'Employment, work involvement and mental health in less qualified young people', *Journal of Occupational Psychology* 53, 291–304.

Stephens, E. (1982) 'Out of the closet into the courts', in *Spare Rib Reader*, Harmondsworth, Penguin.

Stevenson, H.W. and Stewart, T. (1958) 'A developmental study of race awareness in young children', *Child Development* 29, 399–409.

Stonequist, E.V. (1937) *The Marginal Man*, New York, Scribners.

Strauss, A.L. (1959) *Mirrors and Masks*, Glencoe, Ill., Free Press.

Strickland, L. (1979) (ed.) *Soviet and Western Perspectives in Social Psychology*, Oxford, Pergamon.

Stroebe, W. and Stroebe, M.S. (1984) 'When love dies: an integration of attraction and bereavement research', in H. Tajfel (ed.) *The Social Dimension*, vol. 1, Cambridge, Cambridge University Press.

Stryker, S. (1980) *Symbolic Interactionism: A Social Structural Version*, Menlo Park, Calif., Benjamin-Cummings.

Stryker, S. (1984) 'Identity theory: development and extensions', paper presented at the BPS Self and Identity Conference, University College, Cardiff, July.

Tagliacozza, D.L. and Manksch, H.O. (1972) 'The patient's view of the patient's role', in E.G. Jaco (ed.) *Patients, Physicians, and Illness*, 2nd edn, New York, Free Press.

Tajfel, H. (1978) (ed.) *Differentiation Between Social Groups*, London, Academic Press.

Tajfel, H. (1981a) *Human Groups and Social Categories*, Cambridge, Cambridge University Press.

Tajfel, H. (1981b) 'Social stereotypes and social groups', in J.C. Turner and H. Giles (eds) *Intergroup Behaviour*, Oxford, Blackwell.

Tajfel, H. (1982) (ed.) *Social Identity and Intergroup Relations*, Cambridge, Cambridge University Press.

Tajfel, H. (1984) (ed.) *The Social Dimension*, vols 1 and 2, Cambridge, Cambridge University Press.

Tajfel, H. and Turner, J.C. (1979) 'An integrative theory of intergroup conflict', in W.G. Austin and S. Worchel (eds) *The Social Psychology of Intergroup Relations*, Monterey, Calif., Brooks/Cole.

Taylor, D.M. and McKirnan, D.J. (1984) 'A five-stage model of intergroup relations', *British Journal of Social Psychology* 23 (4), 291–300.

Taylor, S.E. (1979) 'Hospital patient behaviour: reactance, helplessness or control?', *Journal of Social Issues* 35, 156–84.

Thomas, B. and Madigan, C. (1974) 'Strategy and job choice after redundancy – a case study in the aircraft industry', *Sociological Review* 22, 83–102.

Toch, H. (1966) *The Social Psychology of Social Movements*, London, Methuen.

Trew, K. and Kirkpatrick, R. (1984) *The Daily Life of the Unemployed: Social and Psychological Dimensions*, Belfast, Queen's University.

Tropp Schreiber, C. (1979) *Changing Places*, Cambridge, Mass., Massachusetts Institute of Technology Press.

Turner, J.C. and Giles, H. (1981) (eds) *Intergroup Behaviour*, Oxford, Blackwell.

Turner, R. (1976) 'The real self: from institution to impulse', *American Journal of Sociology* 81, 989–1016.

Turner, R (1978) 'The role and the person', *American Journal of Sociology* 84, 1–23.

Turner, R. (1984) 'Problems in articulating self and social structure', paper presented at the BPS Self and Identity Conference, University College, Cardiff, July.

Turner, R. and Billings, V. (1984) 'The social contexts of self-feeling', paper presented at the BPS Self and Identity Conference, University College, Cardiff, July.

Turner, R. and Killian, L. (1972) *Collective Behavior*, Englewood Cliffs, NJ, Prentice-Hall.

Turner, R. and Schutte, J. (1981) 'The true self method for studying the self-conception', *Symbolic Interaction* 4, 1–20.

Vadher, A. (1983) 'Help-seeking behaviour in leprosy patients', unpublished MSc thesis, University of Surrey.

Vygotsky, L.S. (1978) discussion contribution in M. Cole, V. John-Steiner, S. Scribner and E. Souberman (eds) *Mind in Society*, Cambridge, Harvard University Press.

Waddell, N. and Cairns, E. (1986) 'Situational perspectives on social identity in Northern Ireland', *British Journal of Social Psychology* 25, 25–31.

Wagstaff, G.F. and Quirk, M.A. (1983) 'Attitudes to sex-roles, political conservatism and belief in a just world', *Psychological Reports* 52, 813–14.

Warr, P.B. (1983) 'Work, jobs and unemployment', *Bulletin of the British Psychological Society* 36, 305–11.

Warr, P.B. (1985) 'Twelve questions about unemployment and health', in B. Roberts, R. Finnegan and D. Gallie (eds) *New Approaches to Economic Life*, Manchester, Manchester University Press.

Warr, P.B., Jackson, R. and Banks, M. (1982) 'Duration of unemployment and psychological well-being in young men and women', *Current Psychological Research*, 207–14.

Warr, P.B. and Lovatt, D.J. (1977) 'Retraining and other factors associated with job finding after redundancy', *Journal of Occupational Psychology* 50, 67–84.

Warr, P.B. and Parry, G. (1982) 'Paid employment and women's psychological well-being', *Psychological Bulletin* 91, 498–516.

Watson, G. (1970) *Passing for White*, London, Tavistock.

Watson, J.L. (1977) *Between Two Cultures: Migrants and Minorities in Britain*, Oxford, Blackwell.

Wedderburn, D. (1964) *White Collar Redundancy*, University of Cambridge, Department of Applied Economics Occasional Papers, no. 1.

Wegner, D.M. and Vallacher, R.R. (1980) (eds) *The Self in Social Psychology*, New York, Oxford University Press.

Weinreich, P. (1980) *A Manual for Identity Exploration Using Personal Constructs*, London, SSRC.

Weinreich, P. (1983) 'Emerging from threatened identities', in G.M. Breakwell (ed.) *Threatened Identities*, Chichester, Wiley.

Weinreich-Haste, H. and Locke, D. (1983) (eds) *Morality in the Making*, Chichester, Wiley.

Wells, L.E. and Marwell, G. (1976) *Self-esteem: Its Conceptualisation and Measurement*, Beverly Hills, Calif., Sage.

West, J. (1982) (ed.) *Work, Women and the Labour Market*, London, Routledge & Kegan Paul.

Wheldall, K. (1985) personal communication.

Williams, J.A. (1979) 'Psychological androgyny and mental health', in O. Hartnett, G. Boden and M. Fuller (eds) *Women: Sex-role Stereotyping*, London, Tavistock.

Willis, J. (1976) *Clinical Psychiatry*, Oxford, Blackwell.

Wilkinson, J. and Canter, S. (1982) *Social Skills Training Manual*, Chichester, Wiley.

Wing, J.K. (1978) (ed.) *Schizophrenia: Towards a New Synthesis*, London, Academic Press.

Wrightsman, L.S. and Deaux, K. (1981) *Social Psychology in the 80s*, 3rd edn, Monterey, Calif., Brooks/Cole.

Zavalloni, M. (1983) 'Ego-ecology: the study of interaction between social and personal identities', in A. Jacobson-Widding (ed.) *Identity: Personal and Socio-cultural*, Uppsala, Uppsala University Press.

Ziller, R.C. (1973) *The Social Self*, Oxford, Pergamon Press.

Name index

Abramson, L.Y., 155
Ajzen, I., 42
Alfert, E., 81
Allport, G.W., 13
Althusser, L., 75
Antonovsky, A., 107–8
Apter, M.J., 25, 113–14
Archer, J., 64
Argyle, M., 25
Asch, S.E., 182
Ashton, D.N., 56
Atkinson, P., 45
Atkinson, T., 62

Bakke, E., 159
Bandura, A., 103
Banks, M., 52, 58
Barber, J.G., 52
Bartell, R., 52
Bavelas, J.B., 11
Beck, A.T., 50, 157
Bem, S.L., 139
Berger, P.L., 10, 22, 55
Berger, S.M., 174
Biddle, B.J., 11
Billig, M., 39, 168, 184
Billings, V., 87
Bingham, W.C., 52
Bion, W.R., 90

Bland, K., 58
Blatt, S., 85
Blumer, H., 30
Bourne, E.J., 184
Braginski, B. and D., 121
Breakwell, G.M., 17–18, 59, 62, 65–6, 69, 71, 83–5, 106, 112, 117, 124, 133–4, 137, 145–6, 151, 161, 163–5, 171
Brenner, M., 44
Brenner, O., 52
Brenner, S., 52
Briar, K., 159
Brickman, P., 170
Briggs, S.R., 16
Brown, G.W., 49–50
Brown, J., 45
Brown, L., 183
Brown, R.J., 185
Bulman, R.J., 170
Bunker, N., 104, 109–10, 112
Bunney, W.E., 49
Burman, S., 67
Burns, R.B., 11
Buss, A.H., 16
Butcher, J.N., 44

Cairns, E., 19, 185
Canter, S., 114

Subject index